HOW TO BUY AND SELL YOUR OWN REAL ESTATE
A Minnesota Guidebook

Library of Congress Catalog Card No.: 85-080257
ISBN 0-96077842X

MURRIN METROPOLITAN
ATTORNEYS AT LAW

Office Locations:

3009 Holmes Avenue South
Minneapolis, MN 55408
(612) 827-4666

5740 Brooklyn Blvd.
Suite 208
Brooklyn Center, MN 55429
(612) 560-2560

2499 Rice Street
Roseville, MN 55113
(612) 482-0634

649 Grand Avenue
Saint Paul, MN 55105
(612) 224-1313

201 W. Burnsville Pkwy.
Suite 154
Burnsville, MN 55337
(612) 890-5630

9001 E. Bloomington Frwy.
90th & 35W
Bloomington, MN 55422
(612) 881-0208

or

DIAL L-A-W-Y-E-R-S

This book was written in 1986. The materials and information contained in this book are current for the laws in effect in the State of Minnesota at that time. If you do not plan to use this book in the near future, please check with our offices before using the book to make sure the laws have not changed.

This book is dedicated to my grandparents:

Henry and Billie Bucher

whose high standards for themselves, the family

and real estate have created some very

valuable assets

FOREWORD

Real Estate, fortunately or unfortunately, is a game of knowledge. The person who posseses the most knowledge or information wins or does well. This book provides the reader with this knowledge and information. In the past, the public has relied exclusively on real estate salespersons and lawyers for this information. Recently our society has moved away from total reliance on professionals. Citizens want to participate in doing more things themselves. They want more control over their own affairs and destiny. At the very least, people want to understand the process rather than be told this is how we do it. Too often real estate matters are shrouded in secrecy. This book gives people the knowledge to uncover the secrets and in many cases use little known facts to their tremendous advantage. What is attempted, and I believe accomplished, is a complete explanation of the entire real estate process. When a person is finished reading this book, he or she will understand the principles and intricacies of the real estate business. No longer, after reviewing a book like this, do you have to be helplessly dependent on others to solve your real estate problems.

This book discusses and simplifies all aspects of the real estate process including the marketing function, the lawyering function, the closing function with step by step instructions concerning document preparation and many other things.

The materials included in this book are current through 1986. If you do not use this book in the near future, you would be wise to obtain updated advice. The people at Dial L-A-W-Y-E-R-S can keep you abreast of any changes in the law in this area.

While this book was put together over a period of about six years, it is the result of some tremendous people putting their talents and skills together toward the goal of making this book a readable and informative guide. I would like to extend a special thanks to my friends and confidants who have stood by me during this and other projects, especially Larry Skoglund and Eric Hanson. I am also grateful to my brother, Bob Murrin, who has taken valuable time away from building skyscrapers and shopping centers to design the delightfully funny cartoons and pictures for the book.

Without the tremendous talent and dedication of Jeanene Hayes, the backbone of this and so many of our projects, this book would never have happened. She deserves credit for many aspects of the book, including editing, writing, organizing, and obtaining many of the forms and documents in this book.

This book is also the result of many outstanding lawyers who contributed to this effort and with whom I have the pleasure and honor of being associated . I cannot thank everyone but, I would like to thank Thomas E. Johnson for his help with Chapter VI, Douglas F. McGuire for his help with Chapter IX, Paul Nelson for his help with Chapter X, Steven C. Smith for his help with Chapter XI. I would also like to thank Richard K. Hocking and Clyde E. Eklund for their input throughout this book.

Also, I would like to thank the people at Meyer's Printing and, in particular, Diane Napier for her tremendous assistance in helping us make this a quality book.

Finally, I would like to thank my wife, DeVonna Murrin, who has stood by me through this and other endeavors with her constant faith, confidence and love in me.

TABLE OF CONTENTS

INTRODUCTION

This book is designed to serve as a simple and readable tool for any person needing to deal with or understand a real estate transaction, simple or complex. It will help most people understand the real estate process from beginning to end in the State of Minnesota. To the best of our knowledge, this is the only book on the market written for laymen and concentrating on Minnesota law. It outlines most of the steps necessary to buy or sell real estate, i.e. advertising the real estate, showing the real estate, financing the real estate, preparing and handling the legal documents, filing the legal documents and much more.

A person interested in studying the nuts and bolts process of real estate will benefit by reading this book. It will assist a person in communicating effectively with real estate agents and lawyers and will be a vital supplement to interaction with other real estate professionals. This book can be valuable to a person who decides to sell or buy his/her own real estate without the assistance of a real estate agent and/or attorney. While there may be times when it is necessary to consult an attorney or real estate agent, a person should be able to do most things without assistance.

Compare the cost saving for an $80,000 house between using a real estate agent and not using one.

	House Sold Through Realtor	House Sold by Owner
7% real estate commission	$5,600.00 (7% of $80,000)	-0-
Appraisal	-0-	$150.00
Advertising	-0-	$300.00
Legal Fees	** 300.00	$300.00
	$5,900.00	$750.00

Total Savings

$	5,600.00
-	150.00
-	300.00
-	300.00
	$4,850.00

** The legal fees quoted above are the average fees charged by this office at the date of this printing for total representation of legal matters related to the sale of real estate (preparation of purchase agreement, preparation of deed, preclosing checks and attendance at closing). There are other costs payable no matter which method is chosen such as abstract continuation, recording fees and deed tax. Some real estate companies also charge a closing fee over and above their commission. These things will be discussed in greater detail later.

The buyer's attorney's fees charged by Murrin Metropolitan are $155.00 on the average, which includes title opinion, preclosing checks and attendance at closing.

As will be stated in more detail throughout this book, an attorney may be needed for only parts of the transaction, or perhaps not at all, depending on the buyer's or seller's particular real estate transaction and his or her satisfaction in that particular area.

CHAPTER I
TO SELL QUICKLY, MARKET EFFECTIVELY

HOW TO MARKET YOUR HOME

The first step in marketing your home is to determine the value of the real estate. The value of real estate, like every other value, follows one golden rule: the value is determined by what someone else is willing to pay. This figure can be ascertained in many ways:

1. Compare property values around your area for similar types of structures.
2. Bargain with a prospective purchaser for a price by mutual agreement.
3. Hire the services of a professional appraiser who will, for a charge of approximately $100.00 to $250.00, appraise your property and submit a professional written opinion to you. The appraiser will usually use one of two types of technical methods (or a combination of both methods) in making the appraisal:
   a. Cost approach. The appraiser determines the market price and cost of building a new comparable home and subtracts for depreciation to determine a "fair market value."
   b. Market data approach. The appraiser determines the value of your home by comparing it to homes in your area with similar features which have been sold recently.

TRUTH IN HOUSING INSPECTION

Before you put your real estate on the market, check the ordinances of your city or town to see if a "Truth in Housing Inspection" is required. Both Minneapolis and St. Paul now require a certified truth in housing expert to inspect your house. The inspectors are independent and the fee charged will depend on the evaluator. The average fee is $75.00. The inspector will make a list of serious defects found in the home. A copy of this inspection is given to the seller and a copy is placed on file with the City. There is no requirement that the hazards listed in the inspection report be repaired, only that the potential buyer be made aware of such hazards.

The inspector must submit a copy of his report to the City and to the seller within ten days of his inspection. The seller must then keep a copy of the inspection report on the premises and make it available to all potential buyers, usually at the time of showing.

It is imperative that you check to see if this ordinance is in effect in your area. If you are a seller in an area which requires such a report, you may be guilty of a misdemeanor if you do not comply with the Truth in Housing Rule. Any information you need regarding this inspection can be obtained by calling your city hall. The individuals there are most helpful and will generally give you any information you need, including step by step instructions on the procedure you must follow. The purpose of the Truth in Housing ordinance is to make the buyer aware of any hazards before entering into a purchase agreement. A seller should be sure to display the Truth in Housing form in a conspicuous place whenever the home is being shown to a prospective buyer.

ADVERTISING AND SHOWING YOUR HOME
SURE FIRE TECHNIQUES TO FIND THAT BUYER

If you do not have a ready buyer, it is necessary to advertise and market your own real estate so that the public is aware that the real estate is for sale. The extra money spent in advertising will be worth it to the enthusiastic seller.

Advertising and marketing your own real estate will usually make the time between offering the real estate for sale and the actual sale shorter and may increase the potential selling price if there is competition between interested buyers. Advertising costs will usually average between $200 and $600. Of course, the costs are dependent upon numerous factors, including the size of the ad you place, the type of advertising you choose, and the length of time you run it.

<u>Newspaper Ads</u>

This is the most effective method available. Creativity in writing the ad is very important. If necessary, it is better to over-emphasize the assets than to risk submitting a "boring ad". However, the ad should also be concise and to the point to avoid running an overly expensive ad.

Before writing your ad, review several ads in the newspaper for common abbreviations and information provided.

The following elements of a newspaper ad should be kept in mind when composing your ad:

1. Use a "catchy" title to your ad. As part of this, you may want to capitalize on a single significant factor. This significant factor might be "immediate possession", "comfortable home", or "close to bus, shopping."
2. List the number of bedrooms, the type of house (i.e. split level, rambler, bungalow, etc.)
3. State the special features of the real estate.
4. Give the phone numbers where you can be reached and the time of day you can be reached at each number.
5. List your asking price.
6. Have a closing statement that motivates the buyer to call your number.

Which newspaper you use for your advertisement will depend on where in Minnesota you reside. It is a good idea to place the ad in both the hometown newspaper and the county newspaper, if both are available. If the property is lake property, a hobby farm, etc., it may also pay to place the ad in both the Minneapolis Star and Tribune and the St. Paul Dispatch and Pioneer Press. For those individuals in the Twin City area, the following newspapers, among others, are available:

1. Minneapolis Star and Tribune
2. St. Paul Dispatch and Pioneer Press
3. Sun Newspapers
4. Lillie Suburban Newspapers
5. Various county and individually suburban newspapers

A good description will run approximately eight lines, which can range in price from $5.00 to as much as $50.00 per printing, depending on the newspaper.

<u>Community Bulletins</u>

Other forms of effective advertising may include fliers in your neighborhood and posters in local stores and shops. Word of mouth advertising can also be very effective.

<u>Display a "For Sale by Owner" Sign</u>

A simple sign with the words "For Sale by Owner" is almost a necessity. This sign should be approximately 24" by 36", contain the telephone number in bold, easy to read lettering, and be displayed in the yard so that it is clearly visible. You may wish to add the words "By

Appointment Only" at the bottom to avoid the problem of people knocking at your door at those unexpected, inconvenient hours. (However, be aware that some of this still may occur.) If you own a corner lot, you may wish to display two signs, so that the sign is visible from both streets.

NOTE: Remember, when you are selling your home yourself, you will attract individuals who believe they can benefit by the price savings of by-passing a real estate agent.

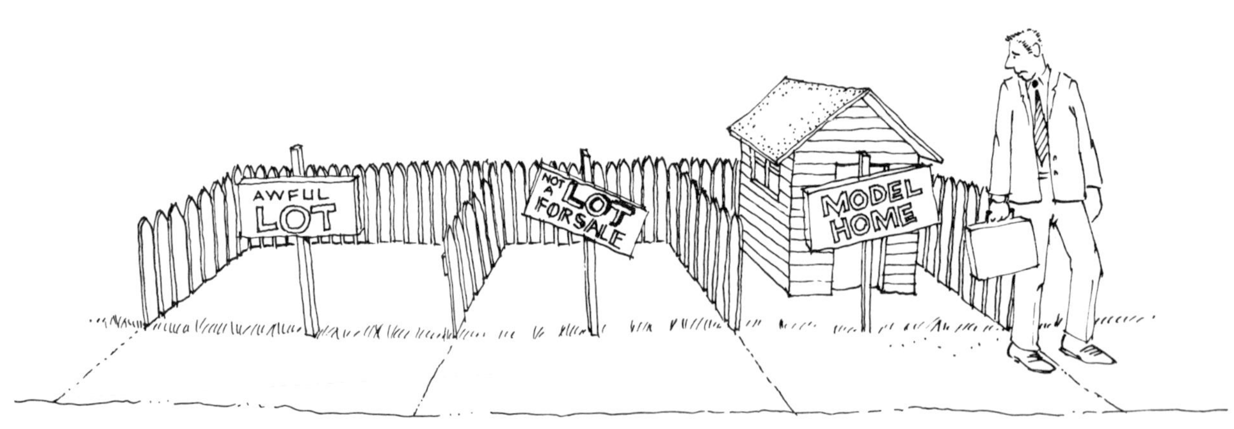

HOW TO PREPARE YOUR HOME FOR SALE

It is very important to freshen up your home and do cosmetic types of improvements which may increase the appeal and salability of your home. A small investment made in this manner could increase the appraised price and thus your sale price substantially. However, excessive improvements will probably not be profitable to you.

The home should be prepared for sale prior to the appraisal. This is especially true if a professional appraiser is used to determine the value of the real estate. Early preparation will help you even if you use a real estate agent because the licensed real estate agent's first impression is vital in affecting the valuing process for selecting potential buyers.

HOME IMPROVEMENT CHECKLIST

A CHECKLIST EVERY SELLER SHOULD HAVE

On the following page is a checklist of improvements which may aid in the salability of your real estate. Check off the items as you complete them. There are additional blank lines available for your use to individualize to your needs. Go through your house as though you were seeing it for the first time and add those items to the checklist that you think should be improved before the real estate is placed on the market or offered for sale.

HOME IMPROVEMENT CHECKLIST

Cross out those items which are not applicable to your home. Place a check mark before the items as you complete them.

	Touch up paint chips and/or scratches on walls and ceilings
	Paint the living room
	Paint the kitchen
	Paint the bedrooms
	Paint the bathroom
	Paint the hallway
	Check walls and floors for cracks and unsightly marks
	Wax and shine floors
	Clean carpets and replace worn spots (or cover with throw rugs)
	Clean cupboards
	Clean and scour kitchen appliances
	Clean and polish furniture
	Scour sink, tub and toilet in bathroom
	Check the basement for water spots and remedy problems if any
	Be sure all rooms are orderly and uncluttered
	Make the lawn look manicured - rejuvinate the greenery
	Clean and patch gutters
	Sidewalks should be in good condition
	Paint any trim that is cracked or peeling; replace or repair loose siding
	Doorbell and all lights are working (no burned out bulbs)
	Clean and unclutter the garage
	Position lawn furniture and other decorative ornaments around the yard to give it a "cozy" look
	Replace or repair missing shingles

SHOWING YOUR PROPERTY

Showings should be handled with diplomacy and delicacy. Be honest and straightforward with the potential buyer. Let your house sell itself, rather than trying to sell the house verbally.

It is a good idea for the children and the pets to be absent from the home during the showings. Further, lights should be on and the television off.

When showing your home, especially at private showings, begin with the most impressive room of the house and end in that room. The potential buyer will have a positive impression at the beginning and at the end.

Remain honest and open concerning all the characteristics of the house. A potential buyer will point out the defects in the house, or some disadvantage about the house or its location. Expect this and do not let it upset you. Combat each defect with a positive attribute of your home or property. You are probably quite aware of the defects and should be expecting comments on them. Remain objective about your house. In discussing it, admit the weaknesses, but also show the comparative value of this house as opposed to other houses. Generally, the best response to "nit-picky" issues is no response. If there is a problem that will be taken care of before the sale it should be explained.

PREPARE A HOME INFORMATION SHEET THAT SELLS

You will find in the appendix of this book a page entitled "Home Information Sheet." It is self-explanatory and should be filled out by you with plenty of copies available for potential buyers to take with them. If you fill out this information, you will be prepared to answer most of the key questions a serious buyer will want to know. Also, you will want the serious buyer to take the sheet with him/her so that it can be used to compare your house with others he/she will see. Note that the Home Information Sheet includes information such as your personal data, where you can be contacted, special features of the house, size of rooms, and most importantly, your purchase price request. Even though there is a sample in the appendix, this is how a home improvement sheet reads:

HOME INFORMATION SHEET

Owner______________________________Res. Ph.______________________
Address____________________________Bus. Ph.______________________
Price____________No. of bedrooms_______Style of Home__________
Exterior__________Sq. footage________Electric (amp)__________
Heat/Fuel System__________Year Built__________________________
Tax Base________________Lot Size________________________________
School District___________Financing Terms______________________

Room	Size	Room	Size
Kitchen	______	Master bedroom	______
Living room	______	Bedroom #2	______
Dining room	______	Bedroom #3	______
Rec. room	______	Basement	______

Central Air	_____	Garbage Disposal	_____
Fireplace	_____	Range & Oven	_____
Dishwasher	_____	Hood Fan	_____
Well Water	_____	Septic Tank	_____
Finished Basement	_____	One Car Garage	_____
Central Vacuum	_____	Two Car Garage	_____
Rec Room	_____	Window Air	_____
Master Bath	_____	220 Volt	_____
Two Baths	_____	110 Volt	_____

Comments____
____
____
____

NEGOTIATING WITH THE POTENTIAL BUYER

The buyer will attempt to negotiate a lower price for the real estate than the seller has set as its value. It is recommended that you be fairly firm in your price. If you are confident in your appraised value, you should not have to come down much in price. However, if you are not confident in the value, your attempt to be conciliatory will probably make a potential buyer "leary."

If the buyer makes an offer, have him/her commit that offer to writing by signing a Purchase Agreement. The Purchase Agreement is a detailed legal document which will be discussed in Chapter VIII.

The Purchase Agreement is not a binding agreement until both the buyer and the seller have signed it and each party has a copy. Therefore, any offers received from potential buyers should be committed to writing. Ideally, you may have several offers from which you can pick and choose. When you sign the Purchase Agreement and both you and the buyer have copies, it becomes a contract and you are bound to it.

WHEN REAL ESTATE AGENTS COME TO CALL

A real estate agent is just that: an agent. If you have hired or anticipate hiring a real estate agent, remember he or she is to follow your instructions. The agent is to represent you and your interest in selling the house.

If you decide not to retain a real estate agent to sell your real estate, be aware of some of the techniques real estate agents may use to obtain you as a client.

Beware of the agent who desires to be helpful and conciliatory, but in reality is looking at you as a potential client. When a real estate agent comes to your house, he may try to intimidate you by asking you if you have had any "firm" offers yet. Do not let this kind of question make you feel insecure or inferior. Many times you will not get a firm offer until you find the "right" buyer and there is nothing wrong with this.

An agent may request a tour of your house, stating he is looking for a house for a client. Be skeptical. Remember, if you have embarked upon selling the house yourself, be firm with the agent and say you are not interested. If that potential buyer is really interested in the house, he can contact you. After all, you have your own "For Sale" sign on the property.

Never tell the real estate agent that you must sell the house quickly. The agent may interpret this to mean that you are "desperate" and continue to attempt to secure you as a client as time runs out on your schedule.

The real estate agent may tell you the benefits you obtain by hiring an agent. He may attempt to entice you with an offer of a free appraisal, the opportunity to be listed on the "multiple listings service", the fact that advertising costs you nothing if he handles your listing. These are nothing more than small carrots or inducements. The real cost to you is usually the 7% real estate commission. That is 7% of the selling price of your real estate. If you are really sincere about selling your real estate yourself, you must remain firm and resist real estate agents.

If you decide to use a real estate agent, it is important to fully understand the listing agreement. A sample listing agreement follows with an explanation of each of its paragraphs. Review this carefully and read in detail any listing agreement provided to you by a real estate agent. If you do not understand some of the terms used, ask for clarification.

SAMPLE LISTING AGREEMENT

Address____
List Price____________________Terms_________________________
To:____, realtor.

In consideration of your efforts, expenditures and your agreement to list in your office the real estate ("property") described hereon and to place this property on the Multiple Listing Service of the St. Paul Area Board of Realtors, Inc., I hereby appoint you my agent and grant the exclusive right to sell the property described hereon for the listing price and terms hereon set forth or such other price and terms which I may hereafter accept.

This agreement and agency shall remain in effect until ________. If, before the expiration of this agreement I receive a written offer consistent with the terms of this listing, or other terms accepted by me, I agree to pay you a commission of _____% of the sale price, whether such is obtained by you, by me, by any member of the Multiple Listing Service of the St. Paul Area Board of Realtors, or any other party.

I further agree to pay you at the same rate of commission should I contract to sell or exchange the property within ______ days after the expiration date of this agreement to any person to whom during the period of this agreement makes inquiry to me regarding this property. However, I shall not be obligated to pay you a commission if during the protection period I have entered into another valid listing agreement pursuant to which I am required to pay a commission to another real estate broker for the contract for sale or exchange of this property.

Permission is granted to you to submit pertinent information concerning this property to the Multiple Listing Service, and upon execution of a purchase agreement for the property, to notify the Multiple Listing Service of such sale and to disseminate sales information to the members of the Multiple Listing Service. The Multiple Listing Service, the listing broker and the selling broker shall not be liable for errors or omissions on the attached data form.

I agree to cooperate with you during the term of this agreement and will directly refer to you the names of all persons or parties making inquiries concerning this property. You shall be given access to the property at reasonable times upon request. Your right to access to the property shall carry no obligation or responsibility for maintenance including the heating of the structure and snow removal, whether the property is occupied or vacant.

You are given permission to place or erect a "For Sale" sign on the property.

Receipt is hereby acknowledged of a copy of this listing agreement.

Date__________________
Owner________________________________Bus. Ph.________________
Address______________________________Res. Ph.________________
BROKER_______________________________By______________________

EXPLANATION OF LISTING AGREEMENT

It is important to understand any legal document you sign. Should you choose to retain a real estate agent to sell your home, he/she will most likely explain the pertinent parts of the listing agreement. But, even so, read the document.

Paragraph 1 - you agree that the agent (and the agency for which that agent works) has the exclusive right to sell your home. You agree to sell at the price listed, or such other price as you may agree. In other words, you cannot decide, after receiving an offer for the listed price, to change your mind and want more for your home. You can accept an offer for less than the listed price. (During periods of low interest rates and high housing demands you may receive more than one offer. You can, of course, choose to accept the offer that is higher than your asking price under those circumstances).

Paragraph 2 - the agent has your home listed until that date filled in on the Agreement. If the home sells during that period of time, you will pay the agent a commission of a certain percent. It doesn't matter who found the buyer. If during that time you found the buyer, you still have to pay the commission.

Paragraph 3 - after the listing agreement expires, the agent still has the right to receive his commission for a certain number of days (he will fill this in; it is usually 30 days) if you sell to anyone the agent talked to while he/she had the home listed. This is to prevent a seller from "cutting a deal" with a prospective buyer who found out about the home through the agent's efforts, but waits until the listing agreement expires to purchase the home. However, if you enter into a listing agreement with another agency, then this paragraphs does not apply.

Paragraph 4 - you agree to allow the agent to put information about your home in a catalog of homes for sale (Multiple Listing) and to give information about your home to other agents who are members of the Multiple Listing Service. Be sure the information the agent puts on his information sheet is accurate. If you knowingly make false statements or omit facts, you could be held liable for those falsities or omissions.

Paragraph 5. You agree to cooperate with your agent and allow him/her to show the property at reasonable times. The agent is not responsible for maintaining your home.

KNOW HOW TO USE A LIMITED LISTING AGREEMENT

The real estate agent may indeed have a buyer who is interested in your property. Under these circumstances, you may offer the real estate agent a Limited Listing Agreement. A listing agreement is nothing more than an agreement where a potential client or owner of a house agrees to let a real estate agent attempt to sell the house for a certain period of time. If the sale is perfected within that period of time, the real estate agent is entitled to collect a commission for his efforts in obtaining the sale.

If the agent has a potential buyer, you and the agent may enter into a Limited Listing Agreement, which states that the real estate agent is entitled to a commission if the real estate is sold to that particular buyer. However, you may want to negotiate the real estate agent's commission under thse circumstancees. A two to three percent commission may be reasonable. (Before signing any agreement, including the Limited Listing Agreement, read it carefully to be sure it states what you believe it should state.)

KNOW HOW THE REAL ESTATE COMMISSION WORKS

The commission is divided amongst the broker, the selling agent and the listing agent. Therefore, no real estate agent ever receives the full commission, unless he is a broker who listed the property (obtained the client) and sold the property.

Remember, when you are trying to sell the property yourself, you are similar to the listing agent. Ask the real estate agent what the usual percentage is for a selling agent or call some real estate agencies and find out. In this way, you will give the real estate agent a fair share of the commission, but also give yourself that part of the "commission" you deserve or what a listing agent would obtain.

THE FULL LISTING AGREEMENT

Should you decide to retain a real estate agent to aid in the sale of your home, you will most likely be required to pay a 7% commission. Again, read the listing agreement carefully to see that it states what you believe it should state. Find out how long a period of time the agent has to sell your home. It is probably a good idea not to allow a listing agreement to last for more than ninety days. This protects you should you find that you and the real estate agent cannot agree on the procedures for selling the real estate or you have any other type of disagreement. Should you sign a listing agreement for any longer period of time, you are obligated to allow the agent to attempt to sell the home for that period of time. Some agents ask for listing agreements for 180 days and the seller does not challenge it. Under those circumstances, six months can prove to be an eternity. (You usually have the option of taking your home off the market during that time, but you cannot re-list with another agency until the expiration of the listing agreement).

Remember, that if the real estate agent has not sold the real estate within the listing period, you have the option of renewing the listing agreement if you feel that the real estate agent is doing a good job, or of finding another real estate agent if you do not feel the agent is doing a good job or you would like to try an agent with a different approach. In many cases, switching real estate agents can make all the difference in the world.

Most real estate agents have listing agreement forms and the potential client usually does not need to provide these forms. However, for your information, a sample Listing Agreement is included in the appendix.

YOU'VE FOUND A BUYER

After the potential buyer has submitted a Purchase Agreement (Earnest Money Contract) along with his Earnest Money (usually $500) and you have decided to accept the offer, the next step is completing the sale:

a. Be sure you have shown the buyer the Truth in Housing Report (if applicable).

b. If a real estate agent is involved, the final steps will probably be taken care of by the agent. If not, you will need to read the following more carefully.

c. Have your abstract updated (this will be discussed in more detail in Part VI).

d. Have the documents prepared and ready to go before the closing date. The buyer may request a copy of the documents to review prior to sale. (See Chapter IV for a more detailed description of the documents required.)

e. At the closing the documents will be signed and money exchanged. NOTE: DO NOT ACCEPT A PERSONAL CHECK AS PAYMENT FOR YOUR REAL ESTATE. ONLY ACCEPT CERTIFIED CHECKS, BANK CHECKS, AND, OF COURSE, CASH. NEVER ACCEPT A PERSONAL CHECK.

f. After you have sold your real estate or during the process of selling your real estate, you may also be looking for new property to purchase. If so, you will probably need to arrange both closings so that they are within a few days or even a few hours of each other. Be sure to arrange the closing of your present property *first* so that you have the finances available to close on your new property.

It is a good idea to have a contingency clause in the Purchase Agreement. If you are the buyer you may want the sale contingent upon obtaining financing or upon the sale of your current home; if you are the seller, you may want the sale contingent upon closing taking place by a certain date.

CHAPTER II
BUYING A HOME THAT YOU CAN ENJOY FOR YEARS TO COME

Although lending institutions will tell you how large a mortgage you qualify for, you must decide for yourself how large a monthly payment you can afford. This will dictate how much you can pay for a house. You should make this decision before you even begin to look at houses.

At the back of this book is a table which shows the monthly payments for homes at various prices and interest rates. Calls to a few lending institutions will tell you what kind of interest rate you will be looking at for your new mortgage. Once you have that information you can look at the tables to see what the monthly payments will be on homes at different prices.

Remember, the amounts in the table are <u>mortgage</u> amounts, not the value of the home you will be buying. It is assumed you have some money you will be using as a down payment (be sure to keep enough for closing costs, though). The amount of your down payment should be added to the amount to be mortgaged to find out what price range you should be looking in for your home.

Mortgage companies will usually approve principal, interest, taxes and insurance payments that average 25% of gross monthly income, (although this can vary) and 33% of gross monthly income, including principal, interest, taxes and insurance and long term debts. For example, if you earn $2,000 per month and have no debts, you should be able to qualify for a mortgage payment of $500.00 per month (plus taxes and insurance, which will be added on top of the mortgage). But do you feel you can afford this? It is now time to sit down with paper and pencil and analyze your budget. After your fixed obligations and the monthly mortgage, what is left? Is that adequate? Or should you be looking for some way to lower the mortgage amount either through creative financing or lowering the price range of the homes you will be viewing. Make this decision now and save yourself disappointment later.

VIEWING THE PROSPECTIVE PROPERTY

HOW TO USE A BUYER'S CHECKLIST TO YOUR ADVANTAGE

On the following page is a checklist of some of the items you should investigate before you purchase a certain house. You may wish to carry this list with you as you view properties so that you are aware of questions to be answered about each prospective property. You may wish to make several copies of the checklist, put the address of the property at the top and check those areas which are applicable to that particular house. Space has been left so that you can make comments about each item. There is also space at the bottom for you to make any other notes you may wish to make.

Property Address______________________

Asking Price_________________________

	1. Try to find out who the builder of the house is. Check his credentials and track record.
	2. Investigate the tax base for the City, County, Town, or Township where the property is located. In addition to your mortgage payments, you must consider your tax payments.
	3. If the neighborhood is new, are there fire hydrants, sidewalks, police protection, good transportation and trash removal.
	4. What is the location of schools, school buses, public transportation, bus stops, etc.
	5. Consider the features of the neighborhood, including shopping centers, public recreation facilities, parks, zoos, tennis courts, community playgrounds.
	6. Consider the feasibility of having the seller certify the property against termites.
	7. Check the repairable status of the house to determine how many repairs will be necessary.
	8. Check utility hookups. Does the house have only electricity for appliances? Or is there also gas available? If your appliances are gas, you may have a problem if there is no gas hookup available.

9. Check the power supply, the wiring; is it at least 60 amp? Preferably 100 amp? Is the wiring up to code? How many outlets are there in each room?
10. Have an insulation inspection. A house which is improperly insulated can cost more in fuel bills than would otherwise be expected.
11. Check the water pipes. Are they the originals? Splicing or variable pipes may be an indication of frozen pipe problems.
12. Is the plumbing up to code?
13. Check the sound level of the house. It is a good idea to have someone walk on the second floor and yell to you on the ground level.
14. If there is well water, have it checked for purity.
15. Check the age and condition of the furnace.
16. Check around the chimney area for leakage (which indicates improper flashing).
17. Check the roof. When was the last time it was reroofed? Are there missing shingles?
18. Check around the sinks and tubs for proper caulking.

19. Check to see that doors hang evenly and properly, especially if the house is older and may have settled.

20. Check for broken windows. Do the windows all work properly?

21. Check the water pressure. What happens if you turn on two faucets - one in the bathroom and one in the kitchen, for example?

22. How old is the water heater? Ask the owners if they have had any problem with it. How large a tank does it have?

23. Check the eaves troughs. Are they adequate and in good condition?

24. Are there outside faucets? Are they located properly?

25. Does the basement show any signs of leakage? Ask the owners if they have had any problems with a wet basement. Look for evidence of water stains.

26. Will there be space for your clothes line and garden?

27. What personal property comes with the house? Do all the drapes stay? What about appliances? Find this out early since this can be a source of conflict between buyer and seller.

Having a checklist like that just provided may help you find what you are looking for in a house and help you to check on things that are easily forgotten in the excitement of a new real estate purchase.

AS A BUYER, WHAT SHOULD YOU KNOW ABOUT INSPECTIONS AND APPRAISALS?

A buyer of real estate will probably find that his lending institution will appraise the property for him to make sure it is of high enough value to secure a loan. This appraisal does not guarantee that the property is free of major defects or that the house's basic systems and structures are adequate.

If you do not live in an area that requires a Truth in Housing Inspection, you may wish to have an independent inspection done on the house. The cost is approximately $75.00.

Do not be embarrassed to ask the seller to allow such an inspection. After all, this will probably be the single most expensive investment in your entire life.

If you do not have an appraisal done through the lending institution, you may want to find out from the seller how he arrived at the asking price for the property. Was there an appraisal done on the property or was the price picked out of the air because it sounded "reasonable?" Find out.

If there is an inspection-appraisal done through the lending institution (most often with FHA or VA mortgages), certain defects may need to be corrected before the final steps of the sale can be completed. If so, this is usually the responsibility of the seller.

If there are certain items you wish to be repaired before buying the property, feel free to set them out in detail in the Purchase Agreement.

YOU'VE FOUND THAT SPECIAL HOME, NOW WHAT?

After you have found the real estate that you believe is right for you, the following steps are usually completed:

a. Make an offer to the seller in the form of a Purchase Agreement. You will accompany your offer by a check for usually $500.00 to $1,000.00. Some sellers may require a larger sum as earnest money.

b. After the seller has accepted your offer, signed the Purchase Agreement and returned a copy to you, check it over carefully. Did he make any changes in your offer? If so, you do not need to accept the counter offer. Be sure that if the seller is married that the spouse has also signed the Purchase Agreement. RULE: IT TAKES ONLY ONE TO BUY, BUT TWO TO SELL.

c. Arrange for financing of the property. You may want to investigate and negotiate financing before signing the purchase agreement or put into the purchase agreement that the purchase is contingent upon obtaining financing at a certain interest rate and for a certain number of points.

When arranging for the financing, be aware that you will be required to pay closing costs and points. Be sure to allow enough money to pay this amount, which is due at closing. A rule of thumb is that closing costs are approximately 2 1/2% to 3% of the purchase price.

d. Check into obtaining Title Insurance. Be sure that if there is title insurance on your new property, that you have it placed in your name also, not just the mortgage company's name.

e. Have an attorney complete a title opinion for you. It will probably take two to four weeks from the time the Purchase Agreement is signed for the seller to have the Abstract of Title brought up to date. In most cases, after the up-dating (continuation) has been completed, it will be delivered to your attorney.

f. Prepare for the closing. Any cash you are to pay at closing must be in the form of a certified check. Personal checks are not accepted.

g. The possession date is set forth in your Purchase Agreement. This may be the date of closing or approximately two days after closing, to give the seller time to move.

h. After the closing it will be your responsibility to see that the conveyance documents are filed. In most cases, the title insurance company will take care of the filing process. The required documents and the filing procedure are set out in Chapter IV of this book.

KNOW ABOUT MARKETABLE TITLE AND HOW TO OBTAIN IT

The definition of marketable title may vary somewhat, depending on the context in which it is used. For purposes of handling the purchase of your own real estate, all you need to know about marketable title is that it is good title, without encumbrances or defects or other difficulties. From your point of view as a purchaser, you want to make sure you buy property that is not "haunted" with hidden legal problems.

There are two ways to assure you, as a prospective purchaser that the property you are purchasing is marketable and not encumbered by any of the defects above mentioned: (1) you may obtain title insurance, and/or (2) have an attorney complete a title opinion.

WHAT IS TITLE INSURANCE

Title insurance is insurance from a special type of company, called a title insurance company. This company insures against legal defects. If you are obtaining a mortgage, it is usually a requirement that title insurance be purchased. Even though you pay for this insurance at the time of closing, the insurance only protects the mortgage company. Therefore, you must request that the title insurance be placed in your name as well if you wish to be protected. This will cost an additional sum of money; however, it is money well spent. If you have a real estate agent, request that he notify the title insurance company that you wish an owner's policy of title insurance. If you do not have a real estate agent, you should be able to obtain the name of the title insurance company from the bank through which you have applied for your mortgage. You may have the real estate agent or bank request the owner's policy on your behalf or you may call the title insurance company yourself and request this policy. You will pay for the insurance at the time of closing. This is a one time payment and insures your title until such time as you sell the property.

You may request a brochure from the title insurance company which will explain their coverage. Chances are that if you have applied for a mortgage, you will receive such a brochure in the mail without requesting one. Read it over, and if you have any questions on the coverage, give the company a call. Just like other insurance companies, coverage may vary from company to company. So be sure that the brochure you obtain is from the company that will be handling your title insurance.

WHAT IS A TITLE OPINION AND WHEN DO YOU NEED IT

You may request a title opinion from an attorney. This will cost you anywhere from $50.00 to $100.00 or more, depending on the attorney's fee schedule. The attorney will review your Abstract of Title and give you his opinion of the encumbrances that exist upon the real estate, inform you of any easements, liens, debts or other difficulties in the title in terms which you should be able to understand so that you can purchase the property with knowledge of any perils which may be present. The attorney will also review the abstract's chain of title to be sure that you will be receiving "good title." The title opinion will probably contain suggestions on how to remedy defects in title, should any be found.

Requesting a title opinion from an attorney does not bind you to any other services which may be offered. If the lawyer offers to perform further services, reserve that decision until you feel having complete legal representation is really in your best interest. You can determine this after the title opinion is written.

A copy of an abbreviated title opinion follows. Realize that the title opinion will be tailored to that piece of property in question.

Sample Title Opinion

Dear Mr. Doe:

I have examined the title to the following described property located in Lyon County, State of Minnesota, to-wit:

Lot Six (6), Block Four (4) Jameson Addition

by examining the Abstract of Title.

From such examination I am of the opinion that as of the above date, title to said premises was good of record in Mary Smith and Joe Smith, husband and wife. That the title is free and clear of all encumbrances of every nature and description except:

1. There is a judgment against Joe E. Smith, entry #215, recorded as document #123456. If Joe Smith and Joe E. Smith are not one and the same person, Joe Smith should file an Affidavit stating such. If Joe Smith and Joe E. Smith are one and the same, a Satisfaction of Judgment or Partial Release of Judgment should be obtained from the creditor and filed prior to the purchase.

2. Mortgage through First National Bank running to Mary Smith and Joe Smith, husband and wife, entry #205, recorded as document #012345 in the amount of $10,456.00.

3. All taxes for the year 1985 and prior years are paid.

4. Subject to the rights of any person or persons in possession of the premises above described.

5. Subject to the right of any person or persons to claim a lien on the premises herein for work performed within the last 120 days.

6. Subject to all encroachments and other matters that might be ascertained by an actual survey and inspection of the premises above described.

7. Subject to existing zoning, building regulations and ordinances.

8. Subject to unpaid installments of special assessments now levied but not yet due and payable.

Marketable title is also discussed in greater detail in Chapter VI of this book.

Once the buyer is assured that the property is free of any clouds and the closing date is set, he/she must obtain financing. It is suggested that this search commence as soon as the purchase agreement is signed and accepted by both parties. Preliminary investigation into financing can be started as soon as you decide to buy a new home, but cannot be finalized until a specific home has been found.

Details of the financing and the closing are dicussed in Chapters III and IV.

CHAPTER III
FINANCING:
NECESSARY FOR THE SELLER WHO WANTS TO SELL AND NECESSARY FOR THE BUYER WHO WANTS TO BUY

Many times financing is the key to a sale of the property. Both the buyer and seller should be flexible in conceiving creative financing ideas. This may be by allowing the buyer to assume the seller's mortgage or by having the seller extend credit to the buyer by way of an installment contract, called a Contract for Deed. There are other types of financing discussed below, but the key to success in this area is FLEXIBILITY.

During periods when inflation and interest rates are low, obtaining financing is usually easy, but during times of high inflation and high interest rates, it is more difficult. Qualifying for a mortgage becomes harder because high interest means high monthly payments. It is during those times that creative financing is really necessary. New types of mortgages surface, new creative ideas take hold. A buyer must investigate these carefully before going ahead to be sure they are the best deals for him/her. Read the articles that appear in the newspapers almost weekly discussing new financing methods. These articles usually detail the pros and cons of these financing opportunities.

STRAIGHT CASH PURCHASE

The easiest form of financing to conceptualize is the cash purchase. Here the buyer simply pays in cash the actual amount of money the seller requests. No credit approvals or inspections are necessary. The problem with this method is that the cost of housing is so high these days that very few people can afford to make a cash outlay in the amount required to buy a house. Therefore, one must look to another type of financing.

CONVENTIONAL FINANCING

Conventional financing is probably the next most popular method of buying a house. This type of financing involves assistance from a bank, savings and loan or mortgage company. The lending institution typically pays seventy to eighty percent of the purchase price, requiring the buyer to pay twenty to thirty percent of the purchase price as a down payment (this amount varies with the availability of mortgage money). The buyer of the house then pays the bank back in monthly installments, plus interest.

Payments are spread over a fifteen to thirty year period. The main sources of this type of loan are the savings and loans, commercial banks, mortgage companies and some credit unions. The lending institution is secured by a mortgage on the real estate, which they can foreclose upon should payments not be met.

INSURED CONVENTIONAL FINANCING

Under this method of financing, the buyer may be able to purchase property without having to come up with twenty or thirty percent down payment. Instead, he may only be required to make a down payment of five to ten percent of the selling price. The interest rates are the same as those for conventional mortgages, but the buyer must pay premiums to a mortgage insurance company. The buyer goes to the same type of lending institution mentioned above. However, the lending institutions are more ready to finance the purchase of the real estate if they know that the payments are insured by a major insurance corporation. For this insurance premium, the buyer must pay an additional fee which is dependent upon the loan relationship to the value of the property.

ARMS (ADJUSTABLE RATE MORTGAGES)

Fixed rate mortgages are only one way to finance the purchase of property. Another method is the adjustable rate mortgage, called ARM. At the present time these rates are around 8 1/2 to 9 1/2 percent. ARMS usually have a guaranteed rate for one year. After that the rates are adjusted annually according to one, three and five year treasury security rates. Most ARMs increase for a set number of years and then stablize at a higher interest rate than when first incurred. Be cautious when agreeing to an ARM. Be sure there is a ceiling on the amount the mortgage can increase in a given year and also over the life of the mortgage. A common ceiling is two percent per year and five percent over the life of the mortgage.

FHA (FEDERAL HOUSING ADMINISTRATION) MORTGAGE

These loans are very similar to the above, except that they are insured by the Federal Housing Administration in much the same way as Insured Conventional Mortgages, and allow buyers to purchase real estate for three to ten percent down payment, with a maximum purchase price. The repayment period is usually up to thirty years. Though the interest rates charged for this type of financing may be lower than for conventional financing, there is an additional charge for this insurance payable either in cash at the time of closing or borrowed and added to the mortgage balance. While the amount varies, it has been averaging 3% of the mortgage amount for a mortgage extending over thirty years. For mortgages that are repaid in a shorter period of time, the charge is somewhat less. Points are also charged at the time of closing. (Points are a percentage of the mortgage amount; one point equals one percent.) The FHA has a ceiling on the amount it can loan. Presently this amount is $90,000.00. This may change periodically so check with a lending institution to find out what is the mortgage limit.

The same lending institutions, including banks, savings and loans, mortgage companies, and some credit unions are qualified to extend FHA loans.

In order for the FHA to insure the mortgage, certain specifications must be met. There must be an inspection of the real estate. Any defects noted on the inspection report must be repaired prior to the closing, with a reinspection conducted. The lending institution will contact the appraiser for the purposes of the inspection. (You should not rely on this inspection to uncover all defects in the property; it does not necessarily do so. Rather, it is just an inspection which meets federal financing requirements.)

Obtaining an FHA mortgage may take longer than a conventional loan because of the time delay required for the inspection. The lending institution must also obtain permission from the Federal Housing Administration to finance the real estate.

VA (VETERAN'S ADMINISTRATION) MORTGAGE

VA loans are similar to FHA loans, except that one of the parties to the purchase must be a veteran of the United States Armed Forces. Please read the above section for details about how this program works. The loan is guaranteed by the Veteran's Administration. The terms of the loan allow no down payment and repayment of the loan for up to thirty years. Interest rates are governed by a maximum set by law, plus additional amounts for insurance premiums as discussed above. There is no prepayment penalty for this kind of loan and it is lower than most other types of financing. These loans are still limited to an amount of $110,000.00.

FIFTEEN VS. THIRTY YEAR MORTGAGES

When thinking about purchasing a home, most people automatically assume the mortgage will extend over thirty years. The general rule of thumb has been that the higher your tax bracket, the better off you are with a thirty year mortgage because the interest can be deducted over a longer period of time.

A mortgage can be shortened to as little as fifteen years, which adds about fifteen percent to the monthly payment over the thirty year mortgage, but it does have its advantages. The principal is repaid faster, so that the total cost of the home is less than if the mortgage is extended over thirty years. There is also a peace of mind that accompanies early repayment of a mortgage especially for someone approaching retirement age. Also, those electing to repay their mortgage over fifteen years instead of thirty years may actually find that the lending institution will give them a lower rate of interest.

Whether a thirty year mortgage or a fifteen year mortgage is best is up to you. Decide whether you want extra cash now that you can use for investment or whether you would rather repay the mortgage over a shorter period of time at a somewhat higher monthly payment, but have it paid off in half the time.

MORTGAGES AVAILABLE TO LOW AND MODERATE INCOME PEOPLE

Loans are made available by the same lending institutions mentioned above and are designed to aid low and moderate income people in the purchase of real estate. These are available through the Department of Housing and Urban Development (HUD). A call to their office should let a prospective buyer know if any programs are currently available. The terms of these loans usually include low down payment set at the discretion of the lending institution, but usually lower than those required for conventional mortgages. The down payments on these mortgages usually average about ten percent of the total purchase price.

There is usually a thirty year repayment, with the interest rate the same as those for FHA mortgages, a maximum which is set by law. These loans are insured through the VA, too.

GRADUATED PAYMENT MORTGAGES

This arrangement, known as the graduated payment plan, is available to buyers who can show that they have a potential for income increases. Loans made under this plan are made by the same lenders mentioned above. The loans are insured by the Federal Housing Administration There are several plans which may be used. Basically, these plans provide for a low down payment, reduced payments which increase over a five to ten year period and stabalize after approximately seven to ten years at a set monthly payment which is paid at that set rate until the mortgage is paid off in full. The person who qualifies under this type of financing gets the benefit of graduated payments which coincide with his/her earning increases. There is a maximum mortgage amount which should be investigated by the buyer. There is no prepayment penalty, except that if the house is sold before the reduced payment is over, an additional interest payment would have to be made to the lender at the time of closing.

A drawback to this type of financing is the fact that the loan balance actually increases the first few years. If the owner wishes to sell during that time period, he could end up owing more than the original loan amount. Once the initial years are past, this is no longer a problem. Therefore, a person considering this type of financing needs to analyze whether he plans on owning the home for a long time.

To qualify for these loans, a buyer must show that his/her income will be increasing about nine percent a year to meet the increased payment burdens required.

BUYDOWN OF CONVENTIONAL MORTGAGE

Another possible way to finance a home is to buydown the interest rate. This requires a payment at the time of closing based on the percentage that the mortgage is to be bought down. If the buyer has enough cash to take advantage of this, it is an excellent way to reduce future mortgage payments. However, it does require a larger down payment.

MINNESOTA HOUSING FINANCING AGENCY LOANS

At times there are state programs which allow lower income persons to purchase new construction or affordable existing homes. The down payment requirements vary. There are extra closing costs and origination fees which amount to approximately 2 1/2% of the loan which must be paid at the time of purchase. The annual interest rate is usually lower than those that can be found in other methods described above.

CONTRACT FOR DEED

A Contract for Deed is simply an installment arrangement of payment or a loan which the seller of the property usually makes available to a prospective buyer. It is usually used when regular financing is not available to a prospective buyer or when there is a shortage between the down payment and an assumed mortgage. The down payment is negotiable between the buyer and seller. There is no minimum or maximum amount of money that can be financed under the Contract for Deed. There is a limit on the amount of interest that can be charged based upon the usury laws.

It is up to the seller of the real estate to investigate whether or not the potential buyer will be able to meet the monthly obligations of the Contract for Deed. When a bank is involved, it will check into the credit background of the potential buyer, and his income. The rule of thumb is that the mortgage (or contract for deed) payments should not exceed 25% of the buyer's gross monthly income.

A common form of constructing a Contract for Deed is to allow set payments for a certain number of years, after which a balloon or lump sum payment is required of the amount due. If that is the case, a buyer should be aware that he will be required to obtain alternative financing after that period and should make arrangements well in advance of the due date of the balloon payment. Many buyers have lost the property because they could not come up with financing within the time period required. Sellers are in a good position if payment is not made because they can cancel or foreclose on the Contract for Deed if the payments are not made as agreed.

A seller should also be aware of tax consequences of the balloon or lump sum payment and should discuss these consequences with his accountant or tax attorney before entering into a Contract for Deed.

Under this type of financing, the buyer must complete all payments and meet the provisions of the loan repayment in the Contract for Deed. After payments are completed, the seller then, and only then, has to convey the deed to the property. This is usually a simple matter of filling out the deed and conveying it to the buyer.

Since a Contract for Deed is usually a private financing device between two individuals, it is a good idea for the parties to retain an attorney to review the documents and make sure that all the matters are in good order. When the parties have the assistance of a lending institution in the purchase of real estate, there are already available to them trained professionals to review the documents and the need for a private attorney is not as great.

Note that the Contract for Deed is only a contract and actual ownership of the property is still with the seller until the Contract for Deed is paid off. Therefore, there is no proof of the sale unless the Contract for Deed is in fact recorded. Minnesota law now requires that the Contract for Deed be recorded within six months of the time it is signed although it is not uncommon to find unrecorded Contracts for Deed from past transactions.

How to Compute the Monthly Contract for Deed Payments

The following is a table which can be used to compute Contract for Deed payments. Remember, usury laws may allow a maximum interest rate to be charged on a Contract for Deed. Generally, what is legal for a lending institution to charge on a mortgage, it is legal for individuals to charge. The usury rate may fluctuate with the economy so this should be checked before entering into a Contract for Deed.

CONSTANT ANNUAL PERCENTAGE AMORTIZATION TABLE

Table of percent needed to amortize a principal amount, calculated on a monthly basis. Divide by 12 to determine amount of monthly payments. (Example: Annual amount of principal and interest necessary to amortize $100,000 loan; 25 years; 9½% interest. $100,000 x .1049 = $10,490. $10,490 ÷ 12 = $874.16 per month principal and interest).

RATE	8	$8\frac{1}{4}$	$8\frac{1}{2}$	$8\frac{3}{4}$	9	$9\frac{1}{4}$	$9\frac{1}{2}$	$9\frac{3}{4}$	10	$10\frac{1}{4}$	$10\frac{1}{2}$	$10\frac{3}{4}$	11	$11\frac{1}{4}$	$11\frac{1}{2}$	$11\frac{3}{4}$
Years																
5	24.34	24.48	24.62	24.77	24.92	25.06	25.21	25.35	25.50	25.66	25.80	25.94	26.10	26.24	26.40	26.54
6	21.04	21.19	21.34	21.49	21.64	21.78	21.93	22.09	22.24	22.39	22.54	22.69	22.85	23.00	23.16	23.32
7	18.71	18.86	19.01	19.16	19.31	19.46	19.62	19.77	19.93	20.09	20.24	20.40	20.56	20.71	20.87	21.02
8	16.97	17.12	17.28	17.43	17.59	17.74	17.90	18.06	18.21	18.37	18.54	18.70	18.85	19.02	18.18	19.34
9	15.63	15.78	15.94	16.10	16.26	16.42	16.58	16.74	16.90	17.06	17.23	17.39	17.56	17.72	17.89	18.06
10	14.56	14.72	14.88	15.04	15.21	15.37	15.53	15.70	15.86	16.03	16.20	16.37	16.54	16.70	16.87	17.05
11	13.70	13.87	14.03	14.19	14.36	14.52	14.69	14.86	15.03	15.20	15.37	15.54	15.72	15.89	16.07	16.25
12	12.99	13.16	13.33	13.49	13.66	13.83	14.00	14.17	14.35	14.52	14.70	14.87	15.05	15.23	15.41	15.59
13	12.40	12.57	12.74	12.71	13.08	13.25	13.43	13.60	13.78	13.96	14.14	14.32	14.50	14.68	14.87	15.05
14	11.90	12.07	12.24	12.42	12.59	12.77	12.95	13.12	13.30	13.49	13.67	13.85	14.04	14.22	14.41	14.59
15	11.47	11.65	11.82	12.00	12.18	12.36	12.54	12.72	12.90	13.08	13.27	13.45	13.64	13.84	14.03	14.22
16	11.10	11.28	11.46	11.64	11.82	12.00	12.18	12.37	12.56	12.74	12.94	13.13	13.32	13.51	13.70	13.90
17	10.78	10.96	11.14	11.33	11.51	11.70	11.88	12.07	12.26	12.46	12.65	12.84	13.03	13.22	13.43	13.62
18	10.50	10.69	10.87	11.06	11.24	11.43	11.62	11.81	12.00	12.19	12.40	12.59	12.79	12.98	13.19	13.39
19	10.26	10.44	10.63	10.82	11.01	11.20	11.39	11.58	11.78	11.98	12.18	12.37	12.58	12.78	12.98	13.19
20	10.04	10.23	10.42	10.61	10.80	11.00	11.19	11.39	11.59	11.78	11.99	12.19	12.40	12.60	12.80	13.01
21	9.85	10.04	10.33	10.43	10.62	10.82	11.01	11.21	11.41	11.62	11.82	12.02	12.23	12.44	12.65	12.86
22	9.68	9.87	10.07	10.26	10.46	10.66	10.86	11.06	11.26	11.46	11.68	11.88	12.08	12.30	12.40	12.72
23	9.53	9.72	9.92	10.12	10.32	10.52	10.72	10.93	11.13	11.33	11.54	11.75	11.96	12.18	12.29	12.61
24	9.39	9.59	9.79	9.99	10.19	10.39	10.60	10.81	11.01	11.22	11.44	11.65	11.87	12.07	12.30	12.52
25	9.27	9.47	9.67	9.87	10.08	10.28	10.49	10.70	10.91	11.12	11.34	11.56	11.77	11.99	12.20	12.42
26	9.16	9.36	9.56	9.77	9.97	10.18	10.39	10.60	10.82	11.03	11.24	11.46	11.68	11.89	12.01	12.34
27	9.06	9.26	9.47	9.67	9.88	10.09	10.31	10.52	10.73	10.94	11.16	11.39	11.60	11.82	11.94	12.28
28	8.97	9.17	9.38	9.59	9.80	10.01	10.23	10.44	10.66	10.88	11.10	11.32	11.54	11.77	11.99	12.22
29	8.88	9.09	9.30	9.51	9.73	9.94	10.16	10.38	10.59	10.81	11.04	11.26	11.48	11.71	11.94	12.17
30	8.81	9.02	9.23	9.45	9.66	9.88	10.10	10.31	10.54	10.76	10.98	11.21	11.44	11.66	11.89	12.12

CONSTANT ANNUAL PERCENTAGE AMORTIZATION TABLE

RATE	12	$12\frac{1}{4}$	$12\frac{1}{2}$	$12\frac{3}{4}$	13	$13\frac{1}{4}$	$13\frac{1}{2}$	$13\frac{3}{4}$	14	$14\frac{1}{4}$	$14\frac{1}{2}$	$14\frac{3}{4}$	15
5	26.70	26.86	27.00	27.16	27.36	27.47	27.61	27.77	27.92	28.08	28.24	28.39	28.55
6	23.47	23.63	23.78	23.94	24.10	24.25	24.41	24.58	24.73	24.89	25.06	25.21	25.38
7	21.19	21.36	21.52	21.67	21.84	22.00	22.16	22.33	22.50	22.66	22.82	22.99	23.16
8	19.51	19.68	19.84	20.00	20.17	20.34	20.51	20.68	20.86	21.02	21.19	21.37	21.54
9	18.23	18.40	18.56	18.74	18.91	19.08	19.26	19.43	19.61	19.79	19.96	20.14	20.32
10	17.22	17.40	17.57	17.75	17.93	18.10	18.28	18.46	18.64	18.82	19.00	19.19	19.37
11	16.42	16.60	16.78	16.96	17.14	17.32	14.50	17.69	17.87	18.06	18.24	18.43	18.61
12	15.77	15.95	16.13	16.32	16.50	16.69	16.87	17.06	17.26	17.44	17.63	17.82	18.01
13	15.23	15.42	15.60	15.79	15.98	16.18	16.36	16.56	16.75	16.94	17.14	17.33	17.53
14	14.78	14.98	15.17	15.36	15.55	15.74	15.94	16.14	16.33	16.54	16.73	16.93	17.14
15	14.41	14.60	14.80	14.99	15.19	15.38	15.59	15.78	15.98	16.19	16.39	16.60	16.80
16	14.09	14.29	14.48	14.69	14.88	15.08	15.29	15.49	15.70	15.90	16.12	16.32	16.52
17	13.82	14.02	14.22	14.42	14.63	14.83	15.04	15.25	15.46	15.66	15.88	16.09	16.30
18	13.58	13.79	14.00	14.21	14.41	14.62	14.83	15.04	15.25	15.47	15.67	15.89	16.10
19	13.39	13.60	13.80	14.02	14.22	14.44	14.65	14.87	15.07	15.29	15.50	15.72	15.95
20	13.22	13.43	13.64	13.85	14.06	14.28	14.50	14.71	14.93	15.14	15.36	15.59	15.80
21	13.07	13.28	13.50	13.72	13.93	14.15	14.36	14.58	14.80	15.02	15.24	15.47	15.70
22	13.08	13.15	13.37	13.58	13.80	14.03	14.24	14.46	14.69	14.92	15.13	15.36	15.59
23	12.96	13.04	13.26	13.48	13.70	13.92	14.15	14.36	14.59	14.82	15.05	15.28	15.50
24	12.73	12.95	13.18	13.39	13.62	13.84	14.06	14.29	14.52	14.75	14.98	15.20	15.43
25	12.65	12.86	13.09	13.32	13.54	13.76	13.99	14.22	14.49	14.68	14.92	15.14	15.37
26	12.66	12.79	13.01	13.24	13.46	13.69	13.92	14.16	14.39	14.62	14.86	15.08	15.31
27	12.59	12.72	12.95	13.18	13.40	13.64	13.87	14.10	14.33	14.57	14.81	15.04	15.28
28	12.44	12.67	12.90	13.13	13.37	13.60	13.82	14.06	14.29	14.53	14.77	15.00	15.24
29	12.40	12.62	12.85	13.10	13.32	13.55	13.79	14.02	14.26	14.50	14.74	14.96	15.20
30	12.35	12.58	12.82	13.04	13.28	13.51	13.75	13.99	14.22	14.46	14.70	14.94	15.18

Using the above table, let's compute, for example, the monthly payments of principal and interest on an $80,000.00 real estate purchase where the Contract for Deed will be paid over a period of fifteen years at 8% interest, with a balloon payment due at the end of that period of $40,000.00.

1. Because there will be a balloon payment of $40,000.00 due at the end of the fifteen year period, the buyer will need to pay only $40,000.00 for the first fifteen years.

2. Look at the year line for the 15th year and go across on that line to the 8% rate line. You will see that the schedule shows an 11.47% repayment rate.

3. 40,000.00 x .1147 = $4,588.00 ÷ 12 months = $382.33 per month.

4. Therefore, the buyer will pay $382.33 per month plus taxes and insurance for a period of fifteen years. At the end of that period, the buyer will obtain a mortgage and pay the balance of $40,000.00.

Perhaps a seller will wish to have a steady monthly income and have no desire for a balloon payment plan. A seller can then to finance the entire purchase price. This is usually financed over a period of 25 to 30 years, depending on the purchase price. If you wish to finance an $80,000.00 real estate purchase for a period of 25 years, you would follow the same steps above, except use the schedule on the chart across from the 25th year line:

$80,000 x .0927 = 7,416.00 ÷ 12 = $618.00

Very rarely, if ever, would the seller be financing the entire purchase price. Usually the buyer will make a down payment of some type. How much of a down payment is to be determined by the seller.

If a seller chooses to finance the real estate purchase through a Contract for Deed, he will need to keep a Contract for Deed payment book, as will the buyer. These can be purchased from most office supply stores. A page from the book is shown below, with the steps to compute payments outlined. The seller keeps the book current at all times. The buyer will enter the date of payment, the payment amount in his book, and send the book to the seller along with the monthly payment. The seller then initials the righthand side of the page indicating

Example of a Contract for Deed Payment Book:

DATE PAID 19	AMOUNT PAID	TAX DEPOSIT	F. H. A. INSURANCE	INSURANCE DEPOSIT		INTEREST	APPLIED ON PRINCIPAL	BALANCE	RECEIVED BY

payment. Whether the buyer or seller computes the interest and principal payments is between the parties, but it is usually done by the seller. Instead of transferring a book, a bank or law office can keep a running account for you. That is more professional, but will cost additional money.

How to Compute Contract for Deed Principal and Interest Payments

Figuring the principal and interest on a Contract for Deed, once a monthly payment has been arrived at, is not difficult. Follow these five easy steps:

(1) First, multiply the total principal owed by the amount of interest charged (8% in our example).

(2) Second, divide this amount by 12 (the number of months in a year). This will give you the amount of interest to be charged for the particular month.

(3) This amount should be subtracted from the monthly payment which was arrived at by using the amortization scheduled (see "Computing the Monthly Contract for Deed Payment" just discussed). What is left is the principal to be paid for that month.

(4) The principal paid for the month is then subtracted from the total balance owing.

(5) This balance is then used for the next month, and the steps are repeated.

Again using the purchase price of $80,000.00 over a period of 25 years at 8% interest, the principal and interest payments come to $618.00 per month.

(1) Compute the yearly interest charge:

$80,000 x .08 = $6,400.00.

(2) Divide this amount by 12 (the number of months in a year):

$6,400 ÷ 12 = $533.33.

(3) Subtract the above figure from the total monthly payment to find the principal payment for the month:

$618.00 - $533.33 = $84.67.

(4) Subtract the principal paid from the total amount owed:

$80,000.00 - $84.67 = $79,915.33.

(5) Repeat steps one through four, this time using $79,915.33 as the beginning balance:

1. $79,915.33 x .08 = 46,393.22
2. $6,393.22 ÷ 12 = $532.77
3. $618.00 - $532.77 = $85.23
4. $79,915.33 - $85.23 = $79,830.10.

You will note that each month, assuming the same monthly payment, more principal than interest is reduced.

Computing Tax and Insurance Payments

The tax and insurance payments are added to the buyer's monthly obligation, so the Contract for Deed payments may fluctuate from year to year, depending on whether or not the tax and/or insurance liability for that particular year went up, down, or stayed at the same level as the year before.

One-twelfth of the estimated taxes and insurance payable for the year is added to the monthly payments. For example, if using the hypothetical sale above, the taxes for the year may be $600.00 and the insurance $240.00 per year. One-twelfth of the taxes would be $50.00 per month and one-twelfth of the insurance payments would be $20.00 per month. Since the monthly payments on the principal and interest are $618.00, one-twelfth of the taxes and insurance would be added to this monthly obligation, bringing the total amount owed per month to $688.00 ($618.00 + $50.00 + $20.00). The obligation for the taxes and insurance would be subtracted from the amount paid before computing the principal and interest payment. The principal and interest would still be calculated on the $618.00 figure.

Of course, if there was an assumption of a previous mortgage in addition to the Contract for Deed, the lender may be escrowing taxes and insurance. In that case, the Contract for Deed payments would not need to include the taxes and insurance amounts.

ASSUMPTION OF PRIOR MORTGAGE

In many situations the seller of the property has a mortgage which he is paying off. In this situation, the interest rate to the seller may be lower than it would be on a new mortgage (for example, in 1978, interest rates were approximately 9.5%). Under these circumstances, the buyer may wish to assume the existing mortgage rather than apply for a new mortgage. The buyer will make a down payment of the difference between the selling price of the real estate and the amount of the mortgage. Frequently the assumption of mortgage and Contract for Deed payment plans are combined.

Not all mortgages are assumable, but if they are, this is often a desirable financing method. The closing costs are lower than for new mortgages (often $25.00 to $75.00 instead of the thousands sometimes paid in closing costs and points). The advantages to the buyer are the lower interest rates and the lower monthly payments available. Also the lower closing costs is a plus factor. The disadvantage is that a larger down payment is usually required, or a combination of a down payment, Contract for Deed, and assumption of mortgage.

Before an assumption of the mortgage is arranged, the lending institution must be contacted. The mortgagee (the bank) may require a credit check on the potential buyer. It will also forward all necessary assumption of mortgage papers for the buyer to sign. Generally, the banks are not permitting assumptions on recent mortgages, but as to mortgages written before 1980, there are clauses in the mortgages permitting assumption that can be enforced against the bank. This should be analyzed because assuming a low interest mortgage can be very profitable to a buyer of real estate.

The lending institution should also confirm the amount due on the expected date of closing and the total amount of any escrowed taxes, property insurance and FHA insurance (if applicable) that may be held by the bank or financial institution. Also, it is important to find out what the per diem (per day) interest rate is so that it can be calculated should the closing not take place on the expected date. This per diem would then be added to the total amount due which was calculated only to the expected date of closing.

The per diem is also important since most interest on loans and mortgages is not prepaid, and the buyer may be paying for the seller's interest to the end of the month set for closing. Therefore, the buyer, under these circumstances, would need to be credited for that amount of interest paid from the first of the month to the date of closing so that he isn't required to pay the seller's portion of the mortgage interest.

UNDERSTAND TAX CONSIDERATIONS WHEN BUYING OR SELLING REAL ESTATE

The basic principal of real estate taxation is that taxes are paid on the gain from the sale of real estate. This gain is computed as the difference between the purchase price (basis) of the real estate and the selling price. However, both the purchase price and the sale price can be adjusted. For example, the purchase price may be adjusted by certain improvements and repairs made to the premises. Therefore it is important that receipts be kept from the date of purchase through the date of sale on the real estate, so that an accountant or tax attorney can compute the adjusted purchase price. The sale price may also be adjusted by subtracting reasonable repair expenses incurred within ninety days of the date of sale. The gain on the sale of the real estate is the difference between this adjusted sale price and the adjusted purchase price.

However, if you should purchase another piece of real estate within twenty-four months at a higher price, then the tax on the gain can be deferred and rolled into the new property. This can defer taxes indefinitely.

If, however, a person purchases a residence which is lower in price than the gain received from the sale of the old residence, tax may be payable on the difference between the sale and purchase price.

Should you be required to pay taxes on the gain, Section 453 of the Internal Revenue Code does provide an optional method for payment of taxes. Under this method, the taxpayer may prorate his profit on a sale over a period of time. The amount of the gross profit in any year is determined by the percentage of gross profit on the sale times the amount of payments received that year.

The major requirement is that the installment method can only be used if the seller received no payment or payments of thirty percent or less of the total selling price during the year of sale.

For example, the gross profits from the sale of real estate amount to $200,000.00 on an installment sale with the sale occuring during the year 1977. During that year, the seller receives $140,000.00, or seventy percent of the total sale price. The seller, under these circumstances could not use the installment method of tax payment, and would be required to pay the total amount of the tax owing.

However, if the seller had received only $60,000.00 during 1977, or 30% of the total purchase price, he may qualify for the installment plan of tax payment.

If there is going to be a sale of real estate involving over $100,000.00, it is advisable to consult with an accountant or tax attorney prior to placing the property on the market to get a clear picture of any tax consequences which may be involved. The above installment sale tax rules are changed periodically, so one must check out the status of the law at the time of sale.

KNOW ABOUT THE ONCE-IN-A-LIFETIME TAX EXEMPTION

There is also available a once-in-a-lifetime exemption from payment of these taxes. A person must have reached age 55 before selling his/her homestead. An accountant or tax attorney can provide more detail. The IRS may also be able to send you a free booklet explaining this in greater detail. This is actually as simple as stated above, so selling one's home can be tax free if one is over fifty-five years of age.

KNOW ABOUT STATE HOMESTEAD TAXES AND HOW THEY WORK

The State of Minnesota offers tax advantages in the area of property taxation for those persons who occupy their homes. Therefore, it is important that the Department of Real Taxation of the County where the property is located be advised as soon as you purchase a new home. There will be a form that you must fill out. It is usually advisable to complete this as soon as possible so that there is no delay in your tax advantage, otherwise known as a homestead credit.

Each year a homeowner must complete and file an Affidavit prior to January 15th of the year for which a homestead credit has been requested. During the month of December (or early January) the homeowner is mailed a statement entitled "Homeowner Declaration", which is the Affidavit to be signed by the homeowner and returned to the Taxation Department. If this document is not signed and returned by the deadline, the property will no longer be qualified as homestead property and the tax base will increase for the next year. By signing the Affidavit, the owner swears that he/she occupied the premises as of either Janury 2nd or June 30th of the preceding year. Since it is probable that a new homeowner's address is not on file with the county, it is advisable for a buyer's first homestead credit filing on that house be done in person at the courthouse.

There is also a tax credit available for permanently disabled persons which has a higher base. To qualify for this a person must be totally and permanently disabled and derive 90% of his income from disability income, such as Social Security. Should the disabled person be married to a non-disabled person, only 50% of the tax base will be adjusted to the disability credit.

CHAPTER IV
THE CLOSING:
THE FINAL STEP IN A REAL ESTATE PURCHASE OR SALE

At the closing the buyer and seller will both receive closing statements showing the amount owed by each. There are certain costs payable by both the buyer and seller over and above the purchase price of the real estate.

COSTS CHARGED TO THE BUYER

The buyer must pay the purchase price of the real estate, plus a recording fee for the deed, mortgage registration tax, cost of a credit report, lender's closing charges, lender's survey report, FHA or VA points, etc. A sample of the buyer's closing statement is given below:

Loan origination fee (usually 1% of the mortgage) 900
Appraisal fee and credit check (usually $180-$300) 300
Lender's inspection fee (usually $50-$75 if not included in the appraisal fee) 75
Mortgage Insurance application fee 100
Settlement or closing fee 100
Title examination (this is usually paid by the buyer prior to the closing) 50
Title insurance binder (usually the title insurance premium is paid in full and no binder is required) —
Title insurance (the cost is approximately $250-$300, depending on the value of the property. If a buyer requests title insurance in his/her name - and he/she should - there is an additional charge for the owner's policy) 250
Special assessment search (usually $10-$15) 15
Plat Drawing (usually $20) 20
Recording fees (varies with value of property, and whether abstract or torrens; usually $10 to $20) 20
Mortgage stamps (varies with the value of the property; mortgage stamps are $.15 per $100 of the mortgage amount) 135
Survey costs (optional at lender's discretion) ~~400~~
Plus one year home insurance paid in advance 200 ~~130~~
Plus two months home insurance reserve 50
Plus tax reserve, required on FHA, VA loans and may also be required on other types of loans 800

SELLER'S CLOSING STATEMENT

The expenses incurred by the seller are deducted from the purchase price received. Costs which may be deducted are as follows:

Real estate commission (usually 7%) ______
Any home improvement loans, special assessments against the property ______
Abstract continuation fee (varies, approx. $100) ______

Recording fees (usually less than $10) ______
Repayment of any mortgage owing (provided the buyer is not assuming the current mortgage) ______
Payment of the year's taxes (pro rata) ______
State Deed Tax which is $1.10 per $500.00 of the amount of the purchase ______

SIGNING THE DOCUMENTS - WHAT TO KNOW WHEN SIGNING THEM

Numerous documents will be signed at the closing. The seller will sign the deed, conveying title to the property to the buyer. If any personal property was sold along with the real estate, the seller will be expected to sign a Bill of Sale. He or she may also be asked to sign a "Certificate of Real Estate Value". This is a document used by the State to evaluate property. He or she will also be asked to sign an "Affidavit of Seller" in which the seller swears he or she has not incurred encumbrances on the property recently, has no judgments or bankruptcies other than those stated on the Affidavit and so forth.

The buyer will sign the mortgage "note" agreeing to pay the lending institution the money he or she is borrowing at a certain rate of interest and the mortgage "deed" which gives the lending institution a lien on the real estate until the mortgage is paid in full.

KNOW WHAT A BILL OF SALE IS AND WHY YOU NEED ONE

If personal property is being transferred, and it usually is, then a Bill of Sale should be signed by the sellers. All personal property which is being transferred to the buyers should be listed. If there is any lien on any personal property, provisions should be made to pay this off.

The language on the standard or form Purchase Agreement is appropriate for this document. A copy of a standard form Purchase Agreement can be found in Chapter VIII. Just eliminate those items not applicable to your situation and add those items of personal property which are involved in the sale is all that is necessary when signing the Bill of Sale. When listing personal property, give the brand names and a description of the personal property:

(example) GE washer, Westinghouse refrigerator.

SELLER'S AFFIDAVIT

This document should be signed by all sellers. If the sellers are not married, it is probably best to use a separate affidavit for each individual seller.

In this document, the seller is stating that he has no judgments against him/her, no bankruptcy proceedings, etc., except those specifically stated in the Affidavit. He is swearing under oath that no labor or materials have been furnished to the real estate within the last 120 days (thereby guaranteeing that no mechanic's liens will be filed against the property), etc. Forms are available at any legal stationary store.

CERTIFICATE OF REAL ESTATE VALUE

This document is required by Minnesota Statute §272.115. It can be obtained from the County Recorder's office or the Minnesota Department of Revenue. The Certificate of Real Estate Value is used by the State to evaluate property values for tax purposes. It is basically a survey tool. A sample is on the next page.

State of Minnesota

Form PE-20
Effective October 1, 1984

Certificate of Real Estate Value

Buyer's Last Name, First, Middle Initial | Present Address

Seller's Last Name, First, Middle Initial | Address

Street Address or Rural Route of Property Purchased | City or Township | County

Legal Description of Property Purchased (Fill in lot number, block number and plat name, or attach 3 copies of the legal description)

Type of Acquisition (check all boxes which apply)

☐ You and seller are relatives or related businesses
☐ You are a religious or charitable organization
☐ You condemned or foreclosed on the property
☐ You purchased partial interest only
☐ You are a unit of government
☐ Property is a gift or inheritance
☐ You received property in a trade
☐ Your name added to or co-owner's name removed from deed (not a sale)
☐ Date purchase agreement signed is over two years ago

If you checked any of the boxes above, skip the rest of this form, and sign and date it.

Type of Property Transferred (check all boxes which apply)

☐ Land Only
☐ Land and Buildings
☐ New building constructed after January 1 of year of sale

Planned Use of Property (check one box)

☐ Residential (single, duplex, triplex)
☐ Apartment (four or more units)
☐ Cabin or Recreational
☐ Agricultural
☐ Commercial-Industrial
☐ Other Use (describe below)

Financial Arrangements

1 Total Purchase Price ______

2 Total Amount of Personal Property (from schedule A on the back of this form) ______

3 Date Purchase Agreement Signed ______

4 Total Down Payment ______

5 Points or Prepaid Interest Paid by Seller ______

6 Points or Prepaid Interest Paid by Buyer ______

Describe each mortgage and contract for deed used to purchase this property

Check if Assumed From Seller	Amount Of Mortgage or Contract for Deed At Purchase	Monthly Payment (Principal and Interest Only)	Interest Rate (In Effect Now)	Total Number Of Payments	Date Of Any Lump Sum (Balloon) Payments
☐ 7					
☐ 8					
☐ 9					

10 If the interest rate of a mortgage or contract for deed is not a variable market rate now and is scheduled to change to a different rate on a fixed date, fill in its line number from above, the month and year of the change, and the rate it will change to:

11 If the dollar amount of the monthly payment is scheduled to change (not as a result of a change in the interest rate), fill in the line number from above, the date of change, and the amount it will change to (or attach payment schedule):

I declare that the information filled in on this form is true, correct and complete to the best of my knowledge and belief.

Your Signature | Phone Number | Date

SWORN CONSTRUCTION STATEMENT AND MECHANIC'S LIEN WAIVERS

A Mechanic's Lien Waiver relates specifically to new construction. It is a waiver which must be filed within 120 days of the date the last work or material was contributed.

Usually the Sworn Statement is obtained from the general contractor involved and will list all subcontractors and materials on the form provided. These are people who provided services on the property. The type and value of their services, etc., is specified on the form. The statement must be signed by the contractor in the presence of a Notary Public. This document should be reviewed prior to the time of closing because many times it is not filled out very well by the contractor and affords no protection. In addition, there must be Sworn Construction Statements or waiver from all subcontractors and materialmen named. Each waiver must specify the value of services and material supplied, the identity of the property and must be signed by each subcontrator in the presence of a Notary Public. The general contractor will usually provide a general lien waiver concerning the balance of the costs of the products not otherwise accounted for in a Sworn Construction Statement. He should also post a bond for that amount. If these items are not accounted for and these people state they have not been paid, then they can file a lien on the real estate which can encumber the property until the claim is settled. Banks and lending institutions will not close pending unsigned waivers for potential services rendered to such real estate.

KNOW HOW TO FILE THE DOCUMENTS

All documents completed at the closing should be filed with the County Recorder. If a mortgage company is involved, the Title Insurance Company will most likely take care of this step. Additional costs will have to be paid for the filing fees, the cost of which are usually deducted at the time of closing. If you will refer to the closing statements discussed previously, you will be able to determine which filing fees are paid by the seller and which are paid by the buyer.

HOW TO CALCULATE STATE DEED TAX - PAID BY THE SELLER

State Deed Tax is calculated $2.20 on the first $1,000.00 or any portion thereof and $1.10 per additional $500.00 or fraction thereof of the purchase price, minus deductions for personal property purchased and minus the mortgage balance. The following table can be used to calculate this tax.

STATE DEED TAX SCHEDULE

1,000 or less	$2.20	20,500	$45.10
1,500	3.30	20,000	46.20
2,000	4.40	21,500	47.30
2,500	5.50	22,000	48.40
3,000	6.60	22,500	49.50
3,500	7.70	23,000	50.60
4,000	8.80	23,500	51.70
4,500	9.90	24,000	52.80
5,000	11.00	24,500	53.90
5,500	12.10	25,000	55.00
6,000	13.20	25,500	56.10
6,500	14.30	26,000	57.20
7,000	15.40	26,500	58.30
7,500	16.50	27,000	59.40
8,000	17.60	27,500	60.50
8,500	18.70	28,000	61.60
9,000	19.80	28,500	62.70
9,500	20.90	29,000	63.80
10,000	22.00	29,500	64.90
10,500	23.10	30,000	66.00
11,000	24.20	30,500	67.10
11,500	25.30	31,000	68.20
12,000	26.40	31,500	69.30
12,500	27.50	32,000	70.40
13,000	28.60	32,500	71.50
13,500	29.70	33,000	72.60
14,000	30.80	33,500	73.70
14,500	31.90	34,000	74.80
15,000	33.00	34,500	75.90
15,500	34.10	35,000	77.00
16,000	35.20	35,500	78.10
16,500	36.30	36,000	79.20
17,000	37.40	36,500	80.30
17,500	38.50	37,000	81.40
18,000	39.60	37,500	82.50
18,500	40.70	38,000	83.60
19,000	41.80	38,500	84.70
19,500	42.90	39,000	85.80
20,000	44.00	39,500	86.90
		40,000	88.00

Add $1.10 per each $500.00 over $40,000.00

HOW TO CALCULATE MORTGAGE REGISTRATION TAX - PAID BY THE BUYER

The mortgage registration tax is figured on $.15 per $100 or fraction thereof for the amount of the mortgage. Note: If a mortgage is being assumed, no mortgage registration tax is due on the assumed mortgage.

WHERE TO DO THE FILING

The documents must first be taken to the Department of Taxation where past taxes are checked, State Deed Tax and Mortgage Registration Taxes are paid. Also, at this point, the Certificate of Real Estate Value is filed. When this is completed, the documents are taken to the County Recorder's Office. Please be aware that some counties will not take personal checks, so be prepared to have a certified check or cash for the payment of the fees (a phone call to your County's tax department will let you know whether or not you can pay by personal check).

After the Department of Taxation has gone over the Deed and any other documents it wishes to check, and all payments for State Deed Tax, Mortgage Registration Taxes and back taxes, if applicable, are made, the County Recorder will place the stamps on the Deed and other notations as to payments. The Deed will be checked for irregularities or defects which can be cured, and if accepted, it will be filed.

If the property is abstract property, the Warranty Deed will be returned to the buyer after it has been filed. This may take a couple of months. If the Deed has been filed by the mortgage company, it may be returned to them for safekeeping until the mortgage is paid off.

If the property is Registered (Torrens) property, the Warranty Deed will not be returned. A new certificate of title will be issued and either sent to the buyer or to the mortgage company.

CHAPTER V
IN THE BEGINNING — OR ALMOST
(LEGAL HISTORY OF THE LAND IN MINNESOTA)

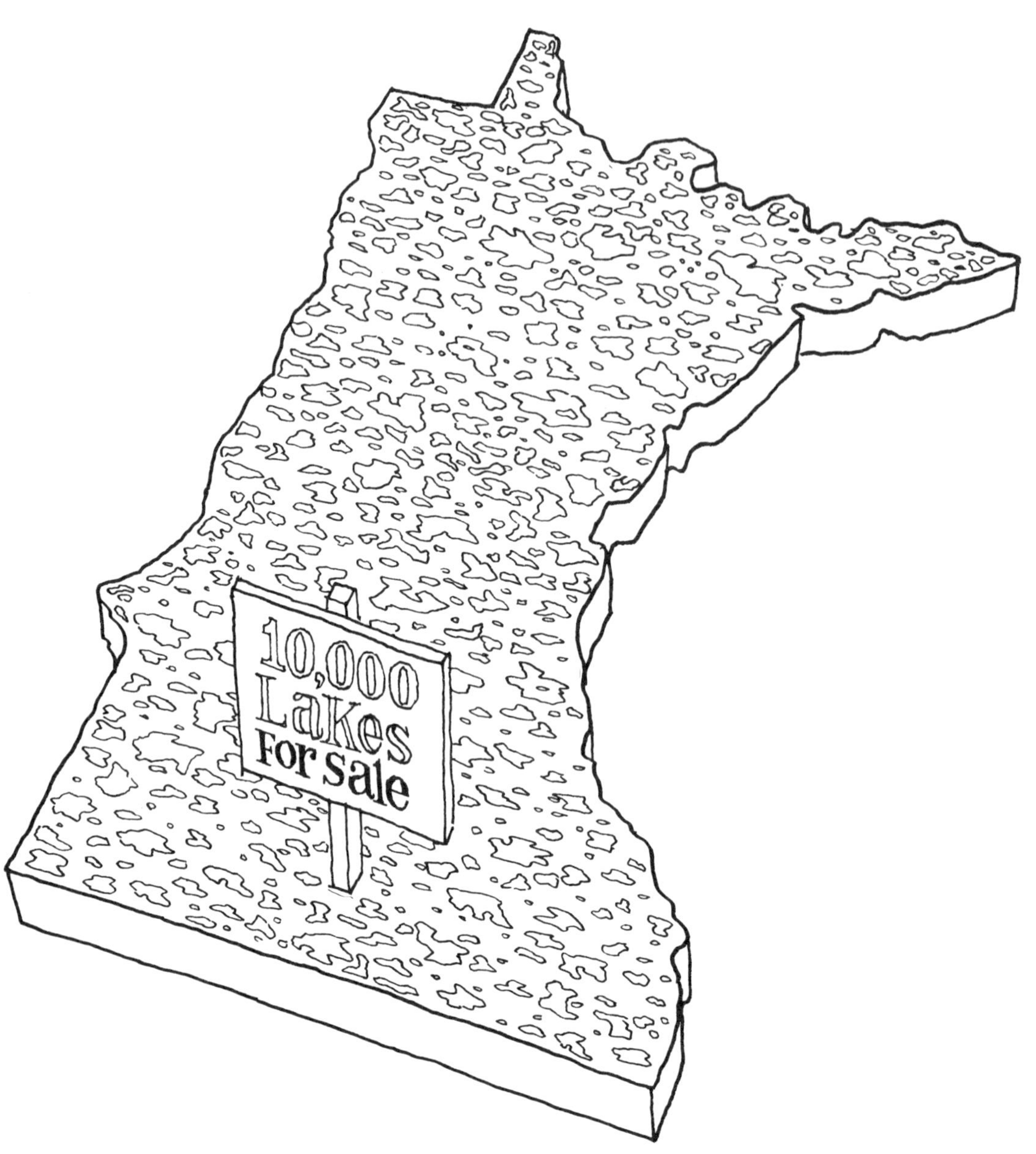

Before going into more complex areas of legal title, legal descriptions or legal documents, it might be appropriate to take time to discuss the history of land in this State.

The legal history of the land in Minnesota is tied to two major themes - politics and cash. Just how the land became part of the United States is tied in with the Revolutionary War, European Politics and Napolean.

Prior to the Revolutionary War most of the land that is now Minnesota was claimed by either France, Spain or Great Britain. The boundaries of the original thirteen colonies were rather vague. They were described in general grants or charters from the King of England and extended in some cases as far west as the Ohio River. After the Revolutionary War, the former colonies were loosely bound together in a confederation of what were in effect separate countries each with power to coin money and wage war. In several cases the boundaries of colonies overlapped. The legislative body for the Confederation was the Continental Congress. In order to give the Continental Congress some central authority and revenue (as it did not have any taxing power) it was determined that the Congress could have both if the State ceded the undeveloped western lands which were mainly west of the Allegheny Mountains to the Continental Congress. The Continental Congress in turn granted land to Revolutinary War Veterans and sold land to raise money. In 1778 a Congressional committee duly proposed the States cede their western land to the federal government. These cessions followed from 1780 to the early 1880's. A number of ordinances were drawn up to regulate the layout and survey of the western lands. The first committee was headed by Thomas Jefferson. The first work of the committee was the Ordinance of 1784 which was never passed into law. Rather it was referred to another committee headed by William Grayson. The results of Grayson's committee were more fruitful. The revised Land Ordinance of 1785 was passed on May 20, 1785. This Ordinance called for the survey of townships. Each township was to be marked into a plat in the lots of one square mile.

KNOW AND UNDERSTAND THE SYSTEM OF SURVEY USED IN THE U.S.A.

The surveys were to be made under the Geographer of the United States. The survey was to start at the intersection of the Ohio River along a line running north from the southwest corner of the State of Pennsylvania and was to extend over seven ranges of townships in the present state of Ohio. The survey started in the summer of 1785, but very little was accomplished the first year. Survey procedures changed greatly over the next fifteen years, 1785-1800, as surveyors, lawyers and owners started to use the system for the location and title of property. The Ordinance of 1785 provided for townships 6 miles square containing 36 one mile square sections. The townships were laid out extending northward from the Ohio River in ranges.

KNOW WHAT A TOWNSHIP AND RANGE MEAN

Townships were numbered from South to North and the Ranges were numbered from East to West. Only the exterior boundaries of the township (that is each of the six mile corners) were surveyed. The minimum size area sold was a lot of one square mile. The Act of May 18, 1796, provided for the appointment of the Surveyor General and changed the section numbering system to the system that is in use today. The Act of May 10, 1800, provided that townships be subdivided into half sections of 320 acres wherever possible by running parallel lines from east to west and from north to south one mile from each other and marking the corners with monuments. The Act of February 11, 1805, directed further subdivision into quarter sections. The boundaries of each of these quarter sections was to be marked with monuments. Finally, the Act of April 5, 1882, directed the subdivision of public lands into quarter-quarters.

In 1803, Thomas Jefferson then President of the United States, concluded the Louisiana Purchase. The land covered in this purchase extended from Canada to the Gulf of Mexico and from the Mississippi to the Rocky Mountains. This land was owned by France who had acquired it from Spain. The price for this vast area of land was $15,000,000.00. The sale was concluded because Napolean needed money to fight his wars in Europe. This land, including most of what is now Minnesota, was eventually included in the Public Land Survey. The original plan was to have Minnesota surveyed using the fifth principal meridian. The initial point for that meridian is in Arkansas. Unfortunately, the best laid plans go awry. The demand for land in the Twin Cities area became too intense long before the land between Arkansas and Minnesota was surveyed. As a result, the Fourth Principal Meridian surveyed in Wisconsin was extended west across the river near Hastings. Part of Minnesota was surveyed using the fourth principal meridian. At a later point the fifth principal meridian met the fourth principal meridian on the South and West.

The men who made the Public Land Surveys varied greatly in technical competence. Some were outstanding and well educated men, some politicians and many frontiersmen. The government surveyor was an independent contractor who worked without any supervision. The government surveyor did his surveys with crude and low accuracy instruments in the wilderness preceding settlement. The government survey was one of the few in history in which land was surveyed before settlement and sold to individuals. The public land survey was a remarkable achievement and quite accurate for its time. Further, the legislation which supported it made the survey useable for all time if the monuments marking the boundaries of the sections and subsections had been preserved. What is more remarkable is that less than 5% of the surveys done prior to 1910 when the survey contract system ended have been proven fraudulent. This figure is more remarkable given the corruption which often went hand in hand with the subsequent sale of the land.

KNOW ABOUT METES AND BOUNDS LEGAL DESCRIPTIONS

The land first generally described and measured by Government Survey was eventually subdivided into even smaller protions of land. These portions were inscribed in two ways.

First, by metes and bounds, which describe the exterior lines of the area in question. Metes and bounds use natural or artificial monuments. The monuments, such as a body of water or a street, may constitute a boundary. If not, it may be used for measurement purposes. These measurements known as courses and distances are run from an identical starting place to a monument or at a stated angel (direction for a stated distance). Metes and bounds usually describe rural land. A sample of a metes and bounds description is as follows:

> That part of the NE 1/4 of the NE 1/4 of Section 8, Township 114, Range 21W of the 4th Principal Meridian, according to the U.S. Government Survey thereof, particularly described as follows:
>
> Commencing at the NE corner of said Section 8; thence West, along the North line of said Section 8 for a distance of 200 feet; thence south, parallel with the East line of said Section 8, for a distance of 250 feet; to the point of beginning; thence West, parallel with the North line of said Section 8, for a distance of 900 feet; thence South parallel with the East line of said Section 8 for a distance of 600 feet; thence East, parallel with the North line of said Section 8 for a distance of 650 feet; thence deflecting to the left 50° for a distance of 300 feet; thence North to the point of beginning.

KNOW WHAT IS MEANT BY LOTS

Urban property is usually surveyed and divided into lots which are numbered on a recorded map or plat. A lot may then be conveyed by describing and by referring to the plat and lot number. This property might be described something like:

Lot 6, Block 2, Baker's Addition to Minneapolis.

KNOW THE DIFFERENCE BETWEEN ABSTRACT AND REGISTERED (TORRENS) PROPERTY

Recording the legal description of the property on a plat also allows ownership of that plat or property to be recorded. The chain of title to the property that is the record of the series of owners of the property is recorded in the document known as an Abstract. An Abstract sets out who the owners are, when they took title and any limitations on their title. An Abstract also states how these limitations on the owners right to the property resolved. The Abstract in effect is a cumulative summary of the legal contracts, law, regulations and encumbrances affecting the land.

There is another form of land registration which is known as the Torrens System. The Torrens System was introduced in Australia in 1858 by Sir Robert Torrens, and was originally used to register title to ships. Under the recording or Abstract system a buyer is required to make a detailed examination of all records in the chain of title. However, what may appear to be a perfect title of record may in fact be a defective title. Under the Torrens System, the Certificate of Title is conclusive as to the state of the title. Registration of Title under the Torrens system is accomplished by a Judicial Proceeding. Upon application for the registration of title, the Court appoints an examiner of title to investigate the pertinent facts respecting the title. Proceedings before the Court are judicial in nature. The Court does not act as a mere administrative tribunal. When the examiner files this report, a

Summons is issued in which all claimants are listed who may have an interest in the land. They are made parties as defendants. Where possible, there is an actual service of process. If after the hearing the Court determines the petitioner is entitled to registration, a Decree is entered ordering the registration. Particulars of all interests and encumbrances are entered upon the record and upon the Certificate of Title. The original Certificate of Title is kept in a register by the Registrar of Titles and a copy is delivered to the owner. This is called the Owner's Duplicate Certificate. A transfer of ownership is accomplished through the surrender of this Owner's Duplicate Certificate of Title to the Registrar and the Registrar's issuance of a new certificate to the new owner.

CHAPTER VI
CHECK OUT CLOUDS ON TITLE AND KNOW THE TRAPS FOR THE UNWARY

Whenever real estate is purchased and title insurance is not purchased, a title opinion should be completed. A title opinion is performed by an attorney. First the attorney reviews the Abstract of Title (a history of ownership of the property or in the case of registered property, a listing of all encumbrances and clouds since the last fee owner took possession) and then gives you his opinion on the marketability of title in writing. This becomes known as the title opinion. Examining an Abstract of Title is a painstaking, difficult process, even for an experienced real estate attorney. The number of potential problems (called "clouds on title") are limitless. A prudent buyer will hire an attorney to prepare a title opinion and also purchase a policy of title insurance, even if he or she attempts to handle the other aspects of the real estate transaction without legal assistance. A new and updated title opinion should be done each time the property is sold.

A word of caution before we begin to look at some of the common title problems and how to deal with them: This chapter is intended as a very basic, general overview of the topic and a general commentary on the manner in which selected title problems can be cured. Each title problem is unique and merits the examination of an experienced real estate attorney. Even if you believe that the title to the property is essentially "clean", based on your conversations with the seller, realtors or others, you should <u>never</u> consider purchasing any real estate without first obtaining an attorney's title opinion and a comprehensive policy of title insurance.

JUDGMENTS AND WHAT TO KNOW BEFORE BUYING PROPERTY WITH JUDGMENTS ON IT

For purposes of this discussion, a judgment is a determination by a Court that money is owed by one person or entity to another person or entity. By law in Minnesota, once a judgment is docketed against an individual, it becomes a lien against all real property in the county owned by him or acquired by him thereafter. The judgment lien expires ten years after it is first docketed, but it can be renewed another ten years.

The easiest way to clear a judgment lien is to have a Satisfaction of Judgment form signed by the judgment creditor and filed in the court where the judgment was entered. As with all legal documents, great care should be exercised to insure that the document is properly filled out. An attorney should be consulted for this purpose.

Alternatively, the judgment creditor can execute a release form, freeing the real estate in question from the judgment. Obviously, the only way a judgment creditor will sign a Satisfaction or a release is if he gets paid! Arrangements will have to be made with your closer to set aside enough money to pay those unpaid judgments at closing, in exchange for the Satisfaction and/or release.

Homestead real estate is "exempt" from judgment liens, meaning that those liens cannot be enforced against one's homestead, provided the property meets the definition of "homestead" under Minnesota law. However, since it is not possible to be certain that a piece of property is a homestead simply by examining an Abstract of Title, a property owner would have to go to court and have a judge determine that the property in question is an exempt homestead and that the lien or judgment does not attach to the property. A certified copy of the

Judgment and Decree of a court determining that the judgment does not constitute a lien on the property is filed with the County Recorder. This then clears up a judgment lien on the property. In practice, this procedure is not used very often because it tends to be too costly and time-consuming for anything but large money judgments. Plus most buyers cannot wait around long enough for the court proceedings to rule on the issue. In the meantime, the title to the property is in limbo.

DIVORCE AND WHAT TO KNOW ABOUT BUYING PROPERTY FROM DIVORCED PERSONS

This area is discussed more fully in Chapter XI. The discussion in this chapter is limited to problems encountered on the Abstract of Title during a title examination, but if the Abstract of Title reveals that your seller originally acquired the property jointly with his or her former spouse, you will need to obtain a deed from the former spouse to your seller and have this deed recorded. In addition, you will need to obtain a certified copy of your seller's divorce Decree from the divorce court and have the Deed recorded. It is necessary to do this even if the property was not owned jointly. Minnesota Title Standards which regulate title in this State permit the Judgment and Decree to transfer title in a divorce proceeding if the wording in the Judgment and Decree is correctly stated. Under those circumstances, the Deed from the former spouse is not necessary.

Special attention should be paid to this situation, as a number of title issues can be raised. For example, frequently a divorce Decree will award title to the real estate to one former spouse, giving the former spouse a lien against the property for a certain amount of money or a certain percentage of the property's equity. In this situation, the person holding the lien will often sign a Quit Claim Deed in favor of the other former spouse, but reserving in the Quit Claim Deed the lien rights set forth in the divorce Decree. Such a Quit Claim Deed does not clear up the problem of the lien, and a second unconditional Quit Claim Deed from the ex-spouse will be needed to clear that cloud on the title. Or, the person holding the lien rights can execute a Satisfaction of Lien form similar to that which a judgment creditor might execute. As is the case with judgments, arrangements must be made with the closer to set aside enough money from the sale proceeds at closing to satisfy the former spouse's lien. Care should be taken by the closer to contact both former spouses and the attorneys involved in the divorce to make sure that there is no misunderstanding as to the amount of money involved or the ex-spouse's willingness to sign any necessary deeds or satisfactions.

BANKRUPTCY AND WHAT TO KNOW IF BUYING PROPERTY OWNED BY A BANKRUPT PERSON

When an individual goes through a Chapter 7 ("straight" or "liquidation") bankruptcy, any real estate owned by that person may or may not be exempt property. Remember the concept of exempt property that we discussed in connection with judgments; the same basic concept applies in bankruptcy, namely, that the bankrupt's interest in, or rights to, the real estate remain vested in him and not subject to any claims by the Bankruptcy Trustee (his creditors).

If the seller has either gone through bankruptcy or is in the midst of one, you will need to obtain a certified copy of an Order or Certificate stating that the property in question has been claimed as exempt by the bankrupt, that no interested party has objected to this claim, and that the proper time period (currently, 30 days) has expired since the date of the bankrupt's first meeting of creditors (or the date on which the bankrupt filed his schedule of exempt property or any amendment to that schedule, whichever date occurs <u>last</u>). The Minnesota Bankruptcy Courts have a standard form for this purpose. Please note that the foregoing applies to the bankruptcy petitions filed on or after October 1, 1979, where the real estate in question has been claimed exempt. A discussion of pre-October 1, 1979, bankruptcies is beyond the scope of this basic outline and the buyer should seek competent legal advice in that situation.

What about real estate which has <u>not</u> been claimed as exempt by the bankrupt? If you are negotiating a purchase of such real estate from the bankrupt (seller) directly, you are probably dealing with the wrong person. If the property has not been claimed as exempt, the Bankruptcy Trustee (creditors) of the bankrupt is the one who "owns" the property. More specifically, the Bankruptcy Trustee succeeds to all the rights and interests of the bankrupt in such property, whatever those rights and interests may be.

Sometimes the Trustee will have no desire to deal with the property, for example, when the real estate has very little equity. Nevertheless, you must obtain a deed from the Trustee relinquishing his rights in the property. Alternatively, you may be able to force the Trustee to "abandon" his rights to the property in the Bankrutpcy Court. "Abandonment" is a term of art in bankruptcy, meaning that the Trustee has given up his claim to the property, either voluntarily by signing a formal Abandonment, or involuntarily by Court Order after a hearing. Either way, this is a rather complicated process for which you should retain the services of an attorney knowledgeable in bankruptcy and real property law.

Once you have taken care of the bankruptcy estate's rights in the property - either through the exemption process or by getting the trustee to relinquish his rights to the property - you may still have to clear any judgment liens against the property. An appropriate order can be obtained from a Bankruptcy Court judge following a hearing, declaring that the judgment liens are null and void (where the real estate is exempt), or that the property should be sold free and clear of any liens (in the case of non-exempt real estate). Once again, the procedures are somewhat complicated, especially in the case of non-exempt real estate, and competent legal advice should be obtained if this situation presents itself. A certified copy of any such Order should be filed with the County Recorder of the county where the real estate is located.

Other Issues. Elsewhere in this book, you will learn about how probate and estate issues affect title to real estate. The following are some other representative clouds on title, together with recommended solutions:

Problem	Solution
a) Mechanic's Lien	Lien expires after a year from the date of the last work was performed on the property, as set forth in his recorded mechanic's lien statement. If less than a year has elapsed, you'll need him to formally execute a Satisfaction of Lien and record this document.
b) Only one of two joint tenants is alive	Record a certified copy of the deceased joint tenant's death certificate, an Affidavit of Survivorship of the remaining joint tenant and a deed from the survivor (and his or her new spouse, if any) to the buyer. Note that depending upon when the deceased joint tenant died you may also have to record documentation showing that there is no inheritance tax owing.
c) Taxes	Obtain a receipt from the appropriate taxing authority showing payment. If a tax lien has been filed against the property, further Discharges, Certificates of Non-Attachment, or Releases will need to be executed. A federal tax lien last

filed or refiled more than six years and thirty days ago can be disregarded.

As with all such time limits, you should always consult an attorney to make sure the law has not been changed.

As a final word of caution, be sure that your Abstract of Title has been certified and updated to within 30 days of the date of closing. An Abstract that was last updated a year or more ago will not be very beneficial to you. Final pre-closing checks should be made to look for any documents recorded between the certified date of the Abstract and the closing date, to make sure that nothing has taken place which could affect title to the property or any of the events above mentioned have occurred.

CHAPTER VII
LEGAL ASPECTS OF THE SALE: UNDERSTANDING THE SMALL PRINT

WHEN DO YOU NEED AN ATTORNEY?

This chapter is probably the most complex. Although many real estate transactions involve a lending institution which will supervise the preparation of the documents, and a title insurance company which will investigate the legality of the title to the property, at times problems arise that need the assistance of an attorney. For example, if the title insurance company, through its investigation, finds problems with the title, it is under no obligation to correct those problems, or even suggest correction (though in many cases, it will do the latter). If the title problems arise, it is the responsibility of the seller to correct the problems. This usually requires the assistance of an attorney.

Should conflicts arise, or the transaction be a complicated one, special attention may be required. Again, it is best to consult an attorney because neither the lending institution nor the title insurance company is required to step in to aid the settlement of these types of problems. An attorney trained in real estate can be a vital tool in any important real estate transaction and may justify his fee many times over. In cases of boundary disputes, mathematical calculations of purchase and selling price, improvements which have not been completed by the time of closing, extra documents, partnership and decedent problems, tax problems and title problems, an attorney should be consulted.

On the other hand, if none of the above problems are involved, and in most cases none of the problems will be involved, you may be able to handle this part of the transaction by yourself. Even if it is necessary for you to consult an attorney, an appointment with an attorney may resolve those issues you are having problems with, and still allow you to proceed with the rest of the transaction on your own. You would incur only a portion of the attorney's fees you might otherwise incur if you retained the attorney to handle the entire process.

Attorneys can be especially valuable to you when processing a part of the real estate transaction. Remember, if you do incur attorney's fees at this point of the transaction, you have still saved a considerable amount of money in real estate fees, which is where most costs are incurred in a real estate transaction. If you have isolated problems, contact the author's lawfirm. For the price of an initial consultation fee, you may find resolutions to these kinds of things.

It is a good idea to consult an attorney if you are in a dilemma trying to decide whether or not an attorney is needed in your case. If at all in doubt, contact an attorney. It is well worth the fee you will be required to pay.

ABSTRACT OR TORRENS PROPERTY?

It is important to find out if the property is abstract property or registered (Torrens) property. We have already discussed and defined the differences between these two types of property. If the property is registered (Torrens) property, then an Owner's Duplicate of the Certificate of Title must be secured from the seller at the time of closing. The legal description on the Deed must conform exactly to the legal description on the Certificate of Title. The names of the sellers must appear exactly as they appear on the Certificate of Title. For example, the Certificate of Title shows the names of the owners as John M. Jones and Mary L. Jones, then the Deed must state John M. Jones and Mary L. Jones.

When registered (Torrens) property is involved, there can be no erasures or "whiteouts" on the deed. (It is advisable that no erasures or "whiteouts" appear on any deed.)

To find out if the property is abstract or Torrens, call the County Recorder's office of the county where the property is located. They will be able to tell you this if you can provide them with a legal description. If the property is Torrens, be sure that the seller has the Owner's Duplicate of the Certificate of Title at the closing. This must be presented to the County Recorder, along with the Affidavit of Purchaser of Registered property, at the time the documents are filed.

KNOW THE DIFFERENT WAYS TO TAKE TITLE TO PROPERTY

Joint Tenancy

There are three principal ways to take title to real property when more than one person or a corporation is involved: joint tenancy, tenancy in common and tenancy by the entirety. In a joint tenancy, each joint tenant is considered the owner of the whole estate and also the undivided part. This is brought about by the fact that there is unity in ownership with respect to time, title and interest in possession. The result is that upon the death of one joint tenant, the surviving joint tenant or tenants continues as owner or owners of the whole estate. The deceased tenant loses any interest in it which could have passed on to others by way of a Will. Minnesota law provides that a creation of a joint tenancy requires an express declaration that the parties are to take title as joint tenants. A sale of joint tenancy property terminates the tenancy unless there is an express provision in the contract of sale. The consideration received is also to be held in joint tenancy. A joint tenancy may be terminated by the death of a joint tenant, by agreement of the parties, by conveyance of an undivided interest, by a valid contract to convey an undivided interest, by execution levied against an interest of a joint tenant and by partition. Partition is where a Court orders that the tenancy be divided. One important consequence of a joint tenancy is that a joint tenant does not have an estate that can be devised or bequethed. A right of testamentary disposition is not a right which goes hand in hand with a joint tenancy interest. Because of the right of survivorship, claims by spouses who were not original joint tenants do not attach in the case of joint tenancy property. The surviving joint tenant acquires his interest at the time the estate was created not at the time of the death or marriage of a joint tenant. In other words, if two men own property as joint tenants, such as a lake cabin, and one of those men dies, his share does not go to his wife, but to the surviving joint tenant.

To own property jointly, the deed must state that the parties take ownership "as joint tenants, not tenants in common" or "with right of survivorship." If one of these is not used, then the property is not considered to be owned jointly, but as tenants in common. Most married people take title to their homestead as joint tenants, unless there are tax reasons for doing otherwise.

When one joint tenant dies, the other becomes the owner of the entire property. The dead owner simply drops away, so to speak, by operation of law. No probate proceedings are needed to clarify title to the land. The survivor (or survivors) must, however, file an Affidavit of Survivorship with the County Recorder of the county where the property is located so that the records reflect the changed circumstances.

The only exception to this is where a person dies while married and owns property jointly with someone other than his or her spouse. As will be described more fully below, a surviving spouse has rights to a share of all real property owned by the last husband or wife, except where consent in writing is given.

Tenancy by Entirety

A tenancy by the entirety is a form of concurrent ownership based upon the common law concept of the unity of husband and wife. The tenancy of the entirety may exist with respect to personal property such as cars, furniture or other household goods. Unless a contrary intention is expressed, the conveyance of the parties who are husband and wife can trace a tenancy by the entirety. This is treated as if they are to take title jointly. The preferred view is that one spouse cannot create a tenancy by the entirety by conveying property to himself and the other spouse. A tenancy by the entirety may be terminated by voluntary partition and may also be terminated by operation of law in case of divorce or death of either spouse.

Tenancy in Common - Know the Difference Between this and Joint Tenancy

Another major form of holding property is tenancy in common. Tenancy in common is a sole and several tenancy without right of survivorship. If two or more persons own undivided possessory interests or estates in property they are presumably tenants in common. This is said to be sole and several because the ownership extends only to an individual's undivided interest. In this respect the tenancy is distinguished from joint tenancy. Tenants in common have an equal right to possession. Upon the death of one tenant in common, his estate or interest passes to his estate or is directed in his Will.

CHAPTER VIII
PREPARATION OF THE REAL ESTATE DOCUMENTS

The following section will deal with the preparation of the necessary documents for a real estate transaction. Samples of each document are provided and you will note a Miller/Davis number in the top center of each document. You may request the documents from any office supply store by requesting the Miller/Davis number (a popular printer in Minnesota) or by requesting the document by name if that particular store does not carry Miller/Davis forms. (The name of the printer will not make any difference in the legality of the document. It just happens that Miller/Davis is one of the larger printers of Minnesota legal documents.)

You must also note how you want to own the property when you take title. That will make a difference in the type of form you purchase. Notice the type of ownership each form sets out. The following form examples are enclosed in full in future chapters of this book.

CONTRACT FOR DEED **Form No. 55-M** Minnesota Uniform Conveyancing Blanks (1978) Miller-Davis Co., Minneapolis
Individual(s) to Joint Tenants

CONTRACT FOR DEED **Form No. 54-M** Minnesota Uniform Conveyancing Blanks (1978) Miller-Davis Co., Minneapolis
Individual Seller

Form No. 11-M—WARRANTY DEED **Minnesota Uniform Conveyancing Blanks (1978)** Miller-Davis Co., Minneapolis
(3) → Corporation or Partnership to Joint Tenants

Form No. 1-M—WARRANTY DEED **Minnesota Uniform Conveyancing Blanks (1978)** Miller-Davis Co., Minnea
(1) → Individual (s) to Individual (s)

Form No. 5-M—WARRANTY DEED **Minnesota Uniform Conveyancing Blanks (1978)** Miller-Davis Co., Minneapolis Miller-Davis Co., Minneapolis
(2) → Individual (s) to Joint Tenants

1. <u>Individual to Individual</u> - this method of transfer is usually used when the property is being sold to one person, two or more persons who are not husband and wife, or when a husband and wife do not want the right of survivorship in that particular piece of property. There are inheritance issues which should be looked into when deciding which method of transfer of property to use.

2. <u>Individual to Joint Tenants</u> - this method is most commonly used when a husband and wife purchase property. Under this type of title, the surviving spouse or joint tenant will automatically have sole ownership of the property upon the death of the other joint tenant. This type of ownership excludes the decedent's heirs and devisees. This type of title transfer is also used between individuals who want to hold property together in joint tenancy other than husband and wife, and again, it depends on what type of survivor rights the parties want from the property and the tax considerations of this type of transfer.

Determining which type of title is best for your situation may be a question you wish to discuss with your attorney. Whichever way you wish to take title, be sure to use the correct form. Should you wish to have the property in joint tenancy, but do not have the "Individual to Joint Tenants" form, you can accomplish the same purpose by adding the words "as joint tenants and not tenants in common" after the buyer's name on the "Individual to Individual form.

3. Corporation to Individual (or Joint Tenants) - this is used many times in new construction where the builder or developer owned the land prior to the sale.

Other methods of transferring property, which are not commonly used in residential sales are those such as Individual to Corporation, Corporation to Corporation, etc. All of these forms are in future chapters of this book. If this sounds confusing, just looking at the choice of the form will readily clear it up.

PURCHASE AGREEMENT (EARNEST MONEY CONTRACT)

(Know How to Use it to Your Advantage)

The purchase agreement is the first document which the parties sign, committing themselves to buying and/or selling a certain piece of real estate. This should not be confused with the deed or conveyancing documents. The purchase agreement is an agreement to convey the real estate at a designated time and place upon certain terms agreed to by both parties. It is an enforceable, binding contract. Therefore, if one of the parties should breach any of the agreements set forth in the purchase agreement, the other party has full legal recourse.

The purchase agreement is not binding until both buyer and seller have signed it. Then copies should be given to each party. The buyer will submit his offer to purchase the real estate on a purchase agreement and submit it along with his deposit, usually $500 to $1,000, to the seller.

If the seller agrees with the terms of the offer, he also signs the purchase agreement and returns a copy to the buyer. The contract is then binding on both parties.

Should the seller make some changes on the document and then sign it, the purchase agreement is not binding on the buyer until he either signs the document again or initials the changes. If he does not agree with the changes, his earnest money will be returned by the seller.

A party can revoke his offer any time prior to its being signed by the other party. This is true after the first party signed it as long as the second party did not.

If you memorize and understand how these rules work, you can control the negotiations and actually use it to your advantage to control price. If you work through an agent, you can buffer yourself from the other party so you can analyze each offer and counter-offer. Generally, each party should make a number of offers and counter-offers before a deal is made. Never be in a hurry or rush. Always stay cool and analytical.

No. 1517½
MILLER-DAVIS Co.
Minneapolis

PURCHASE AGREEMENT

WHITE—Office Copy
YELLOW—Buyer's Copy
GREEN—Seller's Copy
PINK—Buyer's Receipt

Type in City where agreement is signed and date signed

.... Minn., ..., 19........

Type in name of buyer

RECEIVED OF ....

the sum of .... ($ ....) DOLLARS

Type in amount of earnest money paid

.... as earnest money and in part payment for the purchase of property at
(Check, Cash, to be deposited upon acceptance, or Note — State Which)

Type in address of property to be purchased

.... situated in the
County of ...., State of Minnesota, and legally described as follows, to-wit:

Type in legal description

Including all garden bulbs, plants, shrubs and trees, all storm sash, storm doors, detachable vestibules, screens, awnings, window shades, blinds (including venetian blinds), curtain rods, traverse rods, drapery rods, lighting fixtures and bulbs, plumbing fixtures, hot water tanks and heating plant (with any burners, tanks, stokers and other equipment used in connection therewith), water softener and liquid gas tank and controls (if the property of seller), sump pump, television antenna, incinerator, built-in dishwasher, garbage disposal, ovens, cook top stoves and central air conditioning equipment, if any, used and located on said premises and including also the following personal property:

Type in list of personal property to be included with sale

all of which property the undersigned has this day sold to the buyer for the sum of:

Type in amount to be paid for the property

.... ($ ....) DOLLARS,

which the buyer agrees to pay in the following manner:

Type in the amount of earnest money paid

Type in amount of down payment to be paid at closing

Earnest money herein paid $ .... and $ .... cash, on ...., the date of closing.

Type in how rest of money is to be paid (see following pages for wording used for various mortgage types)

Subject to performance by the buyer the seller agrees to execute and deliver a .... Warranty Deed (to be joined in by spouse, if any) conveying marketable title to said premises subject only to the following exceptions:

If a warranty deed is to be received, leave blank; if sold on contract for deed, type in "contract for"

(a) Building and zoning laws, ordinances, State and Federal regulations.
(b) Restrictions relating to use or improvement of premises without effective forfeiture provision.
(c) Reservation of any minerals or mineral rights to the State of Minnesota.
(d) Utility and drainage easements which do not interfere with present improvements.
(e) Rights of tenants as follows: (unless specified, not subject to tenancies)

The buyer shall pay the real estate taxes due in the year 19...... and any unpaid installments of special assessments payable therewith and thereafter. Seller warrants that real estate taxes due in the year 19...... will be .... homestead classification (full, partial or non-homestead — state which)

Type in year of sale

Neither the seller nor the seller's agent make any representation or warranty whatsoever concerning the amount of real estate taxes which shall be assessed against the property subsequent to the date of purchase.

Seller covenants that buildings, if any, are entirely within the boundary lines of the property and agrees to remove all personal property not included herein and all debris from the premises prior to possession date. SELLER WARRANTS ALL APPLIANCES, HEATING, AIR CONDITIONING, WIRING AND PLUMBING USED AND LOCATED ON SAID PREMISES ARE IN PROPER WORKING ORDER AT DATE OF CLOSING.

The seller further agrees to deliver possession not later than .... provided that all conditions of this agreement have been complied with. Unless otherwise specified this sale shall be closed on or before 60 days from the date hereof.

Type in date of closing

In the event this property is destroyed or substantially damaged by fire or any other cause before the closing date, this agreement shall become null and void, at the purchaser's option, and all monies paid hereunder shall be refunded to him.

The buyer and seller also mutually agree that pro rata adjustments of rents, interest, insurance and city water, and, in the case of income property, current operating expenses, shall be made as of ....

Type in date of closing

The seller shall, within a reasonable time after approval of this agreement, furnish an abstract of title, or a Registered Property Abstract certified to date to include proper searches covering bankruptcies, and State and Federal judgments and liens. The buyer shall be allowed 10 days after receipt thereof for examination of said title and the making of any objections thereto, said objections to be made in writing or deemed to be waived. If any objections are so made the seller shall be allowed 120 days to make such title marketable. Pending correction of title the payments hereunder required shall be postponed, but upon correction of title and within 10 days after written notice to the buyer, the parties shall perform this agreement according to its terms.

If said title is not marketable and is not made so within 120 days from the date of written objections thereto as above provided, this agreement shall be null and void, at option of the buyer, and neither principal shall be liable for damages hereunder to the other principal. All money theretofore paid by the buyer shall be refunded. If the title to said property be found marketable or be so made within said time, and said buyer shall default in any of the agreements and continue in default for a period of 10 days, then and in that case the seller may terminate this contract and on such termination all the payments made upon this contract shall be retained by said seller and said agent, as their respective interests may appear, as liquidated damages, time being of the essence hereof. This provision shall not deprive either party of the right of enforcing the specific performance of this contract provided such contract shall not be terminated as aforesaid, and provided action to enforce such specific performance shall be commenced within six months after such right of action shall arise.

It is understood and agreed that this sale is made subject to the approval by the owner of said premises in writing and that the undersigned agent is in no manner liable or responsible on account of this agreement, except to return or account for the earnest money paid under this contract.

The delivery of all papers and monies shall be made at the office of: ....

Type in address of person to receive documents

....

Agent will sign if one is used

By .... Agent

I, the undersigned, owner of the above land, do hereby approve the above agreement and the sale thereby made.

I hereby agree to purchase the said property for the price and upon the terms above mentioned, and subject to all conditions herein expressed.

Seller(s) signs

.... (SEAL)
Seller

.... (SEAL)
Seller

Buyer(s) sign

.... (SEAL)
Buyer

.... (SEAL)
Buyer

THIS IS A LEGALLY BINDING CONTRACT. IF NOT UNDERSTOOD, SEEK COMPETENT ADVICE.

WHAT LANGUAGE SHOULD BE USED IN THE PURCHASE AGREEMENT INCLUDING THE TERMS FOR PURCHASE

The wording for the paragraphs which will specify the terms for payment of the total purchase price will vary, depending on the type of financing that is being arranged. Of course, if the purchase price is being paid in full at the time of closing, nothing more need be added, since the full purchase price will have been paid. However, if a mortgage is being applied, or a Contract for Deed, certain wording must be included in the purchase agreement.

VA MORTGAGE

> ...and $______________ by the buyer placing a GI mortgage in this amount amortized over a period of 30 years. This sale is contingent upon both the property and the purchaser qualifying for said mortgage. Purchaser shall make mortgage application immediately and pay cost of placing such mortgage consistent with this contract and VA regulations. In the event the buyers cannot secure the above mortgage, this agreement shall become null and void and the earnest money paid herein shall be refunded. Seller agrees to pay a mortgage placement not to exceeed __________%* of the mortgage. Seller to pay all special assessments levied, pending or of record as of the date of closing in an amount not to exceed $_____________.** On unassessed (pending) improvements, if any, seller agrees to deposit in escrow funds in an amount considered sufficient by the lending agency to cover costs as assessed; any difference to be refunded to seller. It is expressly agreed that, notwithstanding any provisions of this contract, the purchaser shall not incur any penalty by forfeiture of earnest money or otherwise be obligated to complete the purchase of the property described herein, if the contract purchase price or costs exceeds reasonable value of the property established by the Veterans Administration. The purchaser shall, however, have the privilege and option of proceeding with the consummation of this contract without regard to the amount of reasonable value established by the VA.

FHA MORTGAGES

....and $____________by buyer placing at his expense an FHA mortgage in at least this amount amortized monthly over a period not less than 30 years with interest at no more than ____________% per annum. Application for mortgage is to be made immediately upon acceptance of this purchase agreement by the seller. Buyer agrees to use his best efforts to secure a committment for such financing. In the event the buyer cannot secure a committment for the above mortgage before ________***, this agreement at buyer's option and upon service of written notice within five (5) days of said date, shall become null and void and the earnest money paid herein shall be refunded to buyer minus any expense for appraisal and credit reporting. Maximum points not to exceed________________*.

CONVENTIONAL OR INSURED CONVENTIONAL MORTGAGE

....and $____________by buyer placing at his expense a conventional (or insured conventional) mortgage in at least this amount amortized monthly over a period not less than 30 years with interest at no more than _____________% per annum. Application for mortgage is to be made immediately upon acceptance of this purchase agreement by the seller. Buyer agrees to use his best efforts to secure a committment for such financing. In the event the buyer cannot secure a committment for the above mortgage before _________***, this agreement at buyer's option and upon service of written notice within five (5) days of said date, shall become null and void and the earnest money paid herein shall be refunded to buyer minus any expense for appraisal and credit reporting. Maximum points not to exceed________________*.

----

*there is usually a fee (also called points) payable by the seller. The number of points (or the percentage) being charged when you execute your purchase agreement can be obtained by calling a lending institution. If the points are expected to rise in the near future, it is adviseable to put in the higher number of points.

**If no special assessments, etc. have been levied or are pending, this portion may be left out.

***The buyer should be given at least thirty to forty-five days to obtain a mortgage. Put in a date that will give the buyer enough time to obtain a mortgage. Remember, that FHA will need time to complete a credit investigation and an inspection of the premises.

...$__________together with interest from and after the date hereof at the rate of _________% per annum on the unpaid principal balance from time to time remaining, payable in equal monthly installments of $_______ or more, plus 1/12 taxes and insurance, commencing on the _____ day of ___________, 19_____, and continuing on the ____ day of each and every month thereafter....(choose either (a) or (b) below and add it here, then continue with rest of contract wording set forth in (c)).

Option (a) (if no balloon payment, add)....until paid in full....

Option (b) (if balloon payment, add)....through and including __________, 19____, with a final payment of the entire unpaid principal balance and all accrued interest thereon due and payable on __________, 19____....

(c) (add after either of the above provisions)....Each payment shall be applied first to accrued interest and the remainder shall be applied to principal.

IT IS ADVISABLE TO CONTACT AN ATTORNEY IF A CONTRACT FOR DEED IS INVOLVED, SO THAT THE PROVISION MAY BE CHECK FOR LEGALITY AND TO BE SURE IT SETS FORTH THE AGREEMENT OF THE PARTIES.

WARRANTY DEED

The usual means of transferring property is through a Warranty Deed. It is very rare that any other type of deed will be used in the transfer of residential property. Should the buyer or seller wish to use some other type of deed, then an attorney should probably be consulted first so that both the buyer's and seller's rights are fully protected.

When stating the name of the seller on the deed, the marital status must also be included. Below are the most common circumstances and how the sellers names would be stated in those circumstances.

A single seller:

John A. Jones, a single person

If one spouse purchased the property, the other spouse must still join in the sale of the property. If the husband purchased the property, the names would be stated as follows:

Martin J. Jones and Mary A. Jones, his wife

If the wife had purchased the property:

Mary A. Jones and Martin J. Jones, her husband

If the husband and wife own the property as joint tenants:

Martin J. Jones and Mary A. Jones, husband and wife

An example of a Warrant Deed with instructions follows.

WARRANTY DEED

This particular sample is for "Individual to Joint Tenants." However, this sample will be applicable, with minor differences for the "Individual to Individual" form also.

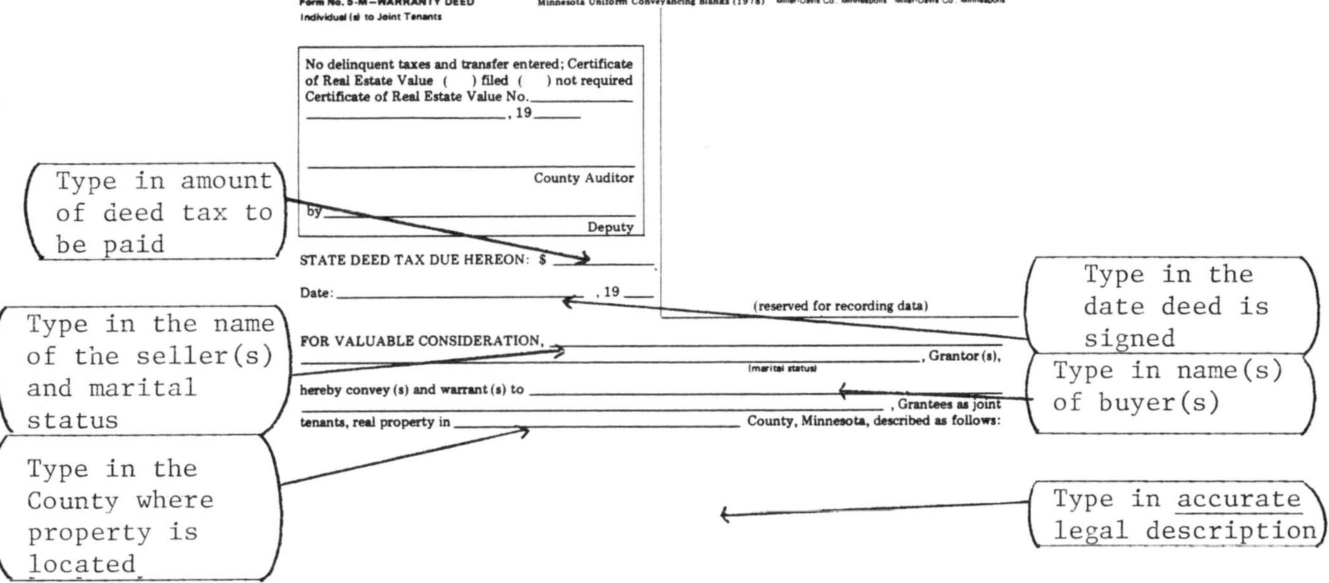

Form No. 5-M—WARRANTY DEED
Individual (s) to Joint Tenants

Minnesota Uniform Conveyancing Blanks (1978) Miller-Davis Co., Minneapolis Miller-Davis Co., Minneapolis

No delinquent taxes and transfer entered; Certificate of Real Estate Value ( ) filed ( ) not required
Certificate of Real Estate Value No.________
____________, 19____

____
County Auditor

by ____________
Deputy

STATE DEED TAX DUE HEREON: $ ________

Date: ____________, 19____

(reserved for recording data)

FOR VALUABLE CONSIDERATION, ____________
____________, Grantor (s),
(marital status)
hereby convey (s) and warrant (s) to ____________
____________, Grantees as joint tenants, real property in ____________ County, Minnesota, described as follows:

(if more space is needed, continue on back)
together with all hereditaments and appurtenances belonging thereto, subject to the following exceptions:

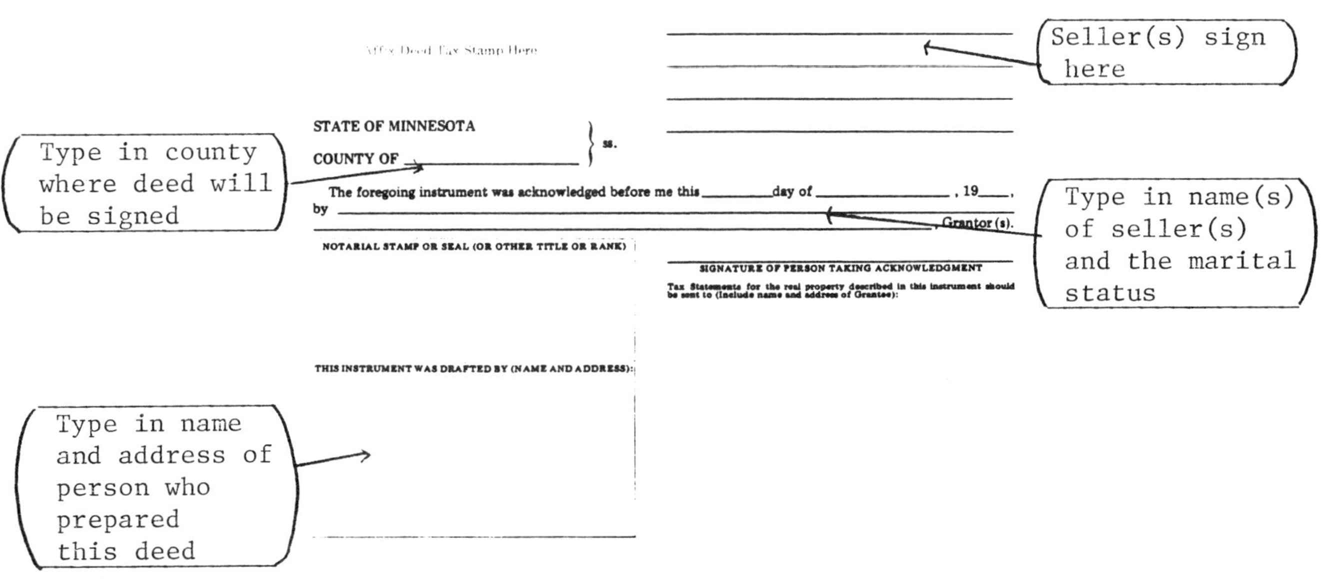

Affix Deed Tax Stamp Here

____
____
____
____

STATE OF MINNESOTA
COUNTY OF ____________ } ss.

The foregoing instrument was acknowledged before me this ______ day of ________, 19____,
by ____________
____________, Grantor (s).

NOTARIAL STAMP OR SEAL (OR OTHER TITLE OR RANK)

____
SIGNATURE OF PERSON TAKING ACKNOWLEDGMENT

Tax Statements for the real property described in this instrument should be sent to (Include name and address of Grantee):

THIS INSTRUMENT WAS DRAFTED BY (NAME AND ADDRESS):

____

CONTRACT FOR DEED - KNOW WHEN AND HOW TO USE ONE

The Contract for Deed, as previously discussed, is only an installment land sales contract. The buyer does not have fee title until the contract has been paid off in full. Though the seller holds legal title, the buyer has equitable title; he has many of the same rights that he would have if the property purchase was financed by a mortgage. The buyer can homestead the property for real estate tax purposes and also deduct the interest paid on the Contract for Deed for Federal and State income tax purposes. Contracts for Deed are good when a person cannot obtain financing. They help both buyers and sellers sell property when there are no alternatives.

A copy of a standard Minneosta form with instructions for filling it out follows.

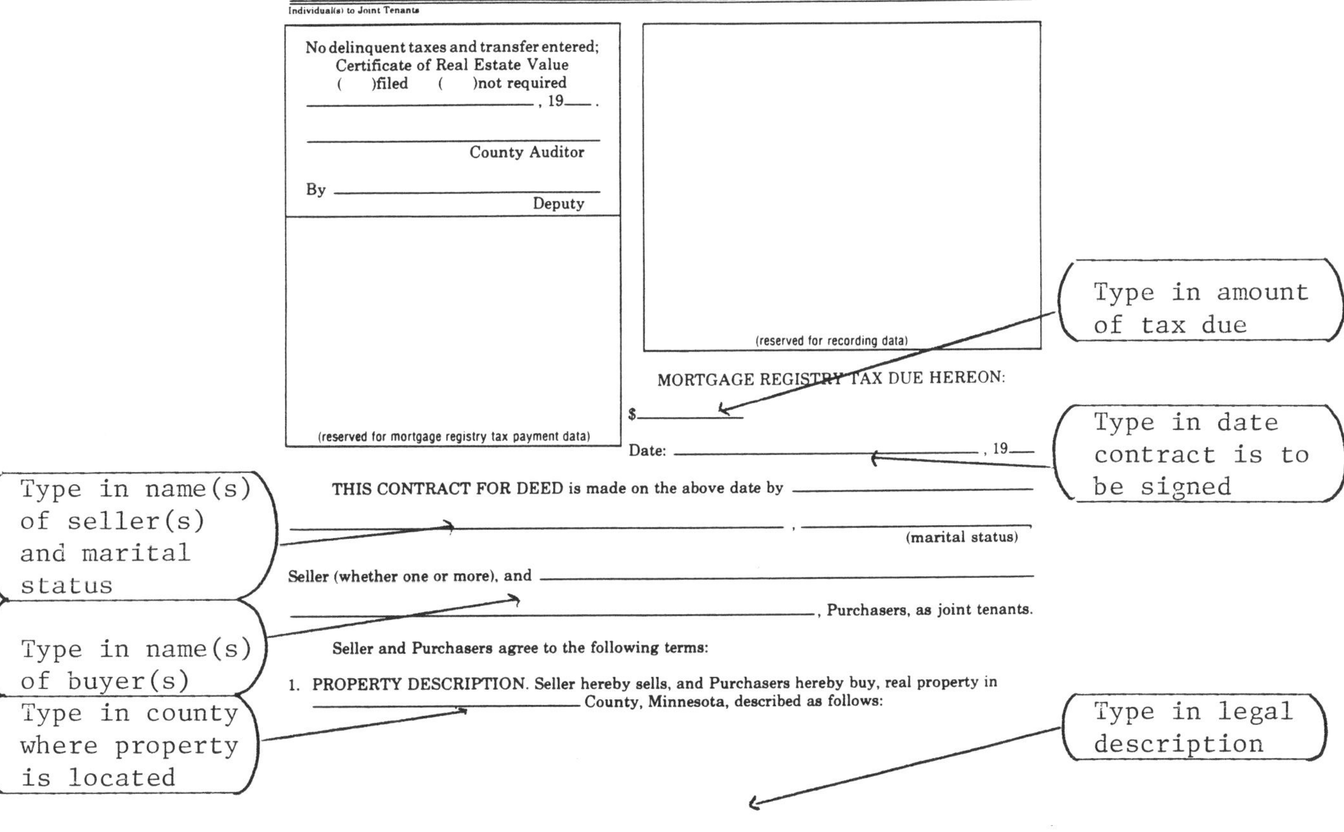

CONTRACT FOR DEED — Form No. 55-M — Minnesota Uniform Conveyancing Blanks (1978) Miller-Davis Co., Minneapolis

Individual(s) to Joint Tenants

No delinquent taxes and transfer entered;
Certificate of Real Estate Value
( )filed ( )not required
____________________, 19____.

____
County Auditor

By ____________________
Deputy

(reserved for mortgage registry tax payment data)

(reserved for recording data)

MORTGAGE REGISTRY TAX DUE HEREON:

$__________

Date: ____________________, 19____

THIS CONTRACT FOR DEED is made on the above date by ____________________

____________________, ____________________
(marital status)

Seller (whether one or more), and ____________________

____________________, Purchasers, as joint tenants.

Seller and Purchasers agree to the following terms:

1. PROPERTY DESCRIPTION. Seller hereby sells, and Purchasers hereby buy, real property in ____________________ County, Minnesota, described as follows:

together with all hereditaments and appurtenances belonging thereto (the Property).

2. TITLE. Seller warrants that title to the Property is, on the date of this contract, subject only to the following exceptions:
   - (a) Covenants, conditions, restrictions, declarations and easements of record, if any;
   - (b) Reservations of minerals or mineral rights by the State of Minnesota, if any;
   - (c) Building, zoning and subdivision laws and regulations;
   - (d) The lien of real estate taxes and installments of special assessments which are payable by Purchasers pursuant to paragraph 6 of this contract; and
   - (e) The following liens or encumbrances:

Type in any mortgages or other liens on the property which will not be paid off on date contract for deed is signed

3. DELIVERY OF DEED AND EVIDENCE OF TITLE. Upon Purchasers' prompt and full performance of this contract, Seller shall:
   - (a) Execute, acknowledge and deliver to Purchasers a ____________________ Deed, in recordable form, conveying marketable title to the Property to Purchasers, subject only to the following exceptions:
     - (i) Those exceptions referred to in paragraph 2(a), (b), (c) and (d) of this contract;
     - (ii) Liens, encumbrances, adverse claims or other matters which Purchasers have created, suffered or permitted to accrue after the date of this contract; and

Type in "Warranty"

(b) PURCHASERS' ELECTION TO REBUILD. If Purchasers are not in default under this contract, or after curing any such default, and if the mortgagees in any prior mortgages and sellers in any prior contracts for deed do not require otherwise, Purchasers may elect to have that portion of such insurance proceeds necessary to repair, replace or restore the damaged Property (the repair work) deposited in escrow with a bank or title insurance company qualified to do business in the State of Minnesota, or such other party as may be mutually agreeable to Seller and Purchasers. The election may only be made by written notice to Seller within sixty days after the damage occurs. Also, the election will only be permitted if the plans and specifications and contracts for the repair work are approved by Seller, which approval Seller shall not unreasonably withhold or delay. If such a permitted election is made by Purchasers, Seller and Purchasers shall jointly deposit, when paid, such insurance proceeds into such escrow. If such insurance proceeds are insufficient for the repair work, Purchasers shall, before the commencement of the repair work, deposit into such escrow sufficient additional money to insure the full payment for the repair work. Even if the insurance proceeds are unavailable or are insufffícient to pay the cost of the repair work, Purchasers shall at all times be responsible to pay the full cost of the repair work. All escrowed funds shall be disbursed by the escrowee in accordance with generally accepted sound construction disbursement procedures. The costs incurred or to be incurred on account of such escrow shall be deposited by Purchasers into such escrow before the commencement of the repair work. Purchasers shall complete the repair work as soon as reasonably possible and in a good and workmanlike manner, and in any event the repair work shall be completed by Purchasers within one year after the damage occurs. If, following the completion of and payment for the repair work, there remain any undisbursed escrow funds, such funds shall be applied to payment of the amounts payable by Purchasers under this contract in accordance with paragraph 8 (a) above.

9. INJURY OR DAMAGE OCCURRING ON THE PROPERTY.

(a) LIABILITY. Seller shall be free from liability and claims for damages by reason of injuries occurring on or after the date of this contract to any person or persons or property while on or about the Property. Purchasers shall defend and indemnify Seller from all liability, loss, costs and obligations, including reasonable attorneys' fees, on account of or arising out of any such injuries. However, Purchasers shall have no liability or obligation to Seller for such injuries which are caused by the negligence or intentional wrongful acts or omissions of Seller.

(b) LIABILITY INSURANCE. Purchasers shall, at their own expense, procure and maintain liability insurance against claims for bodily injury, death and property damage occurring on or about the Property in amounts reasonably satisfactory to Seller and naming Seller as an additional insured.

10. INSURANCE, GENERALLY. The insurance which Purchasers are required to procure and maintain pursuant to paragraphs 7 and 9 of this contract shall be issued by an insurance company or companies licensed to do business in the State of Minnesota and acceptable to Seller. The insurance shall be maintained by Purchasers at all times while any amount remains unpaid under this contract. The insurance policies shall provide for not less than ten days written notice to Seller before cancellation, non-renewal, termination or change in coverage, and Purchasers shall deliver to Seller a duplicate original or certificate of such insurance policy or policies.

11. CONDEMNATION. If all or any part of the Property is taken in condemnation proceedings instituted under power of eminent domain or is conveyed in lieu thereof under threat of condemnation, the money paid pursuant to such condemnation or conveyance in lieu thereof shall be applied to payment of the amounts payable by Purchasers under this contract, even if such amounts are not then due to be paid. Such amounts shall be applied first to unpaid accrued interest and next to the installments to be paid as provided in this contract in the inverse order of their maturity. Such payment shall not postpone the due date of the installments to be paid pursuant to this contract or change the amount of such installments. The balance, if any, shall be the property of Purchasers.

12. WASTE, REPAIR AND LIENS. Purchasers shall not remove or demolish any buildings, improvements or fixtures now or later located on or a part of the Property, nor shall Purchasers commit or allow waste of the Property. Purchasers shall maintain the Property in good condition and repair. Purchasers shall not create or permit to accrue liens or adverse claims against the Property which constitute a lien or claim against Seller's interest in the Property. Purchasers shall pay to Seller all amounts, costs and expenses, including reasonable attorneys' fees, incurred by Seller to remove any such liens or adverse claims.

13. DEED AND MORTGAGE REGISTRY TAXES. Seller shall, upon Purchasers' full performance of this contract, pay the deed tax due upon the recording or filing of the deed to be delivered by Seller to Purchasers. The mortgage registry tax due upon the recording or filing of this contract shall be paid by the party who records or files this contract; however, this provision shall not impair the right of Seller to collect from Purchasers the amount of such tax actually paid by Seller as provided in the applicable law governing default and service of notice of termination of this contract.

14. NOTICE OF ASSIGNMENT. If either Seller or Purchasers assign their interest in the Property, a copy of such assignment shall promptly be furnished to the non-assigning party.

15. PROTECTION OF INTERESTS. If Purchasers fail to pay any sum of money required under the terms of this contract or fail to perform any of their obligations as set forth in this contract, Seller may, at Seller's option, pay the same or cause the same to be performed, or both, and the amounts so paid by Seller and the cost of such performance shall be payable at once, with interest at the rate stated in paragraph 4 of this contract, as an additional amount due Seller under this contract.
If there now exists, or if Seller hereafter creates, suffers or permits to accrue, any mortgage, contract for deed, lien or encumbrance against the Property which is not herein expressly assumed by Purchasers, and provided Purchasers are not in default under this contract, Seller shall timely pay all amounts due thereon, and if Seller fails to do so, Purchasers may, at their option, pay any such delinquent amounts and deduct the amounts paid from the installment(s) next coming due under this contract.

16. DEFAULT. The time of performance by Purchasers of the terms of this contract is an essential part of this contract. Should Purchasers fail to timely perform any of the terms of this contract, Seller may, at Seller's option, elect to declare this contract cancelled and terminated by notice to Purchasers in accordance with applicable law. All right, title and interest acquired under this contract by Purchasers shall then cease and terminate, and all improvements made upon the Property and all payments made by Purchasers pursuant to this contract shall belong to Seller as liquidated damages for breach of this contract. Neither the extension of the time for payment of any sum of money to be paid hereunder nor any waiver by Seller of Seller's rights to declare this contract forfeited by reason of any breach shall in any manner affect Seller's right to cancel this contract because of defaults subsequently occurring, and no extension of time shall be valid unless agreed to in writing. After service of notice of default and failure to cure such default within the period allowed by law, Purchasers shall, upon demand, surrender possession of the Property to Seller, but Purchasers shall be entitled to possession of the Property until the expiration of such period.

17. BINDING EFFECT. The terms of this contract shall run with the land and bind the parties hereto and their successors in interest.

(iii) The following liens or encumbrances:

; and

(b) Deliver to Purchasers the abstract of title to the Property or, if the title is registered, the owner's duplicate certificate of title.

Type in seller(s) address

4. PURCHASE PRICE. Purchasers shall pay to Seller, at ____ , the sum of ____ ($______________), as and for the purchase price for the Property, payable as follows:

Type in amount to be paid under contract

Type in terms of payment

5. PREPAYMENT. Unless otherwise provided in this contract, Purchasers shall have the right to fully or partially prepay this contract at any time without penalty. Any partial prepayment shall be applied first to payment of amounts then due under this contract, including unpaid accrued interest, and the balance shall be applied to the principal installments to be paid in the inverse order of their maturity. Partial prepayment shall not postpone the due date of the installments to be paid pursuant to this contract or change the amount of such installments.

6. REAL ESTATE TAXES AND ASSESSMENTS. Purchasers shall pay, before penalty accrues, all real estate taxes and installments of special assessments assessed against the Property which are due and payable in the year 19__ and in all subsequent years. Real estate taxes and installments of special assessments which are due and payable in the year in which this contract is dated shall be paid as follows:

Type in how taxes for year when contract is signed are to be paid

Type in year buyer(s) is to start making payments of taxes

Seller warrants that the real estate taxes and installments of special assessments which were due and payable in the years preceding the year in which this contract is dated are paid in full.

7. PROPERTY INSURANCE.
   (a) INSURED RISKS AND AMOUNT. Purchasers shall keep all buildings, improvements and fixtures now or later located on or a part of the Property insured against loss by fire, extended coverage perils, vandalism, malicious mischief and, if applicable, steam boiler explosion for at least the amount of ____.
   If any of the buildings, improvements or fixtures are located in a federally designated flood prone area, and if flood insurance is available for that area, Purchasers shall procure and maintain flood insurance in amounts reasonably satisfactory to Seller.
   (b) OTHER TERMS. The insurance policy shall contain a loss payable clause in favor of Seller which provides that Seller's right to recover under the insurance shall not be impaired by any acts or omissions of Purchasers or Seller, and that Seller shall otherwise be afforded all rights and privileges customarily provided a mortgagee under the so-called standard mortgage clause.
   (c) NOTICE OF DAMAGE. In the event of damage to the Property by fire or other casualty, Purchasers shall promptly give notice of such damage to Seller and the insurance company.

Type in amount of insurance to be kept on property

8. DAMAGE TO THE PROPERTY.
   (a) APPLICATION OF INSURANCE PROCEEDS. If the Property is damaged by fire or other casualty, the insurance proceeds paid on account of such damage shall be applied to payment of the amounts payable by Purchasers under this contract, even if such amounts are not then due to be paid, unless Purchasers make a permitted election described in the next paragraph. Such amounts shall be first applied to unpaid accrued interest and next to the installments to be paid as provided in this contract in the inverse order of their maturity. Such payment shall not postpone the due date of the installments to be paid pursuant to this contract or change the amount of such installments. The balance of insurance proceeds, if any, shall be the property of Purchasers.

18. HEADINGS. Headings of the paragraphs of this contract are for convenience only and do not define, limit or construe the contents of such paragraphs.

19. ASSESSMENTS BY OWNERS' ASSOCIATION. If the Property is subject to a recorded declaration providing for assessments to be levied against the Property by any owners' association, which assessments may become a lien against the Property if not paid, then:
   (a) Purchasers shall promptly pay, when due, all assessments imposed by the owners' association or other governing body as required by the provisions of the declaration or other related documents; and
   (b) So long as the owners' association maintains a master or blanket policy of insurance against fire, extended coverage perils and such other hazards and in such amounts as are required by this contract, then:
      (i) Purchasers' obligation in this contract to maintain hazard insurance coverage on the Property is satisfied; and
      (ii) The provisions in paragraph 8 of this contract regarding application of insurance proceeds shall be superceded by the provisions of the declaration or other related documents; and
      (iii) In the event of a distribution of insurance proceeds in lieu of restoration or repair following an insured casualty loss to the Property, any such proceeds payable to Purchasers are hereby assigned and shall be paid to Seller for application to the sum secured by this contract, with the excess, if any, paid to Purchasers.

20. ADDITIONAL TERMS:

Type in any other terms of payment not included above

SELLER(S) PURCHASERS

Seller(s) sign

Buyer(s) sign

State of Minnesota } ss.

County of ____________

Type in county where deed is signed

The foregoing instrument was acknowledged before me this ____ day of ____________, 19____,
by ____________

Type in name(s) of seller(s) and marital status

NOTARIAL STAMP OR SEAL (OR OTHER TITLE OR RANK)

SIGNATURE OF NOTARY PUBLIC OR OTHER OFFICIAL

State of Minnesota } ss.

County of ____________

The foregoing instrument was acknowledged before me this ____ day of ____________, 19____,
by ____________

Type in name(s) of buyer(s)

NOTARIAL STAMP OR SEAL (OR OTHER TITLE OR RANK)

SIGNATURE OF NOTARY PUBLIC OR OTHER OFFICIAL

Tax Statements for the real property described in this instrument should be sent to:

THIS INSTRUMENT WAS DRAFTED BY (NAME AND ADDRESS)

Type in name and address of person who prepared this contract

FAILURE TO RECORD OR FILE THIS CONTRACT FOR DEED MAY GIVE OTHER PARTIES PRIORITY OVER PURCHASERS' INTEREST IN THE PROPERTY.

The buyer on a Contract for Deed has the right to make improvements to the real estate, i.e. decorating, painting, etc. However, if major improvements are going to be made, it is usually required that the fee owner (the seller in most cases) grant permission for these improvements before the work is commenced.

The Contract for Deed Payment Provision

The Contract for Deed must set forth completely the agreement between the buyer and seller as to how the payments will be made on the Contract. This provision should first set forth how much was paid as Earnest Money and how much of a down payment was made at the closing. The provision will next state the monthly payments and if a balloon payment is to be made after a certain length of time, this will also be set forth. Below is a sample provision for the Contract for Deed payment (you will note that it is very similar to the wording used in the Purchase Agreement). However, it is advisable to consult an attorney before any Contract for Deed is signed so that the provision may be checked for legality and be sure that it sets forth the agreement between the buyer and seller.

$__________paid as earnest money and $________paid in cash, receipt of which is hereby acknowledged. The balance of $_______ together with interest from and after the date hereof at the rate of _____% per annum on the unpaid principal balance from time to time remaining, payable in equal monthly installments of $_______ or more, plus 1/12 taxes and insurance, commencing on the ___ day of _________, 19____ and continuing on the ____ day of each and every month thereafter until paid in full (if there will be a balloon payment delete "until paid in full" and add "through and including _________, 19____, with a final payment of the entire unpaid principal balance and all accrued interest thereon due and payable on _______, 19____"). Each payment shall be applied first to accrued interest and the remainder shall be applied to principal.

QUIT CLIAM DEED

KNOW HOW IT IS DIFFERENT FROM A REGULAR DEED

A Quit Claim Deed is not used to transfer title to property under normal circumstances. A Quit Claim Deed does not guarantee title. What it means is "any interest I may have in this property you can have." If the person has no interest, then he has transferred no interest. A Quit Claim Deed is usually used where there is some question of title. When reviewing the Abstract of Title, it may be unclear if a certain individual has some interest in the property. Therefore, the attorney may suggest that a Quit Claim Deed be obtained from that individual.

If the seller is a divorced person, who at one time owned property while married, a Quit Claim Deed is usually obtained from the former spouse to guarantee that the spouse has no interest remaining in the real estate.

It is not advisable to transfer fee ownership of property by way of a Quit Claim Deed. If you have any questions regarding the use of this type of deed, an attorney should be consulted.

A Quit Claim Deed is also used when a party owning property wishes the property to be placed in joint tenancy with his/her spouse. A person contemplating this type of transfer should check with an attorney so that estate tax aspects of the transfer may be investigated. What this does is increase the amount of property in the taxable estate of the spouse who receives the gift. So estate taxes on both spouses for the same piece of property is possible.

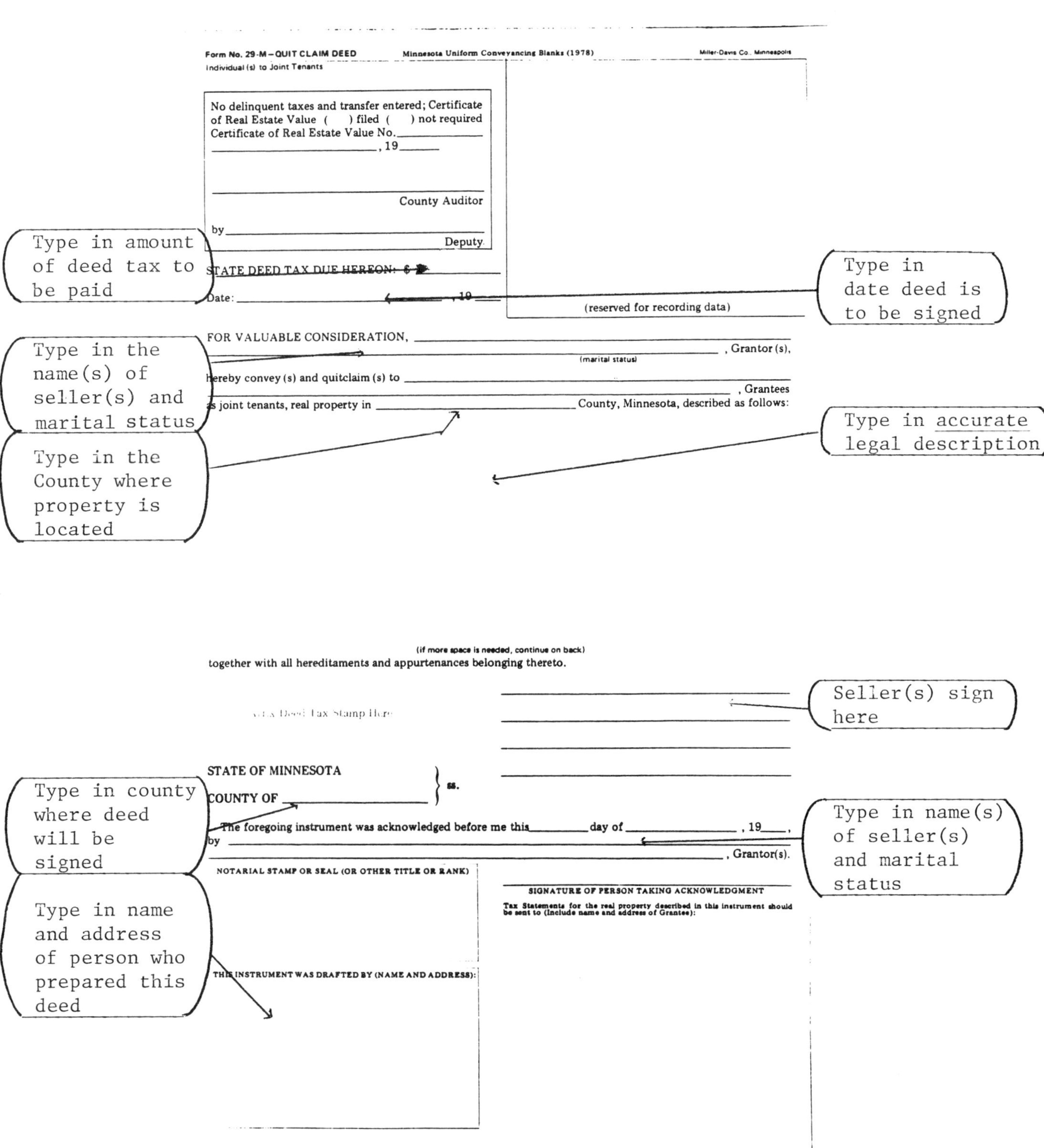

Form No. 29-M — QUIT CLAIM DEED Minnesota Uniform Conveyancing Blanks (1978) Miller-Davis Co., Minneapolis
Individual (s) to Joint Tenants

No delinquent taxes and transfer entered; Certificate of Real Estate Value ( ) filed ( ) not required
Certificate of Real Estate Value No.________
__________, 19____

____
County Auditor

by __________
Deputy

STATE DEED TAX DUE HEREON: $ ________

Date: __________, 19____

(reserved for recording data)

FOR VALUABLE CONSIDERATION, __________
__________, Grantor (s),
(marital status)
hereby convey (s) and quitclaim (s) to __________
__________, Grantees
as joint tenants, real property in __________ County, Minnesota, described as follows:

(if more space is needed, continue on back)
together with all hereditaments and appurtenances belonging thereto.

State Deed Tax Stamp Here

____
____
____
____

STATE OF MINNESOTA
COUNTY OF __________ } ss.

The foregoing instrument was acknowledged before me this _____ day of __________, 19____,
by __________
__________, Grantor(s).

NOTARIAL STAMP OR SEAL (OR OTHER TITLE OR RANK)

SIGNATURE OF PERSON TAKING ACKNOWLEDGMENT

Tax Statements for the real property described in this instrument should be sent to (Include name and address of Grantee):

THIS INSTRUMENT WAS DRAFTED BY (NAME AND ADDRESS):

CHAPTER IX
PROCEDURE FOR CANCELLATION OF CONTRACT FOR DEED

In real estate transactions involving the use of a contract for deed or the conveyance of real estate or an interest in the real estate, a special set of procedures is prescribed by Statute (Minn. Stat. §559.21) when the purchaser fails to make payments under the contract for deed.

A contract for deed is an agreement between the seller of real estate and the purchaser of real estate which typically sets up monthly payments to be applied to principal and interest until a certain date at which time the entire amount financed under the contract becomes due and payable. You will find an example of a Contract for Deed in Chapter VIII.

The procedure for cancelling a contract for deed because of a default by a purchaser is initiated with the form on the following pages. IT IS STRONGLY ADVISED THAT A FORM SUCH AS THIS BE OBTAINED AT A LEGAL STATIONERY STORE AND THAT THE SELLER USE THIS FORM TO PREPARE HIS NOTICE OF CANCELLATION.

The first step in the cancellation procedure is preparation of the form. A number of points are important in the preparation of this document. The form we suggest with instructions for easy completion follows.

NOTICE OF CANCELLATION OF CONTRACT FOR DEED — Form No. 1803 — Miller Davis Co., Minneapolis (8-86)

NOTICE OF CANCELLATION OF CONTRACT FOR DEED

(reserved for recording data)

TO: ______________________________

YOU ARE NOTIFIED:

1. Default has been made in the conditions of that certain Contract for Deed ("Contract"), dated ______________, 19____, recorded ______________, ____, as Document Number ______________ (or in Book ______________ of ______________ Page ______________), in the Office of the (County Recorder) (Registrar of Titles) of ______________ County, Minnesota, in which ______________ as seller ____ sold and agreed to deed to ______________ as purchaser ____ the land and improvements ("Property") in ______________ County, Minnesota, legally described as follows:

(If more space is needed, continue on last page)

2. If applicable, the Contract has not been recorded or registered, but the mortgage registration tax on the Contract in the sum of $ ______________ was paid to the Treasurer of ______________ County, Minnesota, on ______________, 19____, as evidenced by said Treasurer's Receipt No. ______________;

3. That the condition ____ of the Contract which is (are) in default is (are) as follows:

(If more space is needed, continue on last page)

4. For contracts executed after August 1, 1976 and prior to August 1, 1985, the original purchase price for the Property was $ ______________ and the current balance on the purchase price remaining unpaid is $ ______________. Therefore, the purchaser has paid ________ percent of the purchase price, exclusive of interest, and exclusive of any mortgages, prior contracts for deed, taxes or other obligations which were assumed by purchaser.

5. That the conditions contained in Minnesota Statutes § 559.209 have been complied with (or are not applicable).

6. THIS NOTICE IS TO INFORM YOU THAT BY THIS NOTICE THE SELLER HAS BEGUN PROCEEDINGS UNDER MINNESOTA STATUTES, SECTION 559.21, TO TERMINATE YOUR CONTRACT FOR THE PURCHASE OF YOUR PROPERTY FOR THE REASONS SPECIFIED IN THIS NOTICE. THE CONTRACT WILL TERMINATE ____ DAYS AFTER (SERVICE OF THIS NOTICE UPON YOU) (THE FIRST DATE OF PUBLICATION OF THIS NOTICE) UNLESS BEFORE THEN:

(A) THE PERSON AUTHORIZED IN THIS NOTICE TO RECEIVE PAYMENTS RECEIVES FROM YOU:

(1) THE AMOUNT THIS NOTICE SAYS YOU OWE; PLUS

(2) THE COSTS OF SERVICE (TO BE SENT TO YOU); PLUS

(3) $ ____ TO APPLY TO ATTORNEYS' FEES ACTUALLY EXPENDED OR INCURRED; PLUS

(4) FOR CONTRACTS EXECUTED ON OR AFTER MAY 1, 1980, ANY ADDITIONAL PAYMENTS BECOMING DUE UNDER THE CONTRACT TO THE SELLER AFTER THIS NOTICE WAS SERVED ON YOU; PLUS

(5) FOR CONTRACTS EXECUTED ON OR AFTER AUGUST 1, 1985, $ ____ (WHICH IS TWO PERCENT OF THE AMOUNT IN DEFAULT AT THE TIME OF SERVICE OTHER THAN THE FINAL BALLOON PAYMENT, ANY TAXES, ASSESSMENTS, MORTGAGES, OR PRIOR CONTRACTS THAT ARE ASSUMED BY YOU); OR

(B) YOU SECURE FROM A COUNTY OR DISTRICT COURT AN ORDER THAT THE TERMINATION OF THE CONTRACT BE SUSPENDED UNTIL YOUR CLAIMS OR DEFENSES ARE FINALLY DISPOSED OF BY TRIAL, HEARING OR SETTLEMENT. YOUR ACTION MUST SPECIFICALLY STATE THOSE FACTS AND GROUNDS THAT DEMONSTRATE YOUR CLAIMS OR DEFENSES.

IF YOU DO NOT DO ONE OR THE OTHER OF THE ABOVE THINGS WITHIN THE TIME PERIOD SPECIFIED IN THIS NOTICE, YOUR CONTRACT WILL TERMINATE AT THE END OF THE PERIOD AND YOU WILL LOSE ALL THE MONEY YOU HAVE PAID ON THE CONTRACT; YOU WILL LOSE YOUR RIGHT TO POSSESSON OF THE PROPERTY; YOU MAY LOSE YOUR RIGHT TO ASSERT ANY CLAIMS OR DEFENSES THAT YOU MIGHT HAVE; AND YOU WILL BE EVICTED. IF YOU HAVE ANY QUESTIONS ABOUT THIS NOTICE, CONTACT AN ATTORNEY IMMEDIATELY.

Amount of Attorneys fees to be paid

2% of default amount not including taxes, assessments, etc. This is completed ONLY if Contract for Deed signed after 8/1/85

7. YOU MAY BE ELIGIBLE FOR AN EXTENSION OF THE TIME PRIOR TO TERMINATION UNDER MINNESOTA STATUTES SECTIONS 583.01 TO 583.12.

Name and Address of Seller(s) if no Attorney is doing this

NAME OF SELLER OR ATTORNEY:

____

Address: ____________________

____

Phone: ____________________

By ____________________
who is the person authorized by the Seller ____ to receive payments from you under this Notice.

This portion is filled out by the person who serves the Notice of Cancellation; it may be wise to have the sheriff do it to be sure it is done correctly

AFFIDAVIT OF SERVICE

STATE OF MINNESOTA } ss.
County of ____________

____________, being duly sworn, on oath says; that on ____________, 19 ____, I served the foregoing notice upon ____________, the person ____ to whom it is directed, by handing to and leaving with ____________, a true and correct copy thereof.

Subscribed and sworn to before me this ____ day of ____________, 19 ____.

____

Notary Public
____________ County, Minnesota.
My Commission Expires
____________, 19 ____.

____

(Notary Stamp Or Seal)

RETURN OF SERVICE BY SHERIFF

STATE OF MINNESOTA } ss.
County of ____________

I hereby certify and return that on the ____ day of ____________, 19 ____, I served the foregoing notice on ____________, the person ____ to whom it is directed, by handing to and leaving with ____________

____

____

a true and correct copy thereof.

____
Sheriff of ____________ County, Minnesota

BY: ____________
Deputy

Subscribed and sworn to before me this ____ day of ____________, 19 ____.

____

Notary Public
____________ County, Minnesota.
My Commission Expires
____________, 19 ____.

____

(Notary Stamp Or Seal)

AFFIDAVIT OF SERVICE ON OCCUPANT

STATE OF MINNESOTA } ss.
County of ____________

____________, being duly sworn on oath says; that on the ____ day of ____________, 19 ____, I went upon the Property described in the foregoing notice for the purpose of serving the notice on the person ____ in possession of the Property; that on that day and for ____________ prior to that date the Property was and had been, ____________

____
(State whether vacant or occupied, and if occupied, by whom)

____
(If occupied, show service and how made)

____

____

Subscribed and sworn to before me this ____ day of ____________, 19 ____.

____

Notary Public
____________ County, Minnesota.
My Commission Expires
____________, 19 ____.

____

(Notary Stamp Or Seal)

Once the time has lapsed for the buyer(s) to comply and pay the arrearages, this part is filled out (only if the buyer(s) do not pay the amount owing

AFFIDAVIT OF FAILURE TO COMPLY WITH NOTICE

County where seller lives

STATE OF MINNESOTA }
County of ________________ } ss.

Seller's name

type in "the"

________________, being duly sworn, on oath says: that I am ________________ person ________ who signed the notice as ________________; that more than ________ days have elapsed since the service of the notice on ________________ to whom it is directed; that ________________ ha____ not complied with the terms of the notice; that the default set forth in the notice still continues; that no portion of the overdue payments of principal and interest under the contract described in the notice has been paid; nor attorneys' fees of ________; nor, if applicable, two percent of the default in the amount of $ ________; nor costs of service of $ ________. Further, I make this affidavit for the purpose of terminating the contract and recording the notice, the proofs of the service of the contract, and the proof of failure to comply with the terms of the contract.

Type in "seller"

Name of buyer(s)

Type "s" if one buyer; type "ve" if more than one buyer

The number of days since service of Notice of Cancellation

Subscribed and sworn to before me this ______ day of ________________, 19______. ________________

(Notary Stamp Or Seal)

____
Notary Public
________________ County, Minnesota.
My Commission Expires
________________, 19______.

Sign this part and have it notarized - you must sign in the presence of the notary

This instrument was drafted by (Name and Address)

Name and address of the person who completed the Cancellation of Contract for Deed form

First, it is absolutely essential that every aspect of this document be totally correct. If any mistake is made in filling out the cancellation form, it is quite likely that a Minnesota Court would reject the notice as defective and require that service of a corrected notice of cancellation take place. This is frustrating and crucial because it gives the party in possession more free possession and use of the property.

Because the form provides most of the statutory language to proceed with cancellation, it will be necessary only to fill in blanks upon the form (note: the law changes from time to time so it is adviseable to see an attorney or read the current law carefully to be sure your cancellation conforms to current law). The information to be supplied is:

1. Period in which to correct default - in almost all cases this blank will be filled with the number 60 with the only exceptions arising in those situations involving earnest money contracts, purchase agreements and exercised options which can be terminated in a thirty day period. If the exact location of the purchaser is unknown, it is possible to serve notice by publication if ninety days from the first day of publication are allowed for correction of the default under the contract.

2. Default penalty - this amount is the total of a figure which is 2% of the amount in default at the time of service, other than the final balloon payment plus any taxes, assessments, mortgages or prior contracts that are assumed by the purchaser.

3. Attorneys fees - in this blank the amount actually spent or incurred on attorneys fees must be inserted and cannot exceed $125.00 if the amount in default is less than $750.00 or $250.00 if the amount in default is $750.00 or more. No attorneys fees are required to be paid unless some part of the conditions of the default have existed at least thirty days prior to the date of service of the notice of cancellation.

4. Seller or agent of seller - the notice must contain the name, address and telephone number of the individual who is to be contacted in order to correct the default under the contract. If this information is missing from the notice of cancellation and the seller cannot be found (or is not present in the state), then the purchaser can comply with the conditions of the notice by paying to the clerk of the district court in the county where the real estate is located any money due and file a proof of compliance with other defaults in the notice.

5. Contract description - the date and parties to the transaction and a legal description of the property involved must be contained in the notice of cancellation. If there have been any assignments of the Contract for Deed, parties to those assignments, dates and recording data should be included.

6. Mortgage registration tax - to proceed with cancellation, the mortgage registration tax on the involved Contract for Deed, if recorded prior to January 1, 1984, must be paid and the information regarding the county, date and receipt number of this transaction must be included in this notice. That is not a requirement for Contract for Deeds filed after January 1, 1984.
7. Specifics of default - a brief explanation must be included setting forth what the purchaser has failed to do and the total amount due and owing as a result of this default and the period of time allowed to correct the default. Be sure to include all elements of the default since reinstatement can only be made by remedying those items of default specifically mentioned.

SERVE THE NOTICE OF CANCELLATION

Once the notice of cancellation has been prepared and all necessary steps taken to complete the notice of cancellation, it is necessary to serve the notice of cancellation on the purchaser. Service of the notice must be made pursuant to the Minnesota Rules of Civil Procedure which require personal service of the notice upon each of the purchasers by an individual who is not a party to this action.

If the seller cannot personally serve the purchaser, it is adequate for service to occur by delivering the notice of cancellation to someone at the home of the purchaser of reasonable age and discretion and residing at the home of the purchaser.

In the event the address or location of the purchaser is not known, it is possible to proceed by publication of the notice in a legal newspaper for three consecutive weeks. If the premises described in the contract are actually occupied, then personal service of a copy of the notice within ten days of the notice of publication must be made upon the person in possession of the premises. This will be effective service whether the purchaser is within or outside the State of Minnesota. It is important to remember that the purchaser is allowed ninety days from and after the first day of publication of the notice to correct the default set out in the notice of cancellation.

KNOW THE TIME RESTRICTIONS ON TAKING BACK PROPERTY

Once service has occurred, the seller must wait for the period of time set out in the notice of cancellation to elapse. During this period of time, if the seller has incurred costs directly arising from the preparation and service of the notice of cancellation (usually this would include the cost of service if the sheriff or private process server is used), the seller should compile all costs incurred and notify the purchaser, by certified mail at the purchaser's last known address, at least ten days prior to the date of termination set forth in the notice of cancellation. Failure to make this notification will prevent the seller from recovering actual costs expended in the cancellation procedure.

Typically, during the period allowed for reinstatement of the contract, the seller will be contacted by the purchaser to comply with the areas of default in the contract or renegotiate the contract to save the purchaser's equity in the property. If the seller accepts any partial payment of the defaulted amounts, the cancellation is terminated and would have to be reserved if the buyer does not make up the rest of the default.

IF THE BUYER DOES NOT CURE THE DEFAULT, WHAT NEXT?

In the event the purchaser fails to comply with the requirements of reinstatement or does not renegotiate the contract, the purchaser will forfeit all equity accrued in the property. Therefore, if the purchaser is not able to satisfy the conditions of reinstatement, the seller must be satisfied with any proposal made by the purchaser before a new contract could be executed.

Certain conditions have been set out statutorily allowing a purchaser to extend the period allowed for remedying the default on the contract. This will only occur in a situation where the purchaser is living on the property affected by the contract and will not apply to earnest money contracts, purchase agreements or exercised options. The purchaser will be required to prove to the court that the purchaser is unemployed, underemployed, facing catastrophic medical expenses, or facing economic problems due to low farm commodity prices; and as a result is unable to make payments on the contract for deed. If these requirements cannot be met by the purchaser, the court will be required by statute to cancel the contract for deed if there has not been remedy of the default or negotiation of a new agreement satisfactory to the seller. IT IS STRONGLY ADVISED THAT A PURCHASER CONTACT AN ATTORNEY IMMEDIATELY UPON BEING SERVED WITH A NOTICE OF CANCELLATION. THE PURCHASER IS IN A VERY DANGEROUS LEGAL POSITION AND SHOULD NOT WAIT IN REACTING TO THE NOTICE.

As indicated above, the purchaser has four options:

1. Remedy the conditions of default
2. Renegotiate the contract with the seller
3. Seek an extension of the period for remedying the default under the statute, or
4. If a person does nothing he forfeits all interest in the real estate.

The means of successfully resolving this situation is use of option 1 and any other approach should be immediately discussed with an attorney.

At the end of the period allowed to remedy the default, the seller must execute an Affidavit of Non-Compliance and then record the notice of cancellation, Affidavits of Service and/or publication and the Affidavit of Non-Compliance (a portion of the Cancellation of Contract for Deed form), with the county recorder in order to reflect on the public record that the seller has cut off the purchaser's interests in the property. Upon completing this step, the title to the property will be in the name of the seller only.

Problems may arise if the purchaser refuses to vacate the premises after the filing of the notice of cancellation. The seller would be required to bring a complaint for unlawful detainer to obtain an order for the removal of the purchaser. This is another legal procedure more commonly known as an eviction proceeding.

Although the procedure of cancellation focuses on the contract existing between the seller and purchaser, it is important to note that other defaults might be involved which should be investigated. The seller should determine if payments on any other contract or mortgage affecting the real estate are current. In addition, it is strongly advised that the status of property taxes and assessments on the property be reviewed by the seller. Failure to investigate these items may result in legal procedures that may cut off the interest of the seller in the real estate.

Finally, since this procedure is so tightly controlled by statute, any defect in the cancellation procedure will be interpreted against the seller with the cancellation procedure being rejected by the court. The seller will not be prevented from renewing the cancellation procedure, but two months will have been lost by the seller without receiving payments.

CHAPTER X
TRANSFERRING PROPERTY AFTER THE DEATH OF THE OWNER

HOMESTEAD PROPERTY - WHY IS THIS KIND OF PROPERTY DIFFERENT AND SO IMPORTANT?

Homestead property is land on which the owner made his residence--meaning he actually lives there--at the time of his death. There is a limit to the size of property that can be considered homestead property. The ownership size differs depending upon whether the land is a farm or non-farm land.

If the owner of a homestead dies while married, the surviving spouse is guaranteed at least a life estate in that homestead; in other words, the surviving spouse can live there as long as he or she chooses. This is true whether the decedent left a Will or not, and regardless of what the Will provides. Example: A man marries after he has already acquired a homestead. Throughout the marriage title to the property remains in his sole name. He makes a Will leaving his homestead real estate to his brother. He dies. His surviving spouse does not have to accept that provision of the Will (unless she has previously consented to it in writing). She may choose to receive her life interest in the homestead and the Courts must honor her choice.

In the more common case, where the surviving spouse is a joint owner of the property or where it is left to her by Will, she would not have to make any decision about it at all.

In those cases where the surviving spouse receives the life interest in the homestead, when he or she dies or gives up the property, title to it will pass to the person named in the Will, if there was one, or if not then according to law as will be described below. In the example above, it would go to the brother.

When a homestead passes to the surviving spouse who uses it as his or her homestead, the existing mortgages, liens and property taxes remain, but so long as it remains the survivor's homestead, it cannot be taken or foreclosed to pay the debts the decedent left behind.

HOW TO TRANSFER JOINT PROPERTY UPON THE DEATH OF ONE JOINT TENANT

If the husband and wife owned the property as joint tenants, it may only be necessary to file a document called an Affidavit of Survivorship to get the property transferred to the surviving spouse's name. A certified copy of the death certificate is attached to the back of this document and filed with the County Recorder of the County where the property is located.

A copy of an Affidavit of Survivorship as discussed above follows.

THIS FORM IS USED FOR A HOMESTEAD ONLY - THERE ARE OTHER FORMS AVAILABLE FOR NON-HOMESTEAD PROPERTY

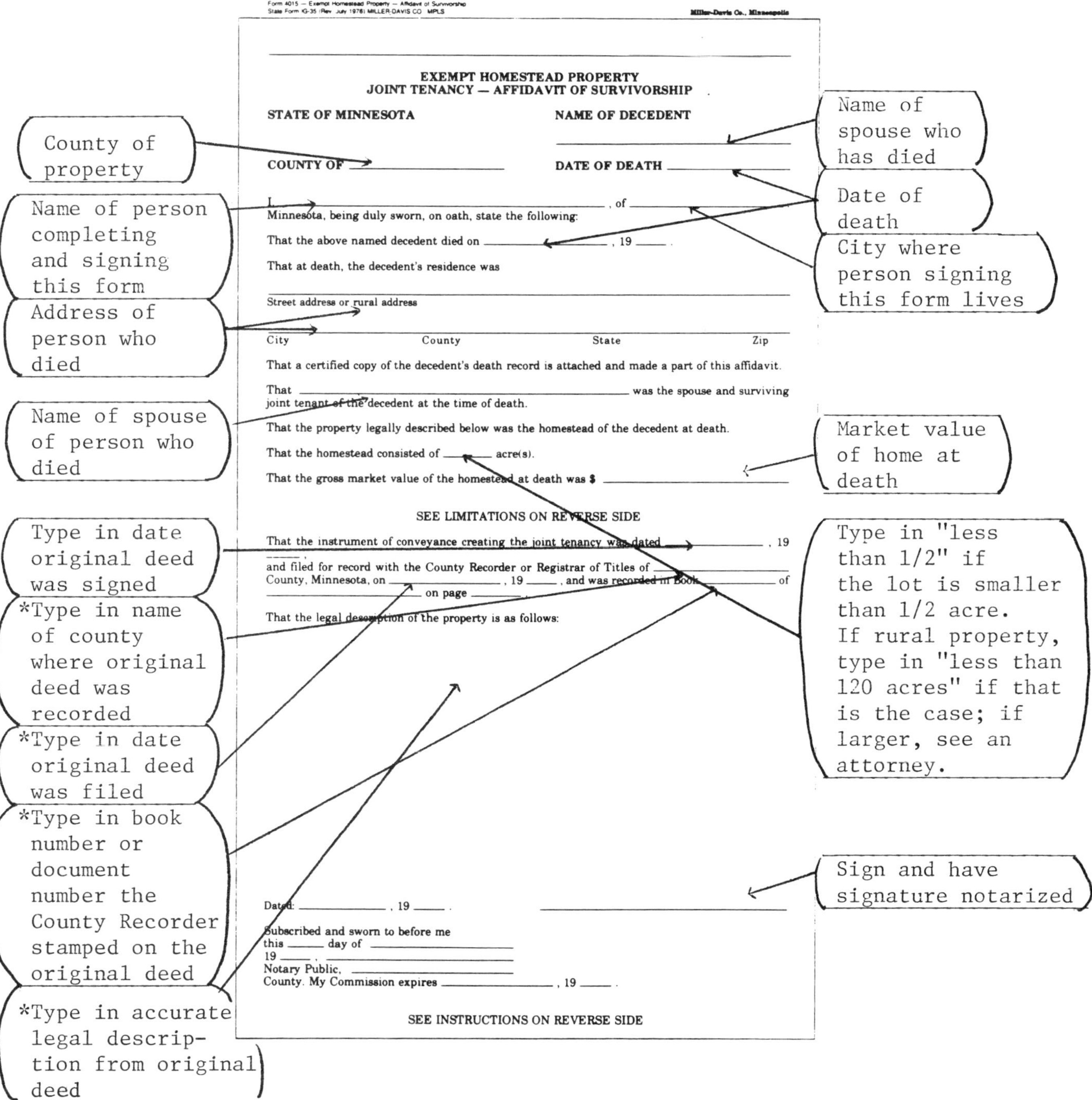

Form 4015 — Exempt Homestead Property — Affidavit of Survivorship
State Form IG-35 (Rev. July 1976) MILLER-DAVIS CO. MPLS

Miller-Davis Co., Minneapolis

EXEMPT HOMESTEAD PROPERTY
JOINT TENANCY — AFFIDAVIT OF SURVIVORSHIP

STATE OF MINNESOTA | **NAME OF DECEDENT** ____________

COUNTY OF ____________ | **DATE OF DEATH** ____________

I, ____________, of ____________ Minnesota, being duly sworn, on oath, state the following:

That the above named decedent died on ____________, 19____.

That at death, the decedent's residence was

____
Street address or rural address

____
City County State Zip

That a certified copy of the decedent's death record is attached and made a part of this affidavit.

That ____________ was the spouse and surviving joint tenant of the decedent at the time of death.

That the property legally described below was the homestead of the decedent at death.

That the homestead consisted of ____ acre(s).

That the gross market value of the homestead at death was $ ____________

SEE LIMITATIONS ON REVERSE SIDE

That the instrument of conveyance creating the joint tenancy was dated ____________, 19____, and filed for record with the County Recorder or Registrar of Titles of ____________ County, Minnesota, on ____________, 19____, and was recorded in Book ____________ of ____________ on page ____________.

That the legal description of the property is as follows:

Dated: ____________, 19____. ____________

Subscribed and sworn to before me this ____ day of ____________, 19____.

____
Notary Public, ____________ County. My Commission expires ____________, 19____.

SEE INSTRUCTIONS ON REVERSE SIDE

*All this information can be obtained from the County Recorder if the original deed cannot be located.

ATTACH A CERTIFIED COPY OF THE DEATH CERTIFICATE TO THE BACK OF THIS FORM AND FILE IT WITH THE COUNTY RECORDER.

KNOW THE RIGHTS OF SURVIVING SPOUSES, CHILDREN AND SPOUSES BY REMARRIAGE UPON DEATH OF AN OWNER

As noted above, the law gives special treatment to homestead real estate where the deed owner left a surviving spouse (assuming the homestead is not in joint tenancy with the spouse). That spouse cannot be put out of his/her home without his/her consent, no matter what the Will says. If the decedent's Will gives the homestead to someone else, probate proceedings will cause title to pass to that third person, but subject to the spouse's right to live there. When he/she dies or renounces that right, the person named in the Will can take possession of the property and then use it as he or she pleases.

A surviving spouse also has claims in non-homestead property which the decedent had an interest in during the marriage and to the transfer of which he/she did not consent. If the decedent left no children or grandchildren, or just one child, the surviving spouse is entitled to receive one-half of all the non-homestead real estate. If the decedent left two or more children (or grandchildren from two or more deceased children) the surviving spouse gets one-third of the non-homestead land. Example: Mr. X was married and had two children. His first wife died. He then made a Will leaving everything, including two pieces of non-homestead land, to his two children. Later he married again, but had no more children. Then he died. Despite the terms of the Will, the second wife has the right to receive one-third of the non-homestead real estate. If she made this choice, the probate court would decree that she and the two surviving children would each own a one-third interest in each of the two non-homestead parcels, as tenants in common.

Now assume that Mrs. Y is married and has two children. She inherits, in her sole name, an apartment building in another town. She and her husband separate, but do not get divorced. She makes a Will leaving the apartment building to the two children in equal shares. One of the children dies, without children of her own. Then Mrs. Y dies. Mr. Y is entitled to receive one-half interest in the apartment building.

The results of both of these examples could be different if the surviving spouse had consented in writing to the terms of the Will. Also, a valid pre-marital agreement can limit a surviving spouse's inheritance rights. Of course, a formal divorce would change the results as well.

If there is no Will and no surviving spouse, homestead real property and other real estate are treated the same. If the decedent left children, the property goes to them in equal shares as tenants in common. If the decedent had a child who had died before he did, the result may be different. Example: Mr. Q had three children. One of them died leaving two children of her own. Then Mr. Q dies. Mr. Q's real estate passes as follows: one-third to each living child and one-sixth to each of the grandchildren. The rule is that grandchildren divide equally the share that would have gone to their deceased parent.

If the property owner left no spouse or children or grandchildren, the land passes to the next of kin according to a formula set by law. First in line would be the decedent's parents; then brothers and sisters. If there are none of these, then the family tree must be traced to find "the next of kin in equal degree", meaning the nearest blood relative - uncles and aunts, then cousins, and so on. Kin of "equal degree" means closeness by blood. They would share equally in the property. If no kin can be found, all of the decedent's property will pass to the State.

REAL ESTATE OUTSIDE MINNESOTA - WHAT LAW IS APPLIED

If the real estate is owned outside the State of Minnesota, the interest will pass according to the laws of that State.

As a general rule, the laws of Minnesota only apply to land within the State. Land in other states owned by a Minnesota resident will be governed by the law of the state where the land is located. If probate proceedings are needed they must be done in that state for that land; thus sometimes two or more probate proceedings will have to be done at once to clear up all the real estate problems. The laws of the states vary significantly. A Will valid in Minnesota will be valid in all states, but provisions dealing with real estate may not be honored if they conflict with the law of the other state.

A FINAL WORD

This chapter simplifies somewhat the intricate law of the passage of land upon death. Individual circumstances will often not fall clearly under the general rules and principles described here. If you become involved in any question of title to or interest in real estate, consult a lawyer familiar with this area of law.

CHAPTER XI
DIVORCE AND HOW IT AFFECTS REAL ESTATE

If you are contemplating selling your home because of a dissolution of your marriage, then this chapter may be of assistance to you.

How to divide up the real estate is one of the issues that causes the most disagreement between divorcing couples. Who should live in the home? Who should pay the expenses of the home? When should it be sold? Who gets the equity from the home and when? These are all problems that are part of divorce. We cannot attempt to answer these questions in det here because each situation is different. However, we will g you an overview which may help you decide how to proceed in y particular case.

Real estate owned by one spouse individually or b spouses together becomes an issue in a dissolution of marri action. The attorney(s) handling the divorce action will need to know when the property was purchased, the purchase price, the down payment and closing costs (and how these funds were obtained, i.e. marital or non-marital property), the mortgage and other encumbrances on the property, whether the property is abstract or Registered (Torrens) Property, whose name appears on the deed, any improvements made to the real property since it was purchased and by whom made, the current amount of the mortgage and real estate taxes. The attorney may also request that an appraisal be done to determine the current market value of the home.

Once this information has been obtained, the attorney will advise you of options available to you and your spouse.

AN OUTRIGHT AWARD OF THE REAL ESTATE TO ONE PARTY

Usually this is done in circumstances where the spouse receiving the property owned it prior to marriage and the marriage has not been a long one or the person receiving the property is able to either pay his/her spouse cash for the non-receiving spouse's interest in the property or that spouse receives some other property of similar value.

THE REAL ESTATE IS SOLD

The real estate is sold and the net proceeds (sale price less mortgage and other encumbrances, closing costs and sale costs) is divided between the parties as they have agreed or the Court has ordered.

THE PROPERTY IS AWARDED TO ONE SPOUSE AND THE OTHER SPOUSE IS GRANTED A LIEN ON THE PROPERTY

This is used quite frequently when there are children and the parties want the children's lives to stay as stable as possible. The children and the custodial spouse (the spouse who receives physical custody of the children) remain in the home. That spouse is usually given ownership of the home and the non-custodial spouse is given a lien. That lien then becomes payable when a certain event occurs. This could be the remarriage of the custodial spouse, the sale of the home, if the custodial spouse moves out of the home, or the youngest child reaches age eighteen. Other events can trigger the sale, too. It all depends on what the parties want or what the Court orders.

When one of the triggering events happens, the property is either sold and the lien paid or the custodial spouse must somehow find the money to pay the lien, either through borrowing or saving towards that date.

A LIEN FORMULA THAT IS FAIR TO BOTH PARTIES

What kind of lien the non-custodial spouse receives will depend on the agreement of the parties or the order of the Court. There is a formula that is often used, which, though it looks cumbersome, can be a fair division:

From the sale price of the home are deducted the following:

- the balance of any existing encumbrances of record
- financing costs related to sale
- real estate broker's commission
- special assessments.

The balance that remains is then divided between the parties as follows:

- to the party who lived in the home (assuming he/she also made the mortgage payments) the difference between the balances of encumbrances of record as of the date of the divorce Decree and the present date;
- the balance after that deduction is divided equally between the parties.

The parties are dividing current equity in the home so if there has been a period of high inflation between the time the parties were divorced and the time the home was sold, the spouse who received the lien would receive half of the appreciated value. On the other hand, that spouse's lien had not been receiving any interest during those years. Conversely, should there be a period of deflation, there is the possibility that the lien would have little value at the time of sale.

Another lien method often used is the fixed-dollar lien. The spouse receiving a lien is awarded that lien based upon the equity in the home at the time of the divorce. Interest may or may not be added to this lien, depending upon the wishes of the parties or the order of the Court.

How all of this is decided depends on a number of things. If any part of the property is non-marital, which means one of the spouses owned it (or the money used to purchase the home) before marriage or had received it as a gift, bequest, devise or inheritance or acquired it in exchange for property that fell into one of the above categories, then the Court will view it differently than property acquired during marriage. Other things that can affect the award of the real estate is if the property was acquired after a Decree of Legal Separation or if the property was excluded by a valid Antenuptial Agreement.

The Court may also look at the other assets of the parties. If there are other assets (stocks, bonds, a business, etc.) which are of value, the Court may award the real estate to one and assets equal to that value to the other spouse.

TITLE PROBLEMS

Numerous title problems can result because of a divorce action when real estate is involved. The first and probably most common problem is the inaccurate legal description. Many times a person assumes that the legal description obtained from the property tax statement is sufficient. This is only an abbreviated form for the tax department's own use and is not accurate. If you cannot find your deed, an accurate legal description can be obtained from the County Recorder of the county where the property is located. Having this done correctly in the beginning will save a lot of headaches when it comes to selling the property.

A spouse's lien on the property must be paid off at the time of sale and a Satisfaction of Lien and Quit Claim Deed obtained from the spouse. The money and Satisfaciton of Lien should be exchanged at the same time - don't plan on getting the Satisfaction at a later date.

If your spouse is uncooperative and will not sign a Quit Claim Deed even though you have been awarded the property, you can still transfer clear title if the wording in the divorce Decree is correctly set out (and assuming your spouse has no lien. If he/she does, then you need to contact an attorney for a solution to the problem).

HOW TO AVOID PROBLEMS

Be sure that an accurate legal description appears in all divorce documents.

Be sure that the divorce Decree allows for transfer of title by the Decree, especially if your spouse is uncooperative.

File a certified copy of the divorce Decree with the County Recorder of the county where the property is located and, if at all possible, obtain a Quit Claim Deed from your spouse and file that, too.

Obtain a Satisfaction of Lien and Quit Claim Deed from your spouse when the property is sold and the lien paid off.

If these steps are followed, you should be able to avoid many of the divorce-related problems in selling your real estate.

CHAPTER XII
REFINANCING — SHOULD YOU DO IT?

Refinancing is done for several reasons. Some homeowners find that they have a large amount of equity tied up in their homes. Inflation has increased the value of the home, and repayment of the existing mortgage has also added to the equity. Should that homeowner incur another, larger, mortgage? How does the owner decide when this is appropriate?

There must first be a reason for wanting to refinance the home. One reason is to get the cash out of the real estate. In times of high interest rates, there is profit in using the equity money for investments which return a higher rate of interest than the mortgage interest rate incurred by refinancing. Another reason refinancing is often used is to finance a child's education or to pay health costs.

An obvious reason overlooked by many homeowners is that refinancing may offer a better rate of interest than the original mortgage. Although the homeowner must again pay points and closing costs, the lower monthly payment may far exceed those costs and be well worth the time, money and effort expended in obtaining the refinancing.

Before deciding whether refinancing is an appopriate step, the homeowner should investigate the interest rates. If the rates are two percent lower than the current mortgage, then there would be an advantage to the refinancing. The homeowner should also review the refinancing to see if the closing costs and points paid divided by the amount saved each month over the old interest rate exceed thirty-six months. If it does, then the refinancing is probably not advantageous.

Homeowners often refinance the real estate to improve the chances of selling the home. Many times the assumable mortgage on the property is so low that a huge down payment is required by any buyer interested in the property or requires the buyer to obtain a new mortgage which is much costlier than assuming a mortgage. The homeowner who refinances for this reason must be very sure that the new mortgage is also assumable for he has negated any advantage to the refinancing.

BEFORE REFINANCING, KNOW THE FACTS

A lending institution will look at many factors when deciding whether to refinance a property including the credit worthiness of the homeowner, the income level of the owner and the long terms debts owed by the homeowner. These items must meet the ratios of income to debts required by the lending institution. For example, if the homeowner is looking at conventional financing, 25-33% of the owners income may go to repayment of a mortgage; including any long term debts, this ratio would be 33-38%. If the mortgage amount plus long term debt uses more than this amount of the income, then the lending institution will probably deny the application for refinancing.

HOW TO KNOW WHAT MORTGAGE RATES ARE AVAILABLE

Each week the Minneapolis and Saint Paul papers publish the current interest rates being charged by various lending institutions. Even the number of points being charged is included. This is a very good thermometer for the homeowner investigating the possibility of refinancing. A call to a lending institution will yield the same informatin.

WHAT WILL THE LENDING INSTITUTION REQUIRE UPON REFINANCING?

The first requirement, after the homeowner has met the income requirements, is an up-to-date appraisal of the home to determine its current value. The lending institution may require the owner to make critical repairs, such as updating wiring, replacing the roof, fixing windows, etc.

There may have to be an updated abstract of title completed by a title insurance company. It may be wise to use the title insurance company that did the first update so that no new charges for title insurance are required.

If there are any liens on the property, these will have to be paid at closing.

Because of the cost of purchasing a new home, many individuals are choosing to remain in their old homes and remodel instead. Should you decide to keep your present home and repair and remodel it, you may be able to use one of the following financing methods:

HOME IMPROVEMENT LOANS

A home improvement loan is different from refinancing. The old mortgage remains on the property. A second mortgage may be taken out to cover the costs of the improvements. Though there may be costs involved, they are not usually as high as refinancing costs and are repayable over a shorter period of time.

Most lending institutions handle home improvement loans. There are some special programs available for low to middle income individuals and also for individuals who live in certain parts of the State or city.

1. <u>Loan and Grant Programs</u>

If you live in certain areas of Minneapolis or Saint Paul, there may be federal loans available. There is no income limit, but low and moderate income families have priority for these funds. The loans are repayable over twenty years at lower than normal interest rates and have a maximum loan amount. The homeowner must agree to bring his/her home up to code, but may use funds for general improvements and non-code items as well.

2. <u>Minnesota Housing Finance Agency</u>

Loans, at lower than normal interest rates, depending on income, have a fifteen year repayment and are made to individuals with a home at least fifteen years old, or in need of repairs for health and safety hazards or energy conservation. There are no restrictions on what work can be done with the funds, but all improvements must meet code standards. There is a maximum loan amount and a maximum income level with additional income limits if the improvements are necessary to make the home accessible to a handicapped resident of the home. Grants are useable to correct defects, increase energy efficiency, or bring the property up to code. Whether or not there is money available may depend upon the given year and what the legislature has allotted for these programs.

3. <u>Other Programs</u>

From time to time other financing programs become available. Check with your State and City offices to find out what programs are available for you, what the requirements of the programs are, and what the money can be used for.

4. Bank or Savings and Loans

Most banks and savings and loan institutions have loans available for remodeling and repairing purposes. The interest rate is usually higher than on a mortgage and repayable over a shorter length of time. The bank or savings and loan may take a second mortgage on the property. A usual rule of thumb is that the loan amount and the first mortgage should not exceed 70% of the value of the property.

APPENDIX

HOME INFORMATION SHEET

Owner________________________________Res. Ph.______________________

Address______________________________Bus. Ph.______________________

Price_____________No. of bedrooms________Style of Home___________

Exterior____________Sq. footage________Electric (amp)_____________

Heat/Fuel System____________Year Built_____________________________

Tax Base__________________Lot Size_________________________________

School District______________Financing Terms_______________________

Room	Size	Room	Size
Kitchen	______	Master bedroom	______
Living room	______	Bedroom #2	______
Dining room	______	Bedroom #3	______
Rec. room	______	Basement	______

Central Air	____	Garbage Disposal	____
Fireplace	____	Range & Oven	____
Dishwasher	____	Hood Fan	____
Well Water	____	Septic Tank	____
Finished Basement	____	One Car Garage	____
Central Vacuum	____	Two Car Garage	____
Rec Room	____	Window Air	____
Master Bath	____	220 Volt	____
Two Baths	____	110 Volt	____

Comments____

____

____

____

SAMPLE LISTING AGREEMENT

Address ____

List Price ____________________ Terms ________________________

To: ____, realtor.

In consideration of your efforts, expenditures and your agreement to list in your office the real estate ("property") described hereon and to place this property on the Multiple listing Service of the St. Paul Area Board of Realtors, Inc., I hereby appoint you my agent and grant the exclusive right to sell the property described hereon for the listing price and terms hereon set forth or such other price and terms which I may hereafter accept.

This agreement and agency shall remain in effect until _______. If, before the expiration of this agreement I receive a written offer consistent with the terms of this listing, or other terms accepted by me, I agree to pay you a commission of _____% of the sale price, whether such is obtained by you, by me, by any member of the Multiple Listing Service of the St. Paul Area Board of Realtors, or any other party.

I further agree to pay you at the same rate of commission should I contract to sell or exchange the property within _____ days after the expiration date of this agreement to any person to whom during the period of this agreement makes inquiry to me regarding this property. However, I shall not be obligated to pay you a commission if during the protection period I have entered into another valid listing agreement pursuant to which I am required to pay a commission to another real estate broker for the contract for sale or exchange of this property.

Permission is granted to you to submit pertinent information concerning this property to the Multiple Listing Service, and upon execution of a purchase agreement for the property, to notify the Multiple Listing Service of such sale and to disseminate sales information to the members of the Multiple Listing Service. The Multiple Listing Service, the listing broker and the selling broker shall not be liable for errors or omissions on the attached data form.

I agree to cooperate with you during the term of this agreement and will directly refer to you the names of all persons or parties making inquiries concerning this property. You shall be given access to the property at reasonable times upon request. Your right to access to the property shall carry no obligation or responsibility for maintenance including the heating of the structure and snow removal, whether the property is occupied or vacant.

You are given permission to place or erect a "For Sale" sign on the property.

Receipt is hereby acknowledged of a copy of this listing agreement.

Date ____________________

Owner ______________________________ Bus. Ph. ________________

Address ______________________________ Res. Ph. ________________

BROKER ______________________________ By ____________________

EXPLANATION OF LISTING AGREEMENT

It is important to understand any legal document you sign. Should you choose to retain a real estate agent to sell your home, he/she will most likely explain the pertinent parts of the listing agreement. But, even so, read the document.

Paragraph 1 - you agree that the agent (and the agency for which that agent works) has the exclusive right to sell your home. You agree to sell at the price listed, or such other price as you may agree. In other words, you cannot decide, after receiving an offer for the listed price, to change your mind and want more for your home. You can accept an offer for less than the listed price. (During periods of low interest rates and high housing demands you may receive more than one offer. You can, of course, choose to accept the offer that is higher than your asking price under those circumstances).

Paragraph 2 - the agent has your home listed until that date filled in on the Agreement. If the home sells during that period of time, you will pay the agent a commission of a certain percent. It doesn't matter who found the buyer. If during that time you found the buyer, you still have to pay the commission.

Paragraph 3 - after the listing agreement expires, the agent still has the right to receive his commission for a certain number of days (he will fill this in; it is usually 30 days) if you sell to anyone the agent talked to while he/she had the home listed. This is to prevent a seller from "cutting a deal" with a prospective buyer who found out about the home through the agent's efforts, but waits until the listing agreement expires to purchase the home. However, if you enter into a listing agreement with another agency, then this paragraphs does not apply.

Paragraph 4 - you agree to allow the agent to put information about your home in a catalog of homes for sale (Multiple Listing) and to give information about your home to other agents who are members of the Multiple Listing Service. Be sure the information the agent puts on his information sheet is accurate. If you knowingly make false statements or omit facts, you could be held liable for those falsities or omissions.

Paragraph 5. You agree to cooperate with your agent and allow him/her to show the property at reasonable times. The agent is not responsible for maintaining your home.

GLOSSARY

A SIMPLE AND CONCISE GLOSSARY OF BASIC TERMS NECESSARY TO UNDERSTAND REAL ESTATE TALK

Abstract of Title — A condensed history of the title to the land, consisting of a summary of the conveyancing documents which affect the land, or the liabilities which may affect the land.

Acceleration Clause — A clause in a mortgage note or deed where the entire amount of the loan or debt becomes due.

Acknowledgement — A party who has executed an instrument declares before some officer of the Court or a Notary Public that the execution was of his own voluntary will.

Amortization — Paying off a mortgage in installments with a partial payment of principal and accrued interest at regular intervals for a definite time.

Appraisal — A valuation or estimation of value of property by a disinterested person who is specifically qualified.

Appreciation — Increase in the value of property.

Assignment — A transfer of an interest in property.

Assumption — Transfer of the debt owed to the mortgage lender to the buyer of the property.

Balloon payment — The entire balance due and owing on a certain date must be paid in full as of that date.

Bill of Sale — A written agreement, by which one person transfers title to personal property to another person.

Cancellation clause — A clause within a contract which states under what circumstances the contract may be cancelled.

Certificate of Title — The document which shows fee ownership in Registered (Torrens) property.

Closing Costs — Fees which must be paid by a buyer and/or seller at the time of closing the sale. These include all charges associated with the origination of a new mortgage, including, but not limited to origination fee, appraisal fees, credit report, title work and title insurance for the lender.

Closing Statement — Sets forth the fees to be paid by the buyer and/or seller at the time of closing.

Contract for Deed — A contract entered into by a buyer and seller whereby the buyer is obligated to pay a certain sum of money prior to the transfer of title in the property to the buyer.

Conventional Insured Mortgage — The financing repayment is guaranteed by an insurance company thus allowing a buyer to pay less money down.

Conventional Mortgage — Financing of the purchase of property through a lending institution.

Deed — An instrument, containing a contract or covenant to convey land from a seller to a buyer.

Down Payment — Partial payment of the total purchase price which is paid to the seller at the time of closing.

Earnest Money — Payment of some money when signing a purchase agreement.

Escrow — Money delivered into the hands of a third party usually a bank or title insurance company to be held until a contingency or performance of a condition.

Exclusive Listing Agreement — A contract whereby the owner shall not sell the property through anyone other than the real estate agency to whom the listing contract was given. An example is found in the book.

Fee Title — Actual, legal ownership as opposed to equitable ownership like what one owns when paying on a Contract for Deed.

Float — The buyer is gambling that the interest rate will be less in the future and does not lock in an interest rate when applying for a mortgage.

Foreclosure — A proceeding by which the rights of the mortgage holder of real property are enforced. The property is put up for public sale through an auction, with the mortgage lender receiving out of the proceeds of the sale, the amount of his debt with certain costs. The remaining amount of the sale price is given to the debtor (owner of the property). Should there still be money owed by the debtor to the mortgage lender, there is usually a judgment filed against the debtor for the portion of the monies owed.

Grantee — The person to whom a transfer is made.

Grantor — The person who transferred the property.

Joint Tenancy — Property is owned by two or more persons under the same instrument. The interest of each joint tenant, upon his death, goes to the surviving joint tenant or joint tenants, to the exclusion of the decedent's heirs.

Lender — He from whom the money is borrowed.

Lien — A right of a creditor in certain property owned by the debtor, as security for the debt owed.

Lock — When a buyer locks an interest rate, the lending institution agrees to give the buyer the mortgage at a certain rate of interest upon closing on a certain date. If the lock expires before the closing takes place, then the purchaser could be subjected to a higher rate of interest.

Mechanic's Lien — A lien which exists in favor of persons who have performed work or furnished materials in and for the building.

Mortagee — Creditor, the person who loans the homeowner money.

Mortgagor — Debtor, or homeowner.

Points — Each point is one percent of the mortgage amount and is charged at the time of closing to achieve an interest rate for the homeowner which is lower than what would otherwise be charged.

Principal — That amount of money borrowed for the purpose of the purchase of the property.

Purchase Agreement	A contract between the seller of real estate and the perspective buyer which sets forth the terms upon which the seller agrees to sell the property and the buyer agrees to buy the property.
Quit Claim Deed	Intended to pass any interest the grantor may have in the property, but does not promise that grantor has any interest and contains no warranties of title.
Realty	A general term meaning lands and buildings thereon.
Redemption Period	A length of time, prescribed by law, in which a debtor may pay amounts owing to the mortgagor.
Special Assessment	An amount of money owed by the property owner to the City or County for its installation of water, sewer, storm sewer, etc.
Special Warranty Deed	A clause inserted in the deed by which the grantor forever defends, guarantees and warrants the land against all persons claiming through or under him (instead of all persons in general as is the usual warranty deed).
Tenancy in Common	Each owner in the property has a distinct and separate estate in said property. The surviving owner or owners of the property does not take title to the entire property, but the decedent's interest passes to his heirs.
Title Opinion	A written legal report by a lawyer on the status of the title and any defects of the same.
Torrens Property	Land registered with the government. The buyer is absolutely protected against any liens or outstanding interests not listed on the Certificate of Title. Title is vested in the buyer when a new Certificate of Title is delivered, not when the deed is executed.
Vendee	A purchaser or buyer of real estate.
Vendor	The person selling real property.

Warranty Deed	The conveyancing instrument (deed) to real property by which the grantor warrants and defends title and possession to the real estate against claims of all persons.

MONTHLY PAYMENT SCHEDULES

The following pages will assist you in finding out what your monthly payments will be for homes of various prices and various interest rates. You can even decide whether you would like to pay off the mortgage in less than the normal thirty years by seeing how a shorter mortgage will affect your budget.

The first number on the top left of each page is the interest rate for that particular page. Also across the top row are numbers of years for which mortgage payments are calculated. At the lower interest rates, the chart begins with fifteen years. At the higher interest rates, it starts at twenty years.

Along the left side going down is the amount to be paid beginning with $25.00 and ending at $100,000.00.

To use the charts, choose the interest rate you think you will have to pay; choose the number of years you will be paying the mortgage and choose the amount you will be paying.

If you have a $100,000.00 mortgage at 8% to be paid over 30 years, you can expect principal and interest payments of $734.17. On top of this you will have to pay taxes and insurance. Be sure to allow for these.

If the mortgazge amount is $37,500.00, you can calculate the monthly payment even though the amount isn't on the chart. Let's say you want to pay this off in fifteen years at 8%:

First find the payment for	$35,000.00	$334.54
Then find the amount for	2,000.00	19.12
Lastly, the amount for	500.00	4.78
	$37,500.00	$358.44

MONTHLY PAYMENT

8%

Years	15	16	17	18	19	20	21	22	23	24	25	26	27	28	29	30
Amount																
25	.24	.23	.22	.22	.21	.21	.21	.20	.20	.20	.19	.19	.19	.19	.19	.18
50	.48	.46	.45	.44	.43	.42	.41	.40	.40	.39	.39	.38	.38	.37	.37	.37
75	.72	.69	.67	.66	.64	.63	.62	.61	.60	.59	.58	.57	.57	.56	.56	.55
100	.96	.93	.90	.88	.87	.84	.82	.81	.79	.78	.77	.76	.76	.75	.74	.73
200	1.91	1.85	1.80	1.75	1.71	1.67	1.64	1.61	1.59	1.57	1.55	1.53	1.51	1.50	1.48	1.47
300	2.87	2.78	2.70	2.63	2.57	2.51	2.46	2.42	2.38	2.35	2.32	2.29	2.27	2.24	2.22	2.20
400	3.82	3.70	3.59	3.50	3.42	3.35	3.28	3.23	3.18	3.13	3.09	3.05	3.02	2.99	2.96	2.94
500	4.78	4.63	4.49	4.38	4.28	4.18	4.10	4.03	3.97	3.91	3.86	3.82	3.76	3.74	3.70	3.67
600	5.74	5.55	5.39	5.25	5.13	5.02	4.93	4.84	4.77	4.70	4.64	4.58	4.53	4.49	4.44	4.41
700	6.69	6.48	6.29	6.13	5.99	5.86	5.75	5.65	5.56	5.48	5.41	5.34	5.29	5.23	5.18	5.14
800	7.65	7.40	7.19	7.00	6.84	6.69	6.57	6.45	6.35	6.26	6.18	6.11	6.04	5.98	5.92	5.87
900	8.60	8.33	8.09	7.88	7.70	7.53	7.39	7.26	7.15	7.04	6.95	6.87	6.80	6.73	6.66	6.61
1,000	9.67	9.25	8.98	8.75	8.72	8.37	8.21	8.07	7.94	7.83	7.73	7.63	7.55	7.48	7.40	7.34
2,000	19.12	18.50	17.67	17.50	17.10	16.73	16.42	16.13	15.88	15.65	15.45	15.27	15.10	14.95	14.80	14.68
3,000	28.68	27.75	26.95	26.25	25.65	25.10	24.63	24.20	23.83	23.48	23.18	22.90	22.65	22.43	22.20	22.03
4,000	38.23	37.00	35.93	35.00	34.20	33.47	32.83	32.27	31.77	31.30	30.90	30.53	30.20	29.90	29.60	29.37
5,000	47.79	46.25	44.92	43.75	42.75	41.83	41.04	40.33	39.71	39.13	38.63	38.17	37.75	37.38	37.00	36.71
6,000	57.35	55.50	53.90	52.50	51.30	50.20	49.25	48.40	47.65	46.95	46.35	45.80	45.30	44.85	44.40	44.05
7,000	66.91	64.75	62.88	61.25	59.85	58.57	57.46	56.47	55.59	54.78	54.08	53.43	52.85	52.33	51.80	51.39
8,000	76.47	74.00	71.87	70.00	68.40	66.93	65.67	64.53	63.53	62.60	61.80	61.07	60.40	59.80	59.20	58.73
9,000	86.03	83.25	80.85	78.75	76.95	75.30	73.88	72.60	71.48	70.43	69.53	68.70	67.95	67.28	66.60	66.08
10,000	95.59	92.50	89.84	87.50	87.17	83.67	82.09	80.67	79.42	78.25	77.25	76.34	75.50	74.75	74.00	73.42
15,000	143.38	138.75	134.75	131.25	128.25	125.50	123.13	121.00	119.13	117.38	115.88	114.50	113.25	112.13	111.00	110.13
20,000	191.17	185.00	179.67	175.00	171.00	167.34	164.17	161.34	158.84	156.50	154.50	152.67	151.00	149.50	148.00	146.84
25,000	238.96	231.25	224.58	218.75	213.75	209.17	205.21	201.67	198.54	195.63	193.13	190.83	188.75	186.88	185.00	183.54
30,000	286.75	277.50	269.50	262.50	256.50	251.00	246.25	242.00	238.25	234.75	231.75	229.00	226.50	224.25	222.00	220.25
35,000	334.54	323.75	314.42	306.25	299.25	292.83	287.29	282.33	277.96	273.88	270.38	267.17	264.25	261.63	259.00	256.96
40,000	382.33	370.00	359.33	350.00	342.00	334.67	328.33	322.67	317.67	313.00	309.00	305.33	302.00	299.00	296.00	293.67
45,000	403.13	416.25	404.25	393.75	384.75	376.50	369.38	363.00	357.38	352.13	347.63	343.50	339.75	336.38	333.00	330.38
50,000	477.92	462.50	449.17	437.50	427.50	418.33	410.42	401.25	397.08	391.25	386.25	381.67	377.50	373.75	370.00	367.08
55,000	525.71	508.75	494.08	481.25	470.25	460.17	451.46	441.38	436.79	430.38	424.88	419.83	415.25	411.13	407.00	403.79
60,000	573.50	555.00	539.00	525.00	513.00	502.00	492.50	484.00	476.50	469.50	463.50	458.00	453.00	448.50	444.00	440.50
65,000	621.29	601.25	583.92	568.75	555.75	543.83	533.54	524.33	516.21	508.64	502.13	496.17	490.75	485.88	481.00	477.21
70,000	669.08	647.50	628.83	612.50	598.50	585.67	574.58	564.67	555.92	547.75	540.75	534.33	528.50	523.25	518.00	513.92
75,000	716.88	693.75	673.75	656.25	641.25	627.50	615.63	605.00	595.63	586.88	579.38	572.50	566.25	560.63	555.00	550.63
80,000	764.67	740.00	718.67	700.00	684.00	669.33	656.67	645.33	635.33	626.00	618.00	610.67	604.00	598.00	592.00	587.33
100,000	955.83	925.00	898.33	875.00	771.67	836.67	820.83	806.67	794.17	782.50	772.50	763.33	755.00	747.50	740.00	734.17

MONTHLY PAYMENT

8¼% (left) · 8¼% (right)

8¼% Years	15	16	17	18	19	20	21	22	23	24	25	26	27	28	29	30
25	.24	.24	.23	.22	.22	.21	.21	.21	.20	.20	.20	.20	.19	.19	.19	.19
50	.49	.47	.46	.45	.44	.43	.42	.41	.41	.40	.39	.39	.39	.38	.38	.38
75	.73	.71	.69	.67	.65	.64	.63	.62	.61	.60	.59	59	.58	.57	.57	.56
100	.97	.94	.91	.89	.87	.85	.84	.82	.81	.80	.80	.78	.77	.76	.76	.75
200	1.94	1.88	1.83	1.78	1.74	1.71	1.67	1.65	1.62	1.60	1.58	1.56	1.54	1.53	1.52	1.50
300	2.91	2.82	2.74	2.67	2.61	2.56	2.51	2.47	2.43	2.40	2.37	2.34	2.32	2.32	2.27	2.26
400	3.88	3.76	3.65	3.56	3.48	3.41	3.35	3.29	3.24	3.20	3.16	3.12	3.09	3.06	3.03	3.01
500	4.85	4.70	4.57	4.45	4.35	4.26	4.18	4.11	4.05	4.00	3.95	3.90	3.86	3.82	3.70	3.76
600	5.83	5.64	5.48	5.35	5.22	5.12	5.02	4.94	4.86	4.80	3.95	4.68	4.63	4.59	4.55	4.51
700	6.80	6.58	6.39	6.24	6.09	5.97	5.86	5.76	5.67	5.59	5.52	5.46	5.40	5.35	5.30	5.26
800	7.77	7.52	7.31	7.13	6.96	6.82	6.69	6.58	6.48	6.39	6.31	6.24	6.17	6.11	6.06	6.01
900	8.74	8.46	8.22	8.02	7.83	7.67	7.53	7.40	7.29	7.19	7.10	7.02	6.95	6.88	6.82	6.77
1,000	9.71	9.40	9.13	8.91	8.70	8.53	8.37	8.23	8.10	7.99	7.90	7.80	7.72	7.64	7.58	7.52
2,000	19.42	18.80	18.27	17.82	17.40	17.05	16.73	16.45	16.20	15.98	15.78	15.60	15.43	15.28	15.15	15.03
3,000	29.13	28.20	27.40	26.73	26.10	25.58	25.10	24.68	24.30	23.98	23.68	23.40	23.15	22.93	22.73	22.55
4,000	38.83	37.60	36.53	35.63	34.80	34.10	33.47	32.90	32.40	31.97	31.57	31.20	30.87	30.57	30.30	30.07
5,000	48.54	47.00	45.67	44.54	43.50	42.63	41.83	41.13	40.50	40.00	39.46	39.00	38.58	38.21	37.88	37.58
6,000	58.25	56.40	54.80	53.45	52.20	51.15	50.20	49.35	48.60	47.95	39.46	46.80	46.30	45.85	45.45	45.10
7,000	67.96	65.80	63.93	62.36	60.90	59.68	58.57	57.58	56.70	55.94	55.24	54.60	54.02	53.49	53.03	52.62
8,000	77.67	75.20	73.07	71.27	69.60	68.20	66.93	65.80	64.80	63.93	63.13	62.40	61.73	61.13	60.60	60.13
9,000	87.38	84.60	82.20	80.18	78.30	76.73	75.30	74.03	72.90	71.93	71.03	70.20	69.45	68.78	68.18	67.65
10,000	97.09	94.00	91.34	89.09	87.00	85.25	83.67	82.25	81.00	79.92	78.92	78.00	77.17	76.42	75.75	75.47
15,000	145.63	141.00	137.00	133.63	130.50	127.88	125.50	123.38	121.50	119.88	118.38	117.00	115.75	114.63	113.63	112.75
20,000	194.17	188.00	182.67	178.17	174.00	170.50	167.34	164.50	162.00	159.84	157.84	156.00	164.34	152.84	151.50	150.34
25,000	242.71	235.00	228.33	222.71	217.50	213.13	209.17	205.63	202.50	199.79	197.29	195.00	192.92	191.04	189.38	187.92
30,000	291.25	282.00	274.00	267.25	261.00	255.75	251.00	246.75	243.00	239.75	236.75	234.00	231.50	229.30	227.25	225.50
35,000	339.79	329.00	319.67	311.79	304.50	298.38	292.83	287.88	283.50	279.71	276.21	273.00	270.08	267.46	265.13	263.00
40,000	388.33	376.00	365.33	356.33	348.00	341.00	334.67	329.00	324.00	319.67	315.67	312.00	308.67	305.67	303.00	300.67
45,000	436.88	423.00	411.00	400.88	391.50	383.63	376.50	370.13	364.50	359.63	355.13	351.00	347.25	343.88	340.88	338.25
50,000	485.42	470.00	456.67	445.42	435.00	426.25	418.33	411.25	405.00	399.58	394.58	390.00	385.83	382.08	378.75	375.83
55,000	533.96	517.00	502.33	489.96	478.50	468.88	460.17	452.38	445.50	439.54	434.04	429.00	424.42	420.29	416.63	413.42
60,000	582.50	564.00	548.00	534.50	522.00	511.50	502.00	493.50	486.00	479.50	485.00	468.00	463.00	458.50	454.50	451.00
65,000	631.04	611.00	593.67	579.04	565.50	554.13	543.83	534.63	526.50	519.46	512.96	507.00	501.58	496.71	492.38	488.58
70,000	679.58	658.00	639.33	623.58	609.00	596.75	585.67	575.75	567.00	559.42	552.42	546.00	540.17	534.92	530.25	526.20
75,000	728.13	705.00	685.00	668.13	652.50	639.38	627.50	616.88	607.50	599.38	591.88	585.00	578.75	573.13	568.13	563.75
80,000	776.67	752.00	730.67	712.67	696.00	682.00	669.33	658.00	648.00	639.33	631.33	624.00	617.33	611.33	606.00	601.33
100,000	970.83	940.00	913.33	890.33	870.00	852.50	836.67	822.50	810.00	799.17	781.17	780.00	771.67	764.17	757.50	751.67

MONTHLY PAYMENT

8½% (left), 8½% (above 29)

Years / Amount	15	16	17	18	19	20	21	22	23	24	25	26	27	28	29	30
25	.25	.24	.23	.23	.22	.22	.22	.21	.21	.20	.20	.20	.20	.20	.19	.19
50	.49	.48	.46	.45	.44	.43	.43	.42	.41	.41	.40	.40	.39	.39	.39	.38
75	.74	.72	.70	.68	.66	.65	.65	.63	.62	.61	.60	.60	.59	.59	.58	.58
100	.99	.96	.93	.91	.87	.87	.86	.84	.83	.82	.81	.80	.80	.78	.78	.77
200	1.97	1.91	1.86	1.81	1.77	1.74	1.72	1.68	1.65	1.63	1.61	1.59	1.58	1.56	1.55	1.54
300	2.96	2.87	2.79	2.72	2.66	2.61	2.58	2.52	2.48	2.45	2.42	2.39	2.37	2.35	2.33	2.31
400	3.94	3.82	3.71	3.62	3.54	3.47	3.44	3.36	3.31	3.26	3.22	3.19	3.16	3.13	3.10	3.08
500	4.93	4.78	4.64	4.53	4.29	4.34	4.30	4.20	4.13	4.08	4.03	3.98	3.95	3.91	3.88	3.85
600	5.91	5.73	5.57	5.44	5.32	5.21	5.17	5.04	4.96	4.90	4.84	4.78	4.74	4.69	4.65	4.62
700	6.90	6.69	6.50	6.34	6.20	6.08	6.03	5.87	5.79	5.71	5.64	5.58	5.52	5.47	5.43	5.38
800	7.88	7.64	7.43	7.25	7.09	6.95	6.89	6.71	6.61	6.53	6.45	6.37	6.31	6.25	6.20	6.15
900	8.87	8.60	8.36	8.15	7.97	7.82	7.75	7.55	7.44	7.34	7.25	7.17	7.10	7.04	6.98	6.92
1,000	9.85	9.55	9.28	9.06	8.86	8.68	8.61	8.39	8.27	8.16	8.06	7.97	7.89	7.82	7.75	7.67
2,000	19.70	19.10	18.57	18.12	17.72	17.37	17.22	16.78	16.53	16.32	16.12	15.93	15.78	15.63	15.50	15.38
3,000	29.55	28.65	27.85	27.18	26.58	26.05	25.83	25.18	24.80	24.48	24.18	23.90	23.68	23.45	23.25	23.08
4,000	39.40	38.20	37.13	36.23	35.43	34.73	34.43	33.57	33.07	32.63	32.23	31.87	31.57	31.27	31.00	30.77
5,000	49.25	47.75	46.42	45.29	44.29	43.42	43.04	41.96	41.33	40.79	40.29	39.83	37.46	39.08	38.75	38.46
6,000	59.10	57.30	55.70	54.35	53.15	52.10	51.65	50.35	49.60	48.95	48.35	47.80	47.35	46.90	46.50	46.15
7,000	68.95	66.85	64.98	63.41	62.01	60.78	60.26	58.74	57.87	57.11	56.41	55.77	35.24	54.72	54.25	53.84
8,000	78.80	76.40	74.27	72.47	70.87	69.47	68.87	67.13	66.13	65.27	64.47	63.73	63.13	62.53	62.00	61.53
9,000	88.65	85.95	83.55	81.53	79.73	78.15	77.48	75.53	74.40	73.43	72.53	71.70	71.03	70.35	69.75	69.23
10,000	98.50	95.50	92.83	90.58	88.58	86.83	86.08	83.92	82.67	81.58	80.58	79.67	78.92	78.17	77.50	76.92
15,000	147.75	143.25	139.25	135.88	132.88	130.25	129.13	125.88	124.00	122.38	120.88	119.50	118.38	117.25	116.25	115.38
20,000	197.00	191.00	185.67	181.17	177.17	173.67	172.17	167.83	165.33	163.17	161.17	159.33	157.83	156.33	155.00	153.83
25,000	246.25	238.75	232.08	226.46	221.46	217.08	215.21	209.78	206.67	203.96	201.46	199.17	197.29	195.42	193.75	192.29
30,000	295.50	286.50	287.50	271.75	265.75	260.50	258.25	251.75	248.00	244.75	241.75	239.00	236.75	234.50	232.50	230.75
35,000	344.75	334.25	324.92	317.04	310.04	303.92	301.29	293.71	289.33	285.54	282.04	278.83	276.21	273.58	271.25	269.21
40,000	394.00	382.00	371.33	362.33	354.33	347.33	344.33	335.67	327.33	326.33	322.33	318.67	315.67	312.67	310.00	307.67
45,000	443.25	429.75	417.75	407.63	398.63	390.75	387.38	833.92	372.00	367.13	362.63	358.50	355.13	351.75	348.75	346.13
50,000	492.50	477.50	464.17	452.92	442.92	434.17	430.42	419.58	413.33	407.92	402.92	398.33	394.58	390.83	387.50	384.58
55,000	541.75	525.25	510.58	498.21	487.21	477.58	473.46	461.54	454.67	448.71	443.21	438.17	434.04	429.92	426.25	423.04
60,000	591.00	573.00	557.00	543.50	531.50	521.00	516.50	503.50	496.00	489.50	483.50	478.00	473.50	469.00	465.00	461.50
65,000	640.25	620.75	603.42	588.79	575.79	564.42	559.54	545.46	537.33	530.29	523.79	517.83	512.96	508.08	503.75	499.96
70,000	689.50	668.50	649.83	634.08	620.08	607.83	602.58	587.42	578.67	571.08	564.08	557.67	552.42	547.17	542.50	538.42
75,000	738.75	716.25	696.25	679.38	664.38	651.25	645.63	629.38	620.00	611.88	604.38	597.50	591.88	586.25	581.25	576.88
80,000	788.00	764.00	742.67	724.67	708.67	694.67	688.67	671.33	661.33	652.67	644.67	637.33	631.33	625.33	620.00	615.33
100,000	985.00	955.00	928.33	905.83	885.83	868.33	860.83	839.17	826.67	815.83	805.83	796.67	789.17	781.67	775.00	769.20

MONTHLY PAYMENT

8 3/4% 8 3/4%

Years	15	16	17	18	19	20	21	22	23	24	25	26	27	28	29	30
Amount																
25	.25	.24	.24	.23	.23	.22	.22	.21	.21	.21	.21	.20	.20	.20	.20	.20
50	.50	.49	.47	.46	.45	.44	.43	.43	.42	.42	.41	.41	.40	.40	.39	.39
75	.75	.73	.71	.69	.68	.66	.65	.64	.63	.62	.62	.61	.60	.60	.59	.59
100	1.00	.97	.94	.92	.90	.88	.87	.86	.84	.83	.82	.81	.81	.80	.79	.79
200	2.00	1.94	1.89	1.84	1.80	1.77	1.74	1.71	1.69	1.67	1.65	1.63	1.61	1.60	1.59	1.58
300	3.00	2.91	2.83	2.77	2.71	2.65	2.61	2.57	2.53	2.50	2.47	2.44	2.42	2.40	2.40	2.36
400	4.00	3.88	3.78	3.69	3.61	3.54	3.48	3.42	3.37	3.33	3.29	3.26	3.22	3.20	3.17	3.15
500	5.00	4.85	4.72	4.61	4.51	4.42	4.35	4.28	4.22	4.16	4.11	4.07	4.03	4.00	3.96	3.94
600	6.00	5.82	5.67	5.53	5.41	5.31	5.22	5.13	5.06	5.00	4.94	4,89	4.84	4.80	4.75	4.73
700	7.00	6.79	6.61	6.45	6.31	6.19	6.08	5.99	5.90	5.83	5.76	5.70	5.64	5.59	5.55	5.51
800	8.00	7.76	7.55	7.37	7.21	7.07	6.95	6.84	6.75	6.66	6.58	6.51	6.45	6.39	6.34	6.30
900	9.00	8.73	8.50	8.30	8.12	7.96	7.82	7.70	7.59	7.49	7.40	7.33	7.25	7.19	7.13	7.09
1,000	10.00	9.70	9.44	9.22	9.02	8.84	8.69	8.55	8.43	8.33	8.23	8.14	8.06	7.97	7.93	7.88
2,000	20.00	19.40	18.88	18.43	18.03	17.68	17.38	17.10	16.87	16.65	16.45	16.28	16.12	15.98	15.85	15.75
3,000	30.00	29.10	28.33	27.65	27.05	26.53	26.08	25.65	25.30	24.98	24.68	24.43	24.18	23.98	23.78	23.63
4,000	40.00	38.80	37.77	36.87	36.07	35.37	34.77	34.20	33.73	33.30	32.90	32.57	32.23	31.97	31.70	31.50
5,000	50.00	48.50	47.21	46.08	45.08	44.21	43.46	42.75	42.17	41.63	41.13	40.71	40.29	39.96	39.63	39.38
6,000	60.00	58.20	56.65	55.30	54.10	53.05	52.15	51.30	50.60	49.95	49.35	48.85	48.35	47.95	47.55	47.25
7,000	70.00	67.90	66.09	64.52	63.12	61.89	60.84	59.85	59.03	58.28	57.58	56.99	56.41	55.94	55.48	55.13
8,000	80.00	77.60	75.53	73.73	72.13	70.73	69.53	68.40	67.47	66.60	65.80	65.13	64.47	63.93	63.40	63.00
9,000	90.00	87.30	84.98	82.95	81.15	79.58	78.23	76.95	75.90	74.93	74.03	73.28	72.53	71.93	71.33	70.88
10,000	100.00	97.00	94.42	92.17	90.17	88.42	86.92	85.50	84.34	83.25	82.25	81.42	80.58	79.92	79.25	78.75
15,000	150.00	145.50	141.63	138.25	135.25	132.63	130.38	128.25	126.50	124.88	123.38	122.13	120.88	119.88	118.88	118.13
20,000	200.00	194.00	188.84	184.34	180.34	176.84	173.84	171.00	168.67	166.50	164.50	162.83	161.17	159.83	158.50	157.50
25,000	250.00	242.50	236.04	230.42	225.42	221.04	217.29	213.75	210.83	208.13	205.63	203.54	201.46	199.79	198.13	196.88
30,000	300.00	291.00	283.25	276.50	270.50	265.25	260.75	256.50	253.00	249.75	246.75	244.25	241.75	239.75	237.75	236.25
35,000	350.00	339.50	330.46	322.58	315.58	309.46	304.21	299.25	295.17	291.38	287.88	284.96	282.04	279.71	277.38	275.63
40,000	400.00	388.00	377.67	368.67	360.67	353.67	347.67	342.00	337.33	333.00	329.00	325.67	322.33	319.67	317.00	315.00
45,000	450.00	436.00	424.88	414.75	405.75	397.88	391.13	384.75	379.50	374.63	370.13	366.38	362.63	359.63	356.63	364.38
50,000	500.00	485.00	472.08	460.83	450.83	442.08	434.58	427.50	421.67	416.25	411.25	407.08	402.92	399.58	396.25	393.75
55,000	550.00	533.50	519.29	506.92	495.92	486.29	478.04	470.25	463.83	457.88	452.38	447.79	443.21	439.54	435.88	433.13
60,000	600.00	582.00	566.50	553.00	541.00	530.50	521.50	513.00	506.00	499.50	493.50	488.50	483.50	479.50	475.50	472.50
65,000	650.00	630.50	613.71	599.08	586.08	574.71	564.96	555.75	548.17	541.13	534.63	529.21	523.79	519.46	515.13	511.88
70,000	700.00	679.00	660.92	645.17	631.17	618.92	608.42	598.50	590.33	582.75	575.75	569.92	564.08	559.42	554.75	551.25
75,000	750.00	727.50	708.13	691.13	676.25	663.13	651.88	641.25	632.50	624.38	616.88	610.63	604.38	599.38	594.38	590.63
80,000	800.00	776.00	755.33	737.33	721.33	707.33	695.33	684.00	674.67	666.00	658.00	671.33	644.67	639.33	634.00	630.00
100,000	1000.00	970.00	944.17	921.67	901.67	884.17	869.17	855.00	843.33	832.50	822.50	184.17	805.83	799.17	792.50	787.50

9% Years	15	16	17	18	19	20	21	22	23	24	25	26	27	28	9% 29	30
Amount																
25	.25	.25	.24	.23	.23	.23	.22	.22	.22	.21	.21	.21	.21	.20	.20	.20
50	.51	.49	.48	.47	.46	.45	.44	.44	.43	.42	.42	.42	.41	.41	.41	.40
75	.76	.74	.72	.70	.69	.68	.66	.65	.65	.64	.63	.62	.62	.61	.61	.60
100	1.02	.99	.96	.94	.92	.90	.89	.87	.86	.85	.84	.83	.82	.82	.81	.81
200	2.03	1.97	1.92	1.87	1.84	1.80	1.77	1.74	1.72	1.70	1.68	1.66	1.65	1.63	1.62	1.61
300	3.05	2.96	2.88	2.81	2.75	2.70	2.66	2.62	2.58	2.55	2.52	2.49	2.47	2.45	2.43	2.42
400	4.06	3.94	3.84	3.75	3.67	3.60	3.54	3.49	3.44	3.40	3.36	3.32	3.29	3.27	3.24	3.22
500	5.08	4.93	4.80	4.68	4.59	4.50	4.43	4.36	4.30	4.25	4.20	4.15	4.12	4.08	4.05	4.03
600	6.09	5.91	5.76	5.62	5.51	5.40	5.31	5.23	5.16	5.10	5.04	4.99	4.94	4.90	4.87	4.83
700	7.11	6.90	6.71	6.56	6.42	6.30	6.20	6.10	6.02	5.94	5.88	5.82	5.76	5.72	5.68	5.66
800	8.12	7.88	7.67	7.49	7.34	7.20	7.08	6.97	6.88	6.79	6.72	6.65	6.59	6.53	6.49	6.44
900	9.14	8.87	8.63	8.43	8.26	8.10	7.97	7.85	7.74	7.64	7.56	7.48	7.41	7.35	7.30	7.25
1,000	10.15	9.85	8.59	9.37	9.18	9.00	8.85	8.72	8.60	8.49	8.40	8.31	8.23	8.17	8.11	8.05
2,000	20.30	19.70	19.18	18.73	18.35	18.00	17.70	17.43	17.20	16.98	16.80	16.62	16.47	16.33	16.22	16.10
3,000	30.45	29.55	28.78	28.10	27.53	27.00	26.55	26.15	25.80	25.48	25.20	24.93	24.70	24.50	24.33	24.15
4,000	40.60	39.40	38.37	37.47	36.70	36.00	35.40	34.87	34.40	33.97	33.60	33.23	32.93	32.67	32.43	32.22
5,000	50.75	49.25	47.96	46.83	45.88	45.00	44.25	43.58	43.00	42.46	42.00	41.54	41.17	40.83	40.54	40.25
6,000	60.90	59.10	57.55	56.20	55.05	54.00	53.10	52.30	51.60	50.95	50.40	49.85	49.40	49.00	48.65	48.30
7,000	71.05	68.95	67.14	65.57	64.23	63.00	61.95	61.02	60.20	59.44	58.80	58.16	57.63	57.17	56.76	56.35
8,000	81.20	78.80	76.73	74.93	73.40	72.00	70.80	69.73	68.80	67.93	67.20	66.47	65.87	65.33	64.87	64.40
9,000	81.35	88.65	86.33	84.30	82.58	81.00	79.65	78.45	77.40	76.43	75.60	74.78	74.10	73.50	72.98	72.45
10,000	101.50	98.50	95.92	93.67	91.75	90.00	88.50	87.17	86.00	84.92	84.00	83.09	82.34	81.67	81.09	80.50
15,000	152.25	147.75	143.88	140.50	137.63	135.00	132.75	130.75	129.00	127.38	126.00	124.63	123.50	122.50	121.63	120.75
20,000	203.00	197.00	191.84	187.34	183.50	180.00	177.00	174.34	172.00	169.84	168.00	166.17	164.67	163.34	162.17	161.00
25,000	253.75	246.25	239.79	234.17	229.38	225.00	221.25	217.92	215.00	212.29	210.00	207.71	205.83	204.17	202.71	201.25
30,000	304.50	295.50	287.75	281.00	275.25	270.00	265.50	261.50	258.00	254.75	252.00	249.30	247.00	245.00	243.25	241.25
35,000	355.25	344.75	335.71	327.83	321.13	315.00	309.75	305.08	301.00	297.21	294.00	290.79	288.17	285.83	283.79	281.75
40,000	406.00	394.00	383.67	374.67	367.00	360.00	354.00	348.67	344.00	339.67	336.00	332.33	329.33	326.67	324.33	322.00
45,000	456.75	443.25	431.63	421.50	412.88	405.00	398.25	392.25	387.00	382.13	378.88	373.88	370.50	367.50	364.88	362.25
50,000	507.50	492.50	479.58	468.33	458.75	450.00	442.50	435.83	430.00	424.58	420.00	415.42	411.67	408.33	405.42	402.50
55,000	558.25	541.75	527.54	515.17	504.63	495.00	486.75	479.42	473.00	467.04	462.00	456.96	452.83	449.17	445.96	442.75
60,000	609.00	591.00	575.50	562.00	550.50	540.00	531.00	523.00	516.00	509.50	504.00	498.50	494.00	490.00	486.50	483.00
65,000	659.75	640.25	623.46	608.83	596.38	585.00	575.25	566.58	559.00	551.96	546.00	540.04	535.17	530.83	527.04	523.25
70,000	710.50	689.50	671.42	655.67	642.25	630.00	619.50	610.17	602.00	594.42	588.00	581.58	576.33	571.67	567.58	563.50
75,000	761.25	738.75	719.38	702.50	688.13	675.00	663.75	653.75	645.00	636.88	630.00	623.13	617.50	612.50	608.13	603.75
80,000	812.00	788.00	767.33	749.33	734.00	720.00	708.00	697.33	688.00	679.33	672.00	664.67	658.67	653.33	648.67	644.00
100,000	1015.00	985.00	959.17	936.67	917.50	900.00	885.00	871.67	860.00	849.17	840.00	830.83	823.33	816.67	810.83	805.00

MONTHLY PAYMENT

9¼% Years	15	16	17	18	19	20	21	22	23	24	25	26	27	28	29	9¼% 30
Amount																
25	.26	.25	.24	.24	.23	.23	.23	.22	.22	.22	.21	.21	.21	.21	.21	.21
50	.52	.50	.49	.48	.47	.46	.45	.44	.44	.43	.43	.42	.42	.42	.41	.41
75	.77	.75	.73	.71	.70	.69	.68	.67	.66	.65	.64	.64	.63	.63	.62	.62
100	1.03	1.00	.98	.95	.93	.92	.90	.89	.88	.87	.86	.85	.84	.83	.83	.82
200	2.06	2.00	1.95	1.91	1.87	1.83	1.80	1.78	1.75	1.73	1.71	1.70	1.68	1.67	1.66	1.65
300	3.09	3.00	2.93	2.86	2.80	2.75	2.71	2.67	2.63	2.60	2.57	2.55	2.52	2.50	2.49	2.47
400	4.12	4.00	3.90	3.81	3.73	3.67	3.61	3.55	3.51	3.46	3.43	3.39	3.36	3.34	3.31	3.29
500	5.15	5.00	4.88	4.76	4.67	4.58	4.51	4.44	4.38	4.33	4.28	4.24	4.20	4.17	4.14	4.12
600	6.18	6.00	5.85	5.72	5.60	5.50	5.41	5.33	5.26	5.20	5.14	5.09	5.05	5.01	4.97	4.94
700	7.21	7.00	6.83	6.67	6.53	6.42	6.31	6.22	6.14	6.06	6.00	5.94	5.89	5.84	5.80	5.76
800	8.24	8.00	7.80	7.62	7.47	7.33	7.21	7.11	7.01	6.93	6.85	6.79	6.21	6.67	6.63	6.59
900	9.27	9.00	8.78	8.57	8.40	8.25	8.12	8.00	7.89	7.79	7.71	7.64	7.57	7.51	7.46	7.41
1,000	10.30	10.00	9.75	9.53	9.34	9.17	9.02	8.88	8.77	8.66	8.57	8.48	8.41	8.34	8.28	8.23
2,000	20.60	20.00	19.50	19.05	18.67	18.33	18.03	17.77	17.53	17.32	17.13	16.97	16.82	16.68	16.57	16.47
3,000	30.90	30.00	29.25	28.58	28.00	27.50	27.05	26.65	26.30	25.98	25.70	25.45	25.23	25.03	24.85	24.70
4,000	41.20	40.00	39.00	38.10	37.33	36.67	36.07	35.53	35.07	34.63	34.27	33.93	33.63	33.37	33.13	32.93
5,000	51.50	50.00	48.75	47.63	46.67	45.83	45.08	44.42	43.83	43.29	42.83	42.42	42.04	41.71	41.42	41.17
6,000	61.80	60.00	58.50	57.15	56.00	55.00	54.10	53.30	52.60	51.95	51.40	50.90	50.45	50.05	49.70	49.40
7,000	72.10	70.00	68.25	66.68	65.33	64.17	63.12	62.18	61.37	60.61	59.97	59.38	58.86	58.39	57.98	57.63
8,000	82.40	80.00	78.00	76.20	74.67	73.34	72.13	71.07	70.13	69.27	68.53	67.87	62.09	66.73	66.27	65.87
9,000	92.70	90.00	87.75	85.73	84.00	82.50	81.15	79.95	78.90	77.93	77.10	76.35	75.68	75.08	74.55	74.10
10,000	103.00	100.00	97.50	95.25	93.34	91.67	90.17	88.84	87.67	86.59	85.67	84.84	84.09	83.42	82.84	82.34
15,000	154.50	150.00	146.25	142.88	140.00	137.50	135.25	133.25	131.50	129.88	128.50	127.25	126.13	125.13	124.25	123.50
20,000	206.00	200.00	195.00	190.50	186.67	183.34	180.34	177.67	175.33	173.17	131.34	169.67	168.17	166.84	165.67	164.67
25,000	257.50	250.00	243.75	238.13	233.33	229.17	225.42	222.08	219.17	216.46	214.17	212.08	210.21	208.54	207.08	205.83
30,000	309.00	300.00	292.50	285.75	280.00	275.00	270.50	266.50	263.00	259.75	257.00	254.50	252.25	250.25	248.50	247.00
35,000	360.50	350.00	341.25	333.38	326.67	320.83	315.58	310.92	306.83	303.04	299.83	296.92	294.29	291.96	289.92	288.17
40,000	412.00	400.00	390.00	381.00	373.33	366.67	360.67	355.33	350.67	346.33	342.67	339.33	336.33	333.67	331.33	329.33
45,000	463.50	450.00	438.75	428.63	420.00	412.50	405.75	399.75	394.50	389.63	385.50	381.75	378.38	375.38	372.75	370.50
50,000	515.00	500.00	487.50	476.25	466.67	458.33	450.83	444.17	438.33	432.92	428.33	424.17	420.42	417.08	414.17	411.67
55,000	566.50	550.00	536.25	523.88	513.33	504.17	495.92	488.58	482.17	476.21	471.17	466.58	462.46	458.79	455.58	452.83
60,000	618.00	600.00	585.00	571.50	560.00	550.00	541.00	533.00	526.00	519.50	514.00	509.00	504.50	500.50	497.00	494.00
65,000	669.50	650.00	633.75	619.13	606.67	595.83	586.08	577.42	569.83	562.79	556.83	551.42	546.54	542.21	538.42	535.17
70,000	721.00	700.00	682.50	666.75	653.33	641.67	631.17	621.83	613.67	606.08	599.67	593.83	588.58	583.92	579.83	576.33
75,000	772.50	750.00	731.25	714.38	700.00	687.50	676.25	666.25	657.50	649.38	642.50	636.25	630.63	625.63	621.25	617.50
80,000	824.00	800.00	780.00	762.00	746.67	733.33	721.33	710.67	701.33	692.67	685.33	678.67	672.67	667.33	662.67	658.67
100,000	1030.00	1000.00	975.00	952.50	933.33	916.67	901.67	888.33	876.67	865.83	856.57	848.33	840.83	834.17	828.33	823.33

MONTHLY PAYMENT

9½% Years	15	16	17	18	19	20	21	22	23	24	25	26	27	28	29	9½% 30
Amount																
25	.26	.26	.26	.24	.24	.23	.23	.23	.22	.22	.22	.22	.21	.21	.21	.21
50	.52	.51	.50	.48	.47	.47	.46	.45	.45	.44	.44	.43	.43	.43	.42	.42
75	.78	.76	.74	.73	.71	.70	.69	.68	.67	.66	.66	.65	.64	.64	.64	.63
100	1.05	1.02	.99	.97	.95	.93	.92	.90	.89	.88	.87	.87	.86	.85	.85	.84
200	2.09	2.03	1.98	1.94	1.90	1.87	1.84	1.81	1.79	1.77	1.75	1.73	1.72	1.71	1.69	1.68
300	3.14	3.05	2.97	2.91	2.85	2.80	2.76	2.72	2.68	2.65	2.62	2.60	2.58	2.56	2.54	2.53
400	4.18	4.06	3.96	3.87	3.80	3.73	3.67	3.62	3.57	3.53	3.50	3.46	3.44	3.41	3.39	3.37
500	5.23	5.08	4.95	4.84	4.75	4.66	4.59	4.53	4.47	4.42	4.37	4.33	4.30	4.26	4.23	4.21
600	6.27	6.09	5.94	5.81	5.70	5.60	5.51	5.43	5.36	5.30	5.25	5.20	5.16	5.12	5.08	5.05
700	7.32	7.11	6.93	6.78	6.64	6.53	6.42	6.34	6.25	6.18	6.12	6.06	6.01	5.97	5.93	5.89
800	8.36	8.12	7.92	7.75	7.59	7.46	7.34	7.24	7.15	7.07	6.99	6.93	6.87	6.82	6.77	6.73
900	9.41	9.14	8.91	8.72	8.54	8.39	8.26	8.15	8.04	7.95	7.87	7.79	7.73	7.67	7.62	7.58
1,000	10.45	10.15	9.90	9.68	9.49	9.33	9.18	9.05	8.93	8.83	8.74	8.66	8.59	8.53	8.47	8.42
2,000	20.90	20.30	19.80	19.37	18.98	18.65	18.35	18.10	17.87	17.67	17.48	17.32	17.18	17.05	16.93	16.83
3,000	31.35	30.45	29.70	29.05	28.48	27.98	27.53	27.15	26.80	26.50	26.23	25.98	25.78	25.58	25.40	25.25
4,000	41.80	40.60	39.60	38.73	37.97	37.30	36.70	36.20	35.73	35.33	34.97	34.63	34.37	34.10	33.87	33.67
5,000	52.25	50.75	49.50	48.42	47.46	46.63	45.88	45.25	44.67	44.17	43.71	43.29	42.96	42.63	42.33	42.08
6,000	62.70	60.90	59.40	58.10	56.95	55.95	55.05	54.30	53.60	53.00	52.45	51.95	51.55	51.55	50.80	50.50
8,000	83.60	81.20	79.20	77.47	75.93	74.60	73.40	72.40	71.47	70.67	69.93	69.27	68.73	68.20	67.73	67.33
9,000	94.05	91.35	89.10	87.15	85.43	83.93	82.58	81.45	80.40	79.50	78.67	77.93	77.33	76.73	76.20	75.75
10,000	104.50	101.50	99.00	96.84	94.92	93.25	91.75	90.50	89.30	88.34	87.42	86.59	85.92	85.25	84.67	84.17
15,000	156.75	152.25	148.50	145.25	142.38	139.88	137.63	135.75	134.00	132.50	131.13	129.88	128.88	127.88	127.00	126.25
20,000	209.00	203.00	198.00	193.67	189.84	186.50	183.50	181.00	178.67	176.67	174.84	173.17	171.84	170.50	169.34	168.34
25,000	261.25	253.75	247.50	242.08	237.29	233.13	229.38	226.25	223.33	220.83	218.54	216.46	214.79	213.13	211.67	210.42
30,000	313.50	304.50	297.00	290.50	284.75	279.75	275.25	271.50	268.00	265.00	262.26	259.75	257.75	255.75	254.00	252.50
35,000	365.75	355.25	346.50	388.92	332.21	326.38	321.13	316.75	312.67	309.17	305.96	303.04	300.71	298.38	296.33	294.58
40,000	418.00	406.00	396.00	387.33	379.67	373.00	367.00	362.00	357.33	353.33	349.67	346.33	343.67	341.00	338.67	336.67
45,000	470.25	456.75	445.50	435.75	427.13	419.63	412.88	407.25	402.00	397.50	393.38	389.63	386.63	383.63	381.00	378.75
50,000	522.50	507.50	495.00	484.17	474.58	466.25	458.75	452.50	446.67	441.67	437.08	432.92	429.58	426.25	423.33	420.83
55,000	574.75	558.25	544.50	532.58	522.04	512.88	504.63	497.75	491.33	485.83	480.79	476.21	472.54	468.88	465.67	462.92
60,000	627.00	609.00	594.00	581.00	569.50	559.50	550.50	543.00	536.00	530.00	524.50	519.50	515.50	511.50	508.00	505.00
65,000	679.25	659.75	643.50	629.42	616.96	606.13	596.38	588.25	580.67	574.17	568.21	562.79	558.46	554.13	550.33	547.08
70,000	731.50	710.50	693.00	677.83	664.42	652.75	642.25	633.50	625.33	618.33	611.92	606.08	601.42	596.75	592.67	589.17
75,000	783.75	761.25	742.50	726.25	711.88	699.38	688.13	678.75	670.00	662.50	655.63	649.38	644.38	639.38	635.00	631.25
80,000	836.00	812.00	792.00	774.67	759.33	746.00	734.00	724.00	714.67	706.67	699.33	692.67	687.33	682.00	677.33	673.33
100,000	1045.00	1015.00	990.00	968.33	949.17	932.50	917.50	905.00	893.33	883.33	874.17	865.83	859.17	852.50	846.67	841.67

MONTHLY PAYMENT

9 3/4% | | | | | | | | | | | | | | | 9 3/4%

Years	15	16	17	18	19	20	21	22	23	24	25	26	27	28	29	30
Amount																
25	.27	.26	.25	.25	.24	.24	.23	.23	.23	.23	.22	.22	.22	.22	.22	.21
50	.53	.52	.50	.49	.48	.47	.47	.46	.46	.45	.45	.44	.44	.44	.43	.43
75	.80	.77	.75	.74	.72	.71	.70	.69	.68	.68	.67	.66	.66	.65	.65	.64
100	1.06	1.03	1.01	.98	.97	.95	.93	.92	.91	.90	.87	.88	.88	.87	.87	.86
200	2.12	2.06	2.01	1.97	1.93	1.90	1.87	1.84	1.82	1.80	1.78	1.77	1.75	1.74	1.73	1.72
300	3.18	3.09	3.02	2.95	2.90	2.85	2.80	2.77	2.73	2.70	2.68	2.65	2.63	2.61	2.60	2.58
400	4.24	4.12	4.02	3.94	3.86	3.80	3.74	3.75	3.64	3.60	3.57	3.53	3.51	3.48	3.46	3.44
500	5.30	5.15	5.03	4.92	4.83	4.75	4.67	4.61	4.55	4.50	4.46	4.42	4.38	4.35	4.33	4.30
600	6.36	6.19	6.04	5.91	5.79	5.70	5.61	5.53	5.47	5.41	5.35	5.30	5.26	5.22	5.19	5.16
700	7.42	7.22	7.04	6.89	6.76	6.64	6.54	6.45	6.38	6.31	6.24	6.18	6.14	6.09	6.06	6.01
800	8.48	8.25	8.05	7.87	7.72	7.59	7.47	7.37	7.29	7.21	7.13	7.07	7.01	6.96	6.92	6.87
900	9.54	9.28	9.05	8.86	8.69	8.54	8.41	8.30	8.20	8.11	8.03	7.95	7.87	7.83	7.79	7.73
1,000	10.60	10.31	10.06	9.84	9.65	9.49	9.34	9.22	9.11	9.01	8.92	8.83	8.77	8.70	8.65	8.59
2,000	21.20	20.62	20.17	19.68	19.30	18.98	18.68	18.43	18.22	18.02	17.83	17.67	17.53	17.40	17.30	17.18
3,000	31.80	30.93	30.18	29.53	28.95	28.48	28.03	27.65	27.33	27.03	26.75	26.50	26.30	26.10	25.95	25.78
4,000	42.40	41.23	40.23	39.37	38.60	37.97	37.37	36.87	36.43	36.03	35.67	35.33	35.07	34.80	34.60	34.37
5,000	53.00	51.54	50.29	49.21	48.25	47.46	46.71	46.08	45.54	45.04	44.58	44.17	43.83	43.50	43.25	42.96
6,000	63.60	61.85	60.35	59.05	57.90	56.95	56.05	55.30	54.65	54.05	53.50	53.00	52.60	52.20	51.90	51.55
7,000	74.20	72.16	70.41	68.89	67.55	66.44	65.39	64.52	63.76	63.06	62.42	61.83	61.37	60.90	60.55	60.14
8,000	84.80	82.47	80.47	78.73	77.20	75.93	74.73	73.73	72.87	72.07	71.33	70.67	70.13	69.60	69.20	68.73
9,000	95.40	92.78	90.53	88.58	86.85	85.43	84.08	82.95	81.98	81.08	80.25	79.50	78.90	78.30	77.85	77.33
10,000	106.00	103.08	100.58	98.42	96.50	94.92	93.42	92.17	91.08	90.08	89.17	88.33	87.67	87.00	86.50	85.92
15,000	159.00	154.63	150.88	147.63	144.75	142.38	140.13	138.25	136.63	135.13	133.75	132.50	131.50	130.50	129.75	128.88
20,000	212.00	206.17	201.17	196.83	193.00	189.83	186.83	184.33	182.17	180.83	178.33	176.67	175.33	174.00	173.00	171.83
25,000	265.00	257.71	251.46	246.04	241.25	237.29	233.54	230.42	227.71	225.21	222.92	220.83	219.71	217.50	216.25	214.79
30,000	318.00	309.25	301.75	295.25	289.50	284.75	280.25	276.50	273.25	270.25	267.50	265.00	263.00	261.00	259.50	257.75
35,000	371.00	360.79	352.04	344.46	337.75	332.21	326.96	322.58	318.79	316.46	312.08	309.17	306.83	304.50	302.75	300.71
40,000	424.00	412.33	402.33	393.67	386.00	379.67	373.67	368.67	364.33	360.33	356.67	353.33	350.67	348.00	346.00	343.67
45,000	477.00	463.88	452.63	442.88	434.26	427.13	420.38	414.75	409.88	405.38	401.25	397.50	394.50	391.50	389.25	386.63
50,000	530.00	515.42	502.92	492.08	482.50	474.58	467.08	460.83	455.42	450.42	445.83	441.67	438.33	435.00	432.50	429.58
55,000	583.00	566.96	553.21	541.29	530.75	522.04	513.79	506.92	500.96	495.46	490.42	485.83	482.17	478.50	475.75	472.54
60,000	636.00	618.50	603.50	590.50	579.00	569.50	560.50	553.00	546.50	540.50	535.00	530.00	526.00	522.00	519.00	515.50
65,000	684.13	670.04	653.79	639.71	627.25	616.96	607.21	599.08	592.04	585.54	579.58	574.17	567.83	565.50	562.25	558.46
70,000	742.00	721.58	704.08	688.92	675.50	664.42	653.92	645.17	637.58	630.58	624.17	618.33	613.67	609.00	605.50	601.42
75,000	795.00	773.13	754.38	738.13	723.75	711.88	700.63	691.25	683.13	675.63	668.75	662.50	657.50	652.50	648.75	644.38
80,000	848.00	824.67	804.67	787.33	772.00	579.33	747.33	73.33	728.67	720.67	713.33	706.67	701.33	696.00	692.00	687.33
100,000	1060.00	1030.83	1005.83	984.17	965.00	949.17	934.17	921.67	910.83	900.83	891.67	883.33	976.67	870.00	865.00	859.17

MONTHLY PAYMENT

10% Years	15	16	17	18	19	20	21	22	23	24	25	26	27	28	10% 29	30
Amount																
25	.27	.27	.26	.25	.25	.25	.24	.23	.23	.23	.23	.23	.22	.23	.23	.22
50	.54	.53	.52	.50	.50	.49	.48	.47	.46	.46	.46	.45	.45	.45	.45	.44
75	.81	.79	.77	.75	.74	.73	.72	.70	.70	.69	.69	.68	.67	.67	.67	.66
100	1.08	1.05	1.03	1.00	.99	.97	.96	.94	.93	.92	.91	.90	.89	.89	.89	.88
200	2.15	2.10	2.05	2.00	1.97	1.94	1.91	1.88	1.85	1.84	1.82	1.80	1.79	1.78	1.77	1.76
300	3.23	3.14	3.07	3.00	2.95	2.90	2.86	2.81	2.78	2.76	2.73	2.70	2.68	2.67	2.65	2.64
400	4.30	4.19	4.09	4.00	3.93	3.87	3.81	3.75	3.71	3.67	3.64	3.60	3.58	3.56	3.53	3.52
500	5.38	5.23	5.11	5.00	4.91	4.83	4.76	4.69	4.64	4.59	4.55	4.50	4.47	4.44	4.42	4.39
600	6.45	6.28	6.13	6.00	5.89	5.80	5.71	5.63	5.56	5.51	5.46	5.41	5.36	5.33	5.30	5.27
700	7.53	7.33	7.15	7.00	6.87	6.76	6.66	6.57	6.49	6.43	6.37	6.31	6.26	6.22	6.18	6.15
800	8.60	8.37	8.17	8.00	7.86	7.73	7.51	7.51	7.42	7.34	7.27	7.21	7.15	7.11	7.06	7.03
900	9.68	9.42	9.20	9.00	8.84	8.69	8.56	8.44	8.34	8.26	8.18	8.11	8.05	8.00	7.95	7.90
1,000	10.75	10.46	10.22	10.00	9.82	9.66	9.51	9.38	9.27	9.18	9.09	9.01	8.94	8.88	8.83	8.78
2,000	21.50	20.92	20.43	20.00	19.63	19.31	19.02	18.76	18.54	18.35	18.18	18.02	17.88	17.76	17.65	17.56
3,000	32.24	31.38	30.64	30.00	29.44	28.96	28.53	28.15	27.82	27.53	27.27	27.03	26.82	26.64	26.48	26.33
4,000	42.99	41.84	40.85	40.00	39.26	38.61	38.04	37.53	37.19	36.70	36.35	36.04	35.76	35.52	35.30	35.11
5,000	53.74	52.30	51.07	50.00	49.07	48.26	47.54	46.91	46.36	45.87	45.44	45.05	44.70	44.40	44.13	43.88
6,000	64.48	62.76	61.28	60.00	58.88	57.91	57.05	56.29	55.63	55.05	54.53	54.06	53.65	53.28	52.95	52.66
7,000	75.23	73.22	71.49	69.99	68.69	67.56	66.56	65.68	64.90	64.22	63.61	63.07	62.59	62.16	61.78	61.44
8,000	85.97	83.68	81.70	79.99	78.51	77.21	76.07	75.06	74.17	73.40	72.70	72.08	71.53	71.04	70.60	70.21
9,000	96.72	94.14	91.91	89.99	88.32	86.86	85.58	84.44	83.45	82.57	81.79	81.09	80.47	79.92	79.43	78.99
10,000	107.47	104.60	102.13	99.99	98.13	96.51	95.08	93.82	92.72	91.74	90.88	90.10	89.41	88.80	88.25	87.76
15,000	161.20	156.89	153.19	149.98	147.19	144.76	142.62	140.74	139.08	137.61	136.31	135.15	134.11	133.20	132.38	131.64
20,000	214.93	209.19	204.25	199.97	196.26	193.01	190.16	187.65	185.44	183.48	181.75	180.20	178.82	177.60	176.50	175.52
25,000	268.66	261.48	255.31	249.97	245.32	241.26	237.70	234.56	231.80	299.35	227.18	225.24	223.52	222.00	220.62	219.40
30,000	322.39	313.78	306.37	299.96	294.38	289.51	285.24	281.47	278.15	275.22	272.62	270.29	268.23	266.39	264.75	263.28
35,000	376.12	366.07	357.43	349.95	343.45	337.76	332.78	328.39	324.51	321.09	318.05	315.34	312.93	310.79	308.87	307.16
40,000	429.85	418.37	408.49	399.94	392.51	386.01	380.32	375.30	370.87	366.96	363.49	360.39	357.64	355.19	353.00	351.03
45,000	483.58	470.66	459.55	449.93	441.57	434.26	427.86	422.21	417.23	412.83	408.92	405.44	402.34	399.59	397.12	394.91
50,000	537.31	522.96	510.61	499.93	490.63	482.52	475.40	469.12	463.59	458.70	454.36	450.49	447.05	443.99	441.24	438.79
55,000	591.04	575.25	561.67	549.92	539.70	530.77	522.93	516.04	509.95	504.57	499.79	495.54	491.75	488.38	485.37	482.67
60,000	644.77	627.55	612.73	599.91	588.76	579.02	570.47	562.95	556.31	550.44	545.23	540.58	536.46	532.78	529.49	526.55
65,000	698.50	679.84	663.79	649.90	637.82	627.27	618.01	609.86	602.67	596.31	590.66	585.64	581.16	577.18	573.62	570.43
70,000	753.23	732.14	714.85	699.90	686.89	675.52	665.55	656.77	649.03	642.18	636.10	630.68	625.87	621.58	617.74	614.31
75,000	805.96	784.43	765.91	749.89	735.95	723.77	713.09	703.68	695.39	688.05	681.53	675.73	670.57	665.98	661.86	658.18
80,000	859.69	836.73	816.97	799.88	785.01	772.02	760.63	750.60	741.75	733.92	726.97	720.78	715.28	710.37	705.99	702.06
100,000	1074.61	1045.91	1021.22	999.85	981.26	965.03	950.79	938.25	927.18	917.39	908.71	900.98	894.10	887.97	882.48	877.58

MONTHLY PAYMENT

10¼% Years	15	16	17	18	19	20	21	22	23	24	25	26	27	28	29	30
Amount																
25	.28	.27	.26	.26	.25	.25	.25	.24	.24	.24	.24	.23	.23	.23	.23	.23
50	.55	.54	.52	.51	.50	.50	.49	.48	.47	.47	.47	.46	.46	.46	.46	.45
75	.82	.80	.78	.77	.75	.74	.73	.77	.71	.71	.70	.69	.68	.68	.68	.68
100	1.09	1.07	1.04	1.02	1.00	.99	.97	.96	.94	.94	.93	.92	.91	.91	.91	.90
200	2.18	2.13	2.08	2.04	2.00	1.97	1.94	1.91	1.89	1.87	1.86	1.84	1.82	1.82	1.81	1.80
300	3.27	3.19	3.12	3.05	3.00	2.95	2.91	2.87	2.83	2.81	2.78	2.76	2.74	2.72	2.71	2.69
400	4.36	4.25	4.15	4.07	4.00	3.93	3.88	3.82	3.78	3.74	3.71	3.68	3.65	3.63	3.61	3.59
500	5.45	5.31	5.19	5.08	4.99	4.91	4.84	4.78	4.72	4.68	4.64	4.59	4.56	4.54	4.51	4.49
600	6.54	6.37	6.23	6.10	5.99	5.89	5.81	5.73	5.67	5.61	5.56	5.51	5.47	5.44	5.41	5.38
700	7.63	7.44	7.26	7.12	6.99	6.88	6.79	6.69	6.61	6.55	6.49	6.43	6.39	6.35	6.31	6.28
800	8.72	8.50	8.30	8.13	7.99	7.86	7.75	7.64	7.56	7.48	7.42	7.35	7.30	7.25	7.21	7.17
900	9.81	9.50	9.34	9.15	8.98	8.84	8.71	8.60	8.50	8.42	8.34	8.27	8.21	8.16	8.11	8.07
1,000	10.90	10.62	10.38	10.16	9.98	9.82	9.68	9.55	9.44	9.35	9.27	9.19	9.12	9.07	9.01	8.97
2,000	21.80	21.24	20.75	20.32	19.96	19.64	19.36	19.11	18.89	18.70	18.53	18.38	18.24	18.13	18.02	17.93
3,000	32.70	31.85	31.12	30.48	29.93	29.45	29.03	28.66	28.33	28.05	27.80	27.57	27.36	27.19	27.03	26.89
4,000	43.60	42.47	41.49	40.64	39.91	39.27	38.71	38.21	37.78	37.40	37.06	36.75	36.49	36.25	36.04	35.85
5,000	54.50	53.08	51.86	50.80	49.89	49.09	48.39	47.77	47.22	46.75	46.32	45.94	45.61	45.31	45.05	44.81
6,000	65.40	63.70	62.23	60.96	59.86	58.90	58.06	57.32	56.67	56.10	55.59	55.13	54.73	54.38	54.06	53.77
7,000	76.30	74.31	72.60	71.12	69.84	68.72	67.74	66.87	66.11	65.45	64.85	64.32	63.85	63.44	63.06	62.73
8,000	87.20	84.93	82.97	81.28	79.82	78.54	77.42	76.43	75.56	74.80	74.12	73.51	72.97	72.50	72.07	71.69
9,000	98.10	95.54	93.34	91.44	89.79	88.35	87.09	85.98	85.00	84.14	83.38	82.70	82.09	81.56	81.08	80.65
10,000	109.00	106.16	103.71	101.60	99.77	98.17	96.77	95.53	94.45	93.49	92.64	91.88	91.21	90.62	90.09	89.62
15,000	163.50	159.23	155.57	152.40	149.65	147.25	145.15	143.30	141.70	140.24	138.96	137.83	136.82	135.93	135.13	134.42
20,000	218.00	212.31	207.42	203.20	199.53	196.33	193.53	191.06	188.89	186.98	185.28	138.77	182.43	181.24	180.18	179.23
25,000	272.49	265.38	259.28	254.00	249.42	245.42	241.91	238.83	236.12	233.72	231.60	229.71	228.04	226.55	225.22	224.03
30,000	326.99	318.46	311.13	304.80	299.30	294.50	290.29	286.60	283.34	280.47	277.92	275.65	273.64	271.86	270.26	268.84
35,000	381.49	371.54	362.99	355.60	349.18	343.58	338.68	334.36	330.56	327.21	324.24	321.60	319.25	317.17	315.30	313.64
40,000	435.99	424.61	414.84	406.40	399.06	392.66	387.06	382.13	377.79	373.96	370.54	367.54	364.86	362.48	360.35	358.45
45,000	490.48	477.69	466.70	457.20	448.94	441.74	435.44	429.89	425.01	420.70	416.88	413.48	410.44	407.78	405.39	403.25
50,000	544.98	530.76	518.55	508.00	498.83	490.83	483.82	477.66	472.23	467.44	463.20	459.42	456.07	453.09	450.43	448.06
55,000	599.48	583.84	570.41	558.79	548.71	539.91	532.20	525.43	519.46	514.19	509.52	505.37	501.68	498.40	495.47	492.86
60,000	653.98	636.92	622.26	609.59	598.59	588.99	580.58	573.19	566.68	560.93	555.83	551.31	547.29	543.71	540.52	537.67
65,000	708.47	589.99	674.11	660.39	648.47	638.07	628.97	620.96	613.90	607.67	602.15	597.25	592.89	589.02	585.56	582.47
70,000	762.97	743.07	725.97	711.19	698.35	687.16	677.35	668.72	661.13	654.42	648.47	643.19	638.50	634.33	630.60	627.28
75,000	817.47	796.14	777.82	761.99	748.24	736.24	725.73	716.49	708.35	701.16	694.79	689.13	684.11	679.64	675.65	672.08
80,000	871.97	849.22	829.68	812.79	798.12	785.32	774.11	764.26	755.57	747.91	741.11	735.08	729.72	724.95	720.69	716.89
100,000	1089.96	1061.52	1037.10	1015.99	997.65	981.65	967.64	955.32	944.47	934.88	926.39	918.85	912.14	906.18	900.86	896.11

MONTHLY PAYMENT

10½% Years	15	16	17	18	19	20	21	22	23	24	25	26	27	28	29	30
Amount																
25	.28	.27	.27	.26	.26	.25	.25	.24	.24	.24	.24	.23	.23	.24	.23	.23
50	.56	.54	.53	.52	.51	.50	.50	.49	.48	.48	.48	.47	.47	.47	.46	.46
75	.83	.81	.79	.78	.77	.75	.74	.73	.72	.72	.71	.70	.70	.70	.69	.69
100	1.11	1.08	1.06	1.04	1.02	1.00	.99	.97	.96	.96	.95	.94	.93	.93	.92	.92
200	2.22	2.16	2.11	2.07	2.03	2.00	1.97	1.95	1.92	1.91	1.89	1.87	1.86	1.85	1.84	1.83
300	3.32	3.24	3.16	3.10	3.05	3.00	2.96	2.92	2.89	2.86	2.84	2.81	2.79	2.78	2.76	2.75
400	4.43	4.31	4.22	4.13	4.06	4.00	3.94	3.89	3.85	3.81	3.78	3.75	3.72	3.70	3.68	3.66
500	5.53	5.39	5.27	5.17	5.08	5.00	4.93	4.86	4.81	4.77	4.73	4.68	4.65	4.63	4.60	4.58
600	6.64	6.47	6.32	6.20	6.09	6.00	5.91	5.84	5.77	5.72	5.67	5.62	5.58	5.55	5.52	5.49
700	7.74	7.55	7.38	7.23	7.10	6.99	6.90	6.81	6.42	6.67	6.61	6.56	6.51	6.48	6.44	6.41
800	8.85	8.62	8.43	8.26	8.12	7.99	7.88	7.78	7.69	7.62	7.56	7.49	7.44	7.40	7.36	7.32
900	9.95	9.70	9.48	9.30	9.13	8.99	8.87	8.75	8.66	8.58	8.50	8.43	8.37	8.33	8.28	8.24
1,000	11.06	10.78	10.54	10.33	10.15	9.99	9.85	9.73	9.62	9.53	9.45	9.37	9.30	9.25	9.20	9.15
2,000	22.11	21.55	21.07	20.65	20.29	19.97	19.70	19.45	19.24	19.05	18.89	18.74	18.61	18.50	18.39	18.30
3,000	33.17	32.32	31.60	30.97	30.43	29.96	29.54	29.18	28.86	28.58	28.33	28.10	27.91	27.74	27.59	27.45
4,000	44.22	43.09	42.13	41.29	40.57	39.94	39.39	38.90	38.47	38.10	37.77	37.47	37.21	36.99	36.78	36.59
5,000	55.27	53.87	52.66	51.62	50.71	49.92	49.23	48.63	48.09	47.63	47.21	46.84	46.52	46.23	45.97	45.74
6,000	66.33	64.64	63.19	61.94	60.85	59.91	59.08	58.35	57.71	57.15	56.66	56.21	55.82	55.48	55.17	54.89
7,000	77.38	75.41	73.72	72.26	70.99	69.89	68.93	68.18	64.18	66.68	66.10	65.58	65.12	64.72	64.36	64.04
8,000	88.44	86.18	84.25	82.58	81.14	79.88	78.77	77.80	76.95	76.20	75.54	74.95	74.42	73.97	73.55	73.18
9,000	99.49	96.96	94.78	92.91	91.28	89.86	88.62	87.53	86.57	85.73	84.98	84.31	83.73	83.21	82.75	82.33
10,000	110.54	107.73	105.31	103.23	101.42	99.84	98.46	97.25	96.19	95.25	94.42	93.68	93.03	92.46	91.94	91.48
15,000	165.81	161.59	157.97	154.84	152.13	149.76	147.69	145.88	144.28	142.88	141.63	140.52	139.55	138.68	137.91	137.22
20,000	221.08	215.45	210.62	206.45	202.83	199.68	196.92	194.50	192.37	190.50	188.84	187.37	186.06	184.91	183.87	182.95
25,000	276.35	269.32	263.28	258.06	253.54	249.60	246.15	243.13	240.47	238.13	236.05	234.21	232.58	231.13	229.84	228.69
30,000	331.62	323.18	315.93	309.67	304.25	299.52	295.38	291.75	288.56	285.75	283.26	281.05	279.09	277.36	275.81	274.43
35,000	386.89	377.04	368.58	361.28	354.95	349.44	344.61	340.04	336.65	333.37	330.47	327.89	325.61	323.58	321.77	320.16
40,000	442.16	430.90	421.24	412.90	405.66	399.36	393.84	389.00	384.75	381.00	377.68	374.73	372.12	369.81	367.74	365.90
45,000	497.43	484.76	473.89	464.51	456.37	449.28	443.07	437.63	432.84	428.62	424.89	421.57	418.64	416.03	413.71	411.64
50,000	552.70	538.63	526.55	516.12	507.07	499.19	492.30	486.25	480.93	476.25	472.10	468.42	465.15	462.26	459.68	457.37
55,000	607.97	592.49	579.20	567.73	557.78	549.11	541.53	534.88	529.03	523.87	519.30	515.26	511.67	508.48	505.64	503.11
60,000	663.24	646.35	631.85	619.34	608.49	599.03	590.76	583.50	577.12	571.49	566.51	562.10	558.18	554.71	551.61	548.85
65,000	718.51	700.21	684.51	670.95	659.20	648.95	639.99	632.13	625.21	619.12	613.72	608.94	604.70	600.93	597.58	594.59
70,000	773.78	754.07	737.16	722.56	709.90	698.87	689.22	680.76	641.81	666.74	680.93	655.78	651.21	647.16	643.54	640.32
75,000	829.05	807.94	789.82	774.18	760.61	748.79	738.45	729.38	721.40	714.37	708.14	702.62	697.73	693.38	689.51	686.06
80,000	884.32	861.80	842.47	825.79	811.32	798.71	787.68	778.01	769.49	761.99	755.35	749.46	744.24	739.61	735.48	731.80
100,000	1105.40	1077.25	1053.09	1032.23	1014.14	998.38	984.60	972.51	961.87	952.49	944.19	936.83	930.30	924.51	919.35	914.74

MONTHLY PAYMENT

10 3/4% (left), 10 3/4% (right)

Years / Amount	15	16	17	18	19	20	21	22	23	24	25	26	27	28	29	30
25	.29	.28	.27	.27	.26	.26	.25	.25	.24	.25	.25	.24	.24	.24	.24	.24
50	.57	.55	.54	.53	.52	.51	.51	.49	.49	.49	.49	.48	.47	.48	.47	.47
75	.85	.82	.81	.79	.78	.77	.76	.74	.43	.73	.73	.72	.71	.71	.71	.71
100	1.13	1.10	1.07	1.05	1.04	1.02	1.01	.99	.98	.98	.97	.95	.95	.95	.94	.94
200	2.25	2.19	2.14	2.10	2.07	2.04	2.01	1.98	1.96	1.95	1.93	1.91	1.90	1.89	1.88	1.87
300	3.37	3.28	3.21	3.15	3.10	3.05	3.01	2.97	2.94	2.92	2.89	2.94	2.85	2.83	2.82	2.81
400	4.49	4.38	4.28	4.20	4.13	4.07	4.01	3.96	3.92	3.89	3.85	3.82	3.79	3.78	3.76	3.74
500	5.61	5.47	5.35	5.25	5.16	5.08	5.01	4.95	4.90	4.86	4.82	4.77	4.74	4.72	4.69	4.67
600	6.73	6.56	6.42	6.30	6.19	6.10	6.02	5.94	5.88	5.83	5.78	5.73	5.69	5.66	5.63	5.61
700	7.85	7.66	7.49	7.35	7.22	7.11	7.02	6.93	6.86	6.80	6.74	6.68	6.64	6.61	6.57	6.54
800	8.97	8.75	8.56	8.39	8.25	8.13	8.02	7.92	7.84	7.77	7.70	7.64	7.59	7.55	7.51	7.47
900	10.09	9.84	9.63	9.44	9.28	9.14	9.02	8.91	8.81	8.74	8.66	8.59	8.54	8.49	8.45	8.41
1,000	11.21	10.94	10.70	10.49	10.31	10.16	10.02	9.90	9.79	9.71	9.63	9.55	9.49	9.43	9.38	9.34
2,000	22.42	21.87	21.39	20.98	20.62	20.31	20.04	19.80	19.59	19.41	19.25	19.10	18.97	18.86	18.76	18.67
3,000	33.63	32.80	32.08	31.46	30.93	30.46	30.06	29.70	29.18	29.11	28.87	29.38	28.46	28.29	28.14	28.01
4,000	44.84	43.73	42.77	41.95	41.23	40.61	40.07	39.59	39.18	38.81	38.49	38.20	37.94	37.72	37.52	37.34
5,000	56.05	54.66	53.46	52.43	51.54	50.77	50.09	49.49	48.97	48.51	48.11	47.75	47.43	47.15	46.90	46.68
6,000	67.26	65.59	64.16	62.92	61.85	60.92	60.11	59.39	58.76	58.22	57.73	57.30	56.92	56.58	56.28	56.01
7,000	78.47	76.52	74.85	73.41	72.16	71.07	70.12	69.29	68.56	67.92	67.35	66.85	66.40	66.01	65.66	65.35
8,000	89.68	87.45	85.54	83.89	82.46	81.22	80.14	79.19	78.36	77.62	76.97	76.39	75.89	75.44	75.04	74.68
9,000	100.89	98.38	96.23	94.38	92.77	91.38	90.16	89.08	88.15	87.32	86.59	85.94	85.37	84.87	84.42	84.02
10,000	112.10	109.31	106.92	104.86	103.08	101.53	100.17	98.98	97.94	97.02	96.21	95.49	94.86	94.30	93.80	93.35
15,000	168.15	163.97	160.38	157.29	154.62	152.29	150.26	148.47	146.91	145.53	144.32	143.24	142.29	141.45	140.70	140.03
20,000	224.19	218.62	213.84	209.72	206.15	203.05	200.34	197.97	195.90	194.04	192.42	190.99	189.72	188.59	187.59	186.70
25,000	280.24	273.27	267.30	262.15	257.69	253.81	250.42	247.45	244.85	242.55	240.53	238.73	237.14	235.74	234.49	233.38
30,000	336.29	327.93	320.76	314.58	309.23	304.57	300.51	296.95	391.76	291.06	288.63	293.82	284.58	282.89	281.39	280.05
35,000	392.34	382.58	374.22	367.01	360.77	355.34	350.59	346.43	342.78	339.57	336.74	334.22	332.00	330.03	328.28	326.72
40,000	448.38	437.23	427.68	419.44	412.30	406.10	400.68	395.93	391.80	388.08	384.84	381.97	379.43	377.18	375.18	373.40
45,000	504.43	491.89	481.14	471.87	463.84	456.86	450.76	445.41	440.72	436.59	432.95	429.72	426.86	424.33	422.08	420.07
50,000	560.48	546.54	534.59	524.30	515.38	507.62	500.84	494.91	587.63	485.10	481.05	477.47	474.29	471.47	468.97	466.75
55,000	616.53	601.19	588.05	576.73	566.92	558.38	550.93	544.40	538.66	533.61	529.16	525.21	521.72	518.62	515.87	513.42
60,000	672.57	655.85	641.51	629.16	618.45	609.14	601.01	593.89	685.57	582.12	577.26	572.96	569.15	565.77	562.77	560.09
65,000	728.62	710.50	694.97	681.59	669.99	659.90	651.10	643.38	636.60	630.63	625.37	620.70	616.57	612.92	609.66	606.77
70,000	784.67	765.15	748.43	734.01	721.53	710.67	701.18	692.87	685.57	679.14	673.47	668.45	664.01	660.06	656.56	653.44
75,000	840.72	819.81	801.89	786.44	773.07	761.43	751.26	724.36	734.54	727.65	721.57	716.19	711.43	707.21	703.46	700.12
80,000	896.76	874.46	855.35	838.87	824.60	812.19	801.35	791.85	783.51	776.16	769.68	763.94	758.86	754.36	750.35	746.79
100,000	1120.95	1093.07	1069.18	1048.59	1030.75	1015.23	1001.68	989.81	979.38	970.20	962.10	954.93	948.57	942.94	937.94	933.49

11% Years	15	16	17	18	19	20	21	22	23	24	25	26	27	28	11% 29	30
Amount																
25	.29	.28	.28	.27	.27	.26	.26	.25	.25	.25	.25	.24	.24	.25	.24	.24
50	.57	.56	.55	.54	.53	.52	.51	.50	.50	.50	.50	.49	.48	.49	.48	.48
75	.86	.84	.82	.80	.79	.78	.77	.76	.75	.75	.74	.73	.73	.73	.72	.72
100	1.14	1.11	1.09	1.07	1.05	1.04	1.02	1.01	1.00	.99	.99	.97	.97	.97	.96	.96
200	2.28	2.22	2.18	2.14	2.10	2.07	2.04	2.01	1.99	1.96	1.97	1.95	1.93	1.93	1.92	1.81
300	3.41	3.33	3.26	3.20	3.15	3.10	3.06	3.02	2.99	2.97	2.95	2.92	2.90	2.89	2.87	2.86
400	4.55	4.44	4.35	4.27	4.19	4.13	4.08	4.03	3.99	3.96	3.93	3.89	3.87	3.85	3.83	3.81
500	5.69	5.55	5.43	5.33	5.24	5.17	5.10	5.04	4.99	4.95	4.91	4.89	4.83	4.81	4.79	4.77
600	6.82	6.66	6.52	6.40	6.29	6.20	6.12	6.04	5.98	5.93	5.89	5.84	5.80	5.77	5.74	5.72
700	7.96	7.77	7.60	7.46	7.34	7.23	7.14	7.05	6.98	6.92	6.87	6.81	6.77	6.74	6.70	6.67
800	9.10	8.88	8.69	8.53	8.38	8.26	8.16	8.06	7.98	7.91	7.85	7.79	7.74	7.70	7.66	7.62
900	10.23	9.99	9.77	9.59	9.43	9.29	9.17	9.07	8.97	8.90	8.83	8.76	8.73	8.66	8.61	8.58
1,000	11.37	11.10	10.86	10.66	10.48	10.33	10.19	10.07	9.97	9.89	9.81	9.73	9.67	9.62	9.57	9.53
2,000	22.74	22.19	21.71	21.31	20.95	20.65	20.38	20.15	19.94	19.77	19.61	19.46	19.34	19.23	19.14	19.05
3,000	34.10	33.28	32.57	31.96	31.43	30.97	30.57	30.22	29.91	29.65	29.41	29.19	29.01	28.85	28.70	28.57
4,000	45.47	44.37	43.42	42.61	41.90	41.29	40.76	40.29	39.88	39.53	39.21	38.93	38.68	38.46	38.27	31.10
5,000	56.83	55.46	54.27	53.26	52.38	51.61	50.95	50.36	49.85	49.41	49.01	48.66	48.35	48.08	47.84	47.62
6,000	68.20	66.55	65.13	63.91	62.85	61.94	61.14	60.43	59.82	59.29	58.81	58.39	58.02	57.69	57.40	57.14
7,000	79.57	77.64	75.98	74.56	73.33	72.26	71.33	70.51	69.79	69.17	68.61	68.12	67.69	67.31	66.97	66.67
8,000	90.93	88.73	86.84	85.21	83.80	82.58	81.51	80.58	79.76	79.05	78.41	77.85	77.36	76.92	76.54	76.19
9,000	102.30	99.82	97.69	95.86	94.28	92.90	91.70	90.65	89.73	88.93	88.22	87.58	87.30	86.54	86.10	85.71
10,000	113.66	110.91	108.54	108.51	104.75	103.22	101.89	100.72	99.70	98.81	98.02	97.31	96.70	96.15	95.67	95.24
15,000	170.49	166.36	162.81	159.76	157.12	154.83	152.84	151.08	149.55	148.21	147.02	145.97	145.04	144.23	143.50	142.85
20,000	227.32	221.81	217.08	213.01	208.50	206.44	203.78	201.45	199.41	197.61	196.03	194.63	193.39	192.30	191.33	190.47
25,000	284.15	277.26	271.35	266.27	261.87	258.05	254.72	251.81	249.25	247.01	245.03	243.28	241.74	240.37	239.16	238.09
30,000	340.98	332.71	325.62	319.52	314.24	309.66	305.67	302.17	299.11	296.41	294.04	291.94	290.09	288.45	286.99	285.70
35,000	397.81	388.16	379.89	372.77	366.62	361.27	356.61	352.53	348.95	345.81	343.04	340.59	338.43	336.52	334.83	333.32
40,000	454.64	443.61	434.16	426.02	418.99	412.88	407.55	402.87	398.81	395.22	392.05	389.26	386.78	384.60	382.66	380.93
45,000	511.47	499.06	488.43	479.28	471.36	464.49	458.50	453.25	448.65	444.62	441.06	437.91	435.13	432.67	430.49	428.55
50,000	568.30	554.51	542.70	532.53	523.74	516.10	509.44	503.62	498.51	494.02	490.06	486.57	483.48	480.74	478.32	476.17
55,000	625.13	609.96	596.96	585.78	576.11	567.71	560.38	553.97	548.35	543.42	539.07	535.22	531.82	528.82	526.15	523.78
60,000	68196	665.41	651.23	639.03	628.48	619.32	611.33	604.34	598.21	592.82	588.07	583.88	580.17	576.89	573.98	571.40
70,000	795.62	776.31	759.77	745.54	733.23	722.54	713.21	705.06	697.91	691.62	686.08	681.19	676.87	673.04	669.65	666.63
75,000	852.45	831.76	814.04	798.79	785.60	774.15	764.16	755.42	747.76	741.02	735.09	729.85	725.21	271.11	717.48	714.25
80,000	909.28	887.21	868.31	852.04	837.98	825.76	815.10	805.78	797.61	790.43	784.10	778.51	773.56	769.19	765.31	761.86
100,000	1136.60	1109.01	1085.39	1067.05	1047.47	1032.19	1018.88	1007.22	997.01	988.03	980.12	973.13	966.95	961.48	956.63	952.33

MONTLHY PAYMENT

11¼% Years	15	16	17	18	19	20	21	22	23	24	25	26	27	28	11¼% 29	30
Amount																
25	.29	.29	.28	.28	.27	.27	.26	.26	.25	.26	.25	.25	.25	.25	.25	.25
50	.58	.57	.56	.55	.54	.53	.52	.51	.51	.51	.50	.50	.49	.50	.49	.49
75	.87	.85	.83	.82	.80	.79	.78	.75	.76	.76	.75	.74	.74	.74	.74	.73
100	1.16	1.13	1.11	1.09	1.07	1.05	1.04	1.02	1.01	1.01	1.00	.99	.99	.99	.98	.98
200	2.31	2.26	2.21	2.17	2.13	2.10	2.08	2.05	2.03	2.02	2.00	1.98	1.97	1.97	1.96	1.95
300	3.46	3.38	3.31	3.25	3.20	3.15	3.11	3.07	3.04	3.02	3.00	2.97	2.96	2.95	2.93	2.92
400	4.61	4.51	4.41	4.33	4.26	4.20	4.15	4.10	4.06	4.03	4.00	3.97	3.94	3.93	3.91	3.80
500	5.77	5.63	5.51	5.41	5.33	5.25	5.19	5.12	5.07	5.03	5.00	4.96	4.93	4.91	4.88	4.86
600	6.92	6.76	6.62	6.49	6.39	6.30	6.22	6.15	6.09	6.04	5.99	5.95	5.91	5.89	5.86	5.83
700	8.07	7.88	7.72	7.58	7.46	7.35	7.26	7.17	7.10	7.05	6.99	6.94	6.90	6.87	6.83	6.80
800	9.22	9.01	8.82	8.66	8.52	8.40	8.29	8.20	8.12	8.05	7.99	7.93	7.88	7.85	7.81	7.78
900	10.38	10.13	9.92	9.74	9.58	9.45	9.33	9.22	9.13	9.06	8.99	8.92	8.87	8.83	8.78	8.75
1,000	11.53	11.26	11.02	10.82	10.65	10.50	10.37	10.25	10.15	10.06	9.99	9.91	9.85	9.81	9.76	9.72
2,000	23.05	22.51	22.04	21.64	21.29	20.99	20.73	20.50	20.30	20.12	19.97	19.83	19.71	19.61	19.51	19.43
3,000	34.58	33.76	33.06	32.45	31.93	31.48	31.09	30.74	30.44	30.18	29.95	29.74	29.56	29.41	29.27	29.14
4,000	46.10	45.01	44.07	43.27	42.58	41.98	41.45	40.99	40.59	40.24	39.93	39.66	37.42	39.21	39.02	38.86
5,000	57.62	56.26	55.09	54.09	53.22	52.47	51.81	51.24	50.74	50.30	49.92	49.57	49.27	49.01	48.78	48.57
6,000	69.15	67.51	66.11	64.90	63.86	62.96	62.18	61.49	60.89	60.36	59.90	59.49	59.13	58.81	58.53	58.28
7,000	80.67	76.76	77.12	75.72	74.51	73.45	72.54	71.73	71.03	70.42	69.88	69.40	68.98	68.61	68.28	67.99
8,000	92.19	90.01	88.14	86.53	85.15	83.95	82.90	81.98	81.18	80.48	78.86	79.32	78.84	78.41	78.04	77.71
9,000	103.72	101.26	99.16	97.35	95.79	94.44	93.26	92.23	91.33	90.54	89.85	89.23	88.69	88.22	87.79	87.42
10,000	115.24	112.51	110.17	108.17	106.43	104.93	103.62	102.47	101.47	100.60	99.83	99.14	98.54	98.02	97.55	97.13
15,000	172.86	168.76	165.26	162.25	159.65	157.39	155.43	153.71	152.21	150.90	149.74	148.72	147.81	147.02	146.32	145.69
20,000	230.47	225.01	220.34	216.33	212.86	209.86	207.24	204.95	202.95	201.20	199.65	198.29	197.09	198.03	195.09	194.26
25,000	288.09	281.26	275.43	270.41	266.08	262.32	259.05	256.19	253.69	251.50	249.56	247.86	247.36	245.04	243.86	242.82
30,000	345.71	337.51	330.51	324.49	319.29	314.78	310.86	307.43	304.43	301.79	299.48	297.43	295.63	294.04	292.63	291.38
35,000	403.33	393.77	385.60	378.57	372.51	367.24	362.66	358.66	355.16	352.09	349.39	347.00	344.90	343.05	341.40	339.95
40,000	460.94	450.02	440.68	432.65	425.72	419.71	414.47	409.90	405.90	402.39	399.30	396.58	394.18	392.05	390.17	388.51
45,000	518.56	506.27	495.76	486.73	478.93	472.17	466.28	461.14	456.63	452.69	449.21	446.15	443.44	441.06	438.95	437.07
50,000	576.18	562.52	550.85	540.82	532.15	524.63	518.09	512.38	507.38	502.99	499.12	495.72	492.72	490.07	487.72	485.64
55,000	633.79	618.77	605.93	594.90	585.36	577.10	569.90	563.61	558.11	553.28	549.04	545.29	541.99	539.07	536.49	534.20
60,000	691.41	675.02	661.02	648.98	638.58	629.56	621.71	614.85	608.85	603.58	598.95	894.87	591.26	588.08	585.26	582.76
65,000	749.03	731.28	716.10	703.06	691.79	682.02	673.52	666.08	659.58	653.88	648.86	644.43	640.53	637.08	634.03	631.32
70,000	806.65	787.53	771.19	757.14	745.01	734.48	725.32	717.33	710.32	704.18	698.77	694.01	689.81	686.09	682.80	679.89
75,000	864.26	843.78	826.27	811.22	798.22	786.95	777.13	768.56	761.06	754.48	748.68	743.58	739.07	735.10	731.57	728.45
80,000	921.88	900.03	881.35	865.30	851.44	839.41	828.94	819.80	811.80	804.77	798.60	793.15	788.35	784.10	780.34	777.01
100,000	1152.35	1125.04	1101.69	1081.63	1064.29	1049.26	1036.18	1024.75	1014.74	1005.97	998.24	991.44	985.43	980.13	975.43	971.27

MONTHLY PAYMENT

11½% | | | | | | | | | | | | | | 11½% |

Years	15	16	17	18	19	20	21	22	23	24	25	26	27	28	29	30
Amount																
25	.30	.29	.28	.28	.28	.27	.27	.26	.26	.26	.26	.25	.25	.25	.25	.25
50	.59	.58	.56	.55	.55	.54	.53	.52	.52	.52	.51	.50	.50	.50	.50	.50
75	.88	.86	.84	.83	.82	.80	.80	.78	.77	.77	.77	.76	.75	.75	.75	.75
100	1.17	1.15	1.12	1.10	1.09	1.07	1.06	1.04	1.03	1.03	1.01	1.00	1.00	1.00	1.00	1.00
200	2.34	2.29	2.24	2.20	2.17	2.14	2.11	2.08	2.07	2.05	2.04	2.02	2.01	2.00	1.99	1.99
300	3.51	3.43	3.36	3.30	3.25	3.20	3.17	3.13	3.10	3.08	3.05	3.03	3.01	3.00	2.99	2.98
400	4.68	4.57	4.48	4.40	4.33	4.27	4.22	4.17	4.13	4.10	4.07	4.04	4.02	4.00	3.98	3.97
500	5.85	5.71	5.60	5.50	5.41	5.34	5.27	5.21	5.16	5.13	5.09	5.05	5.02	5.00	4.98	4.96
600	7.01	6.85	6.71	6.59	6.49	6.40	6.33	6.25	6.20	6.15	6.10	6.06	6.02	6.00	5.97	5.95
700	8.18	7.99	7.83	7.69	7.57	7.47	7.38	7.30	7.23	7.17	7.12	7.07	7.03	7.00	6.97	6.94
800	9.35	9.13	8.95	8.79	8.65	8.54	8.43	8.34	8.26	8.20	8.14	8.08	8.03	8.00	7.96	7.93
900	10.52	10.28	10.07	9.89	9.74	9.60	9.49	9.38	9.29	9.22	9.15	9.09	9.04	8.99	8.95	8.92
1,000	11.69	11.42	11.19	10.99	10.82	10.67	10.54	10.42	10.33	10.25	10.17	10.10	10.04	9.99	9.95	9.91
2,000	23.37	22.83	22.37	21.97	21.63	21.33	21.08	20.85	20.65	20.49	20.33	20.20	20.08	19.98	19.89	19.81
3,000	35.05	34.24	33.55	32.95	32.44	32.00	31.61	31.27	30.98	30.73	30.50	30.30	30.12	29.97	29.83	29.71
4,000	46.73	45.65	44.73	43.94	43.25	42.66	42.15	41.70	41.30	40.97	40.66	40.39	40.16	39.96	39.78	39.62
5,000	58.41	57.06	55.91	54.92	54.07	53.33	62.68	52.19	51.63	51.21	50.83	50.49	50.20	49.95	49.72	49.52
6,000	70.10	68.47	67.09	65.90	64.88	63.99	63.22	62.54	61.95	61.45	60.99	60.59	60.24	59.94	59.66	59.42
7,000	81.78	79.89	78.27	76.89	75.69	74.66	73.76	72.97	72.28	71.69	71.16	70.69	70.28	69.93	69.61	69.33
8,000	93.46	91.30	89.45	87.87	86.50	85.32	84.29	83.39	82.61	81.93	81.32	80.78	80.32	79.91	79.55	79.23
9,000	105.14	102.71	100.63	98.85	97.31	95.98	94.83	93.81	92.93	92.17	91.49	90.88	90.36	89.90	89.49	89.13
10,000	116.82	114.12	111.81	109.83	108.13	106.65	105.36	104.24	103.26	102.41	101.65	100.98	100.40	99.89	99.44	99.03
15,000	175.23	171.18	167.72	164.75	162.19	159.97	158.04	156.36	154.89	153.61	152.48	151.48	150.60	149.83	149.15	148.55
20,000	233.64	228.24	223.62	219.66	216.25	213.29	210.72	208.48	206.52	204.81	203.30	201.97	200.80	199.78	198.87	198.06
25,000	292.05	285.30	279.53	274.58	270.31	266.61	263.40	260.59	258.15	256.01	264.12	252.46	251.00	249.72	248.58	247.58
30,000	350.46	342.35	335.43	329.49	324.37	319.93	316.08	312.71	309.77	307.21	304.95	302.95	301.20	299.66	298.30	297.09
35,000	408.87	399.41	391.34	384.41	378.43	373.26	366.76	364.83	361.40	358.41	355.77	353.45	351.40	349.61	348.01	346.61
40,000	467.28	456.47	447.24	439.32	432.49	426.58	421.44	416.95	413.03	409.61	406.59	403.94	401.60	399.55	397.73	396.12
45,000	525.69	513.53	503.15	494.24	486.55	479.90	474.11	469.07	464.66	460.81	457.42	454.43	451.80	499.49	477.45	445.64
50,000	584.10	570.59	559.05	549.15	540.61	533.22	526.79	521.88	516.29	512.01	508.24	504.92	502.00	499.43	497.16	495.15
55,000	642.51	627.65	614.96	604.07	594.67	586.54	579.47	573.31	567.92	563.21	559.06	555.41	552.20	549.38	546.88	544.67
60,000	700.92	684.70	670.86	658.98	648.74	639.86	632.15	625.43	619.55	614.41	609.89	605.91	602.40	599.32	596.59	594.18
65,000	759.33	741.76	726.77	713.90	702.80	693.18	684.83	677.54	671.18	665.61	660.71	656.40	652.61	649.26	646.31	643.69
70,000	817.74	798.82	782.67	768.81	756.86	746.51	737.51	729.66	722.81	716.81	711.53	706.89	702.81	699.21	698.02	693.21
75,000	876.15	855.88	838.58	823.73	810.92	799.83	790.19	781.78	774.44	768.01	762.36	757.38	753.01	749.15	745.74	742.72
80,000	934.56	912.94	894.48	878.64	864.98	853.15	842.87	833.90	826.07	819.21	813.18	807.88	803.21	799.09	795.45	792.24
100,00	1168.19	1141.17	1118.10	1098.30	1081.22	1066.43	1053.58	1042.38	1032.58	1024.01	1016.47	1009.84	1004.01	998.86	994.32	990.30

MONTHLY PAYMENT

11 3/4%														11 3/4%	
Years	15	16	17	18	19	20	21	22	23	24	25	26	27	28	29	30
Amount																
25	.30	.29	.29	.28	.28	.28	.27	.27	.26	.27	.26	.26	.26	.26	.26	.26
50	.60	.58	.57	.56	.55	.55	.54	.53	.53	.53	.52	.51	.51	.51	.51	.50
75	.89	.87	.86	.84	.83	.82	.81	.80	.79	.79	.78	.77	.77	.77	.76	.76
100	1.19	1.16	1.14	1.12	1.10	1.09	1.08	1.06	1.05	1.05	1.04	1.03	1.02	1.02	1.02	1.01
200	2.37	2.32	2.27	2.24	2.20	2.17	2.15	2.12	2.10	2.09	2.07	2.06	2.05	2.04	2.03	2.02
300	3.56	3.48	3.41	3.35	3.30	3.26	3.22	3.18	3.15	3.13	3.11	3.09	3.07	3.06	3.04	3.03
400	4.74	4.63	4.54	4.47	4.40	4.34	4.29	4.24	4.20	4.17	4.14	4.11	4.09	4.08	4.06	4.04
500	5.93	5.79	5.68	5.58	5.50	5.42	5.36	5.30	5.25	5.22	5.18	5.14	5.11	5.09	5.07	5.05
600	7.11	6.95	6.81	6.70	6.59	6.51	6.43	6.36	6.30	6.26	6.21	6.17	6.14	6.11	6.08	6.06
700	8.29	8.11	7.95	7.81	7.69	7.59	7.50	7.42	7.35	7.30	7.25	7.20	7.16	7.13	7.10	7.07
800	9.48	9.26	9.08	8.93	8.79	8.67	8.57	8.48	8.40	8.34	8.28	8.23	8.18	8.15	8.11	8.08
900	10.66	10.42	10.22	10.04	9.89	9.76	9.64	9.54	9.45	9.38	9.32	9.26	9.20	9.16	9.12	9.09
1,000	11.85	11.58	11.35	11.16	10.99	10.84	10.72	10.60	10.51	10.43	10.35	10.28	10.23	10.18	10.14	10.10
2,000	23.69	23.15	22.70	22.31	21.97	21.68	21.43	21.20	21.01	20.85	20.70	20.57	20.45	20.36	20.27	20.19
3,000	35.53	34.73	34.04	33.46	32.95	32.52	32.14	31.80	31.52	31.27	31.05	30.85	30.68	30.54	30.40	30.29
4,000	47.37	46.30	45.39	44.61	43.94	43.35	42.85	42.41	42.02	41.69	41.40	41.13	40.91	40.71	40.54	40.38
5,000	59.21	57.87	56.74	55.76	54.92	54.19	53.56	53.01	52.53	52.11	51.74	51.42	51.14	50.89	50.67	50.48
6,000	71.05	69.45	68.08	66.91	65.90	65.03	64.27	63.61	63.03	62.53	62.09	61.70	61.36	61.07	60.80	60.57
7,000	82.89	81.02	79.43	78.06	76.88	75.86	74.98	74.21	73.54	72.95	72.44	71.99	71.59	71.24	70.94	70.66
8,000	94.74	92.60	90.77	89.21	87.87	86.70	85.69	84.81	84.04	83.38	82.79	82.27	81.82	81.42	81.07	80.76
9,000	106.58	104.17	102.12	100.36	98.85	97.54	96.40	95.41	94.55	93.80	93.14	92.55	92.04	91.60	91.20	90.85
10,000	118.42	115.74	113.47	111.51	109.83	108.38	107.11	106.01	105.06	104.22	103.48	102.84	102.27	101.77	101.33	100.95
15,000	177.62	173.61	170.20	167.27	164.74	162.56	160.87	159.02	157.58	156.33	155.22	154.25	153.40	152.66	152.00	151.42
20,000	236.83	231.48	226.93	223.02	219.66	216.75	214.22	212.03	210.11	208.43	206.96	205.67	204.54	203.54	202.66	201.89
25,000	296.04	289.35	283.66	278.77	274.57	270.93	267.78	265.03	262.63	260.54	258.70	257.09	255.67	254.43	253.33	252.36
30,000	355.24	347.22	340.39	334.53	329.48	325.12	321.33	318.04	315.16	312.65	310.44	308.41	306.81	305.31	303.99	302.83
35,000	414.45	405.09	397.12	390.28	384.39	379.30	374.89	371.04	367.68	364.75	362.18	367.92	357.94	356.20	354.66	353.30
40,000	473.66	462.96	453.85	446.03	439.31	433.49	428.44	424.05	420.21	416.86	413.92	411.34	409.08	407.08	405.32	403.77
45,000	532.86	520.83	510.58	501.79	494.22	487.67	481.99	477.05	472.74	468.97	465.65	462.76	460.21	457.97	455.99	545.24
50,000	592.07	578.70	567.31	557.54	549.13	541.86	535.55	530.06	525.27	521.08	517.40	514.18	511.35	508.85	506.65	504.71
55,000	651.28	626.57	624.04	613.29	604.04	596.04	589.10	583.06	577.79	573.18	569.14	565.59	562.48	559.74	557.32	555.18
60,000	710.48	694.44	680.77	669.05	658.96	650.23	642.66	636.07	630.32	625.29	620.88	617.01	613.61	610.62	607.98	605.65
65,000	769.69	752.31	373.50	724.80	713.87	704.41	696.21	689.07	682.84	677.40	672.62	668.43	664.74	661.50	658.64	656.12
70,000	828.90	810.18	794.23	780.56	768.78	758.60	749.77	742.08	735.37	729.50	724.36	719.85	715.88	712.39	709.31	706.59
75,000	888.10	868.05	850.96	836.31	823.69	812.79	803.32	795.08	787.89	781.61	776.10	771.26	767.01	763.27	759.97	757.06
80,000	947.31	925.92	907.69	892.06	878.61	866.97	856.88	848.09	840.42	833.72	827.84	822.68	818.15	814.16	810.64	807.53
100,000	1184.14	1157.40	1134.61	1115.08	1098.26	1083.71	1071.09	1060.11	1050.60	1042.15	1034.80	1028.40	1022.70	1017.70	1013.30	1009.41

MONTHLY PAYMENT

12% Years	20	21	22	23	24	25	26	27	28	29	12% 30
25	.28	.28	.27	.27	.27	.27	.26	.26	.26	.26	.26
50	.56	.55	.54	.53	.54	.53	.52	.52	.52	.52	.52
75	.83	.82	.81	.80	.80	.79	.79	.78	.78	.78	.78
100	1.11	1.09	1.08	1.07	1.07	1.06	1.05	1.04	1.04	1.04	1.03
200	2.21	2.18	2.16	2.14	2.13	2.11	2.09	2.08	2.08	2.07	2.06
300	3.31	3.27	3.23	3.21	3.19	3.16	3.14	3.12	3.11	3.10	3.09
400	4.41	4.36	4.31	4.27	4.25	4.22	4.19	4.17	4.15	4.13	4.12
500	5.51	5.45	5.39	5.34	5.31	5.27	5.23	5.21	5.19	5.17	5.15
600	6.61	6.54	6.47	6.41	6.37	6.32	6.28	6.25	6.22	6.20	6.18
700	7.71	7.63	7.55	7.48	7.43	7.38	7.33	7.29	7.26	7.23	7.21
800	8.81	8.71	8.62	8.55	8.49	8.43	8.38	8.33	8.30	8.26	8.23
900	9.91	9.80	9.70	9.62	9.55	9.48	9.42	9.37	9.33	9.30	9.26
1,000	11.02	10.89	10.78	10.69	10.61	10.54	10.47	10.41	10.37	10.33	10.29
2,000	22.03	21.78	21.57	21.37	21.21	21.07	20.94	20.83	20.74	20.65	20.58
3,000	33.04	32.67	32.34	32.06	31.82	31.60	31.41	31.24	31.10	30.98	30.86
4,000	44.05	43.55	43.12	42.74	42.42	42.13	41.88	41.66	41.47	41.30	41.15
5,000	55.06	54.44	53.95	53.43	53.02	52.67	52.35	52.07	51.84	51.62	51.44
6,000	66.07	65.33	64.68	64.13	63.63	63.20	62.82	62.49	62.20	61.95	61.72
7,000	77.08	76.21	75.46	74.80	74.23	73.73	73.29	72.90	72.57	72.27	72.01
8,000	88.09	87.10	86.24	85.49	84.84	84.26	83.76	83.32	82.93	82.59	82.29
9,000	99.10	87.99	97.01	96.17	85.44	94.80	94.23	93.73	93.30	92.92	92.58
10,000	110.11	108.87	107.79	106.86	106.04	105.33	104.69	104.14	103.67	103.24	102.87
15,000	165.17	163.31	161.69	160.28	159.06	157.99	157.04	156.22	155.50	154.86	154.30
20,000	220.22	217.74	215.59	213.71	212.08	210.65	209.39	208.29	207.33	206.48	205.73
25,000	275.28	272.18	277.28	267.14	265.10	263.31	261.74	260.36	259.16	258.09	257.16
30,000	330.33	326.61	323.38	320.57	318.12	315.97	314.09	312.43	310.99	309.71	308.59
35,000	385.39	381.05	377.28	374.00	371.14	368.63	366.43	364.51	362.82	361.33	360.02
40,000	440.44	435.48	431.18	427.43	424.16	421.29	418.78	416.58	414.65	412.95	411.45
45,000	495.49	489.92	485.07	480.85	477.18	473.96	471.13	468.65	466.48	464.57	462.88
50,000	550.55	544.35	539.47	534.28	530.20	526.62	523.48	520.72	518.31	516.18	514.31
55,000	605.60	598.79	592.87	587.71	583.22	579.28	575.82	572.80	570.14	567.80	565.74
60,000	660.66	653.22	646.76	641.14	636.23	631.94	628.17	624.87	621.97	619.42	617.17
65,000	715.71	707.66	700.66	694.57	689.25	684.60	680.52	676.94	673.80	671.04	668.60
70,000	770.77	762.09	754.56	748.00	742.27	737.26	732.87	729.01	725.63	722.66	720.03
75,000	825.82	816.53	808.45	801.42	795.29	789.92	785.21	781.09	777.46	774.27	771.46
80,000	880.87	870.96	862.35	854.85	848.31	842.58	837.56	833.16	829.30	825.89	822.90
100,000	1101.09	1088.70	1077.94	1068.57	1060.39	1053.23	1046.95	1041.45	1036.62	1032.36	1028.62

12¼% Years	20	21	22	23	24	25	26	27	28	29	12¼% 30
Amount											
25	.28	.28	.27	.27	.27	.27	.27	.27	.27	.27	.27
50	.56	.56	.55	.54	.54	.54	.53	.53	.53	.53	.53
75	.84	.83	.82	.82	.81	.81	.80	.80	.80	.79	.79
100	1.12	1.11	1.10	1.09	1.08	1.08	1.07	1.06	1.06	1.06	1.05
200	2.24	2.22	2.19	2.17	2.16	2.15	2.13	2.12	2.12	2.11	2.10
300	3.36	3.32	3.29	3.26	3.24	3.22	3.20	3.18	3.17	3.16	3.15
400	4.48	4.43	4.38	4.35	4.32	4.29	4.26	4.24	4.23	4.21	4.20
500	5.60	5.54	5.48	5.43	5.40	5.36	5.33	5.30	5.28	5.26	5.24
600	6.72	6.64	6.58	6.52	6.48	6.44	6.39	6.36	6.34	6.31	6.29
700	7.83	7.75	7.67	7.61	7.56	7.51	7.46	7.42	7.39	7.37	7.34
800	8.95	8.86	8.77	8.69	8.63	8.58	8.53	8.48	8.45	8.42	8.39
900	10.07	9.96	9.86	9.78	9.71	9.65	9.59	9.54	9.51	9.47	9.44
1,000	11.19	11.07	10.96	10.87	10.79	10.72	10.66	10.60	10.56	10.52	10.48
2,000	22.38	22.13	21.92	21.73	21.58	21.44	21.31	21.21	21.12	21.04	20.96
3,000	33.56	33.20	32.88	32.60	32.37	32.16	31.97	31.81	31.67	31.55	31.44
4,000	44.75	44.26	43.83	43.47	43.15	42.87	42.63	42.41	42.23	42.07	41.92
5,000	55.93	55.33	54.79	54.34	53.94	53.59	53.28	53.02	52.79	52.58	52.40
6,000	67.12	66.39	65.75	65.20	64.73	64.31	63.94	63.62	63.34	63.10	62.88
7,000	78.30	77.45	76.71	76.07	75.52	75.03	74.60	74.22	73.90	73.61	73.36
8,000	89.49	88.52	87.67	86.94	86.30	85.74	85.25	84.82	84.45	84.13	83.84
9,000	100.68	99.58	98.63	97.80	97.09	96.46	95.91	95.43	95.01	94.54	94.32
10,000	111.86	110.65	109.59	108.67	107.88	107.18	160.56	106.03	105.57	105.16	104.79
15,000	167.79	165.97	164.38	163.01	161.81	160.77	159.85	159.05	158.35	157.73	157.19
20,000	223.72	221.29	219.17	217.34	215.75	214.35	213.13	212.06	211.13	210.31	209.58
25,000	279.65	276.61	273.96	271.68	269.68	267.94	266.41	265.08	263.91	262.88	261.98
30,000	335.57	331.93	328.76	326.01	323.62	321.53	319.69	318.09	216.69	315.46	314.37
35,000	391.50	387.25	383.55	380.35	377.58	375.12	372.98	371.11	369.47	368.03	368.77
40,000	447.43	442.57	438.34	484.68	431.49	428.70	426.26	424.12	422.25	420.61	419.16
45,000	503.36	497.89	493.14	489.02	455.43	482.29	479.54	477.14	475.03	473.18	471.56
50,000	559.29	553.21	547.94	543.35	539.36	535.88	532.82	530.15	527.82	525.76	523.95
55,000	615.22	608.53	602.73	597.69	593.30	589.46	586.11	583.17	580.60	578.34	576.35
60,000	671.14	663.85	657.52	652.02	647.24	643.05	639.39	636.18	633.38	630.91	628.74
65,000	727.07	719.17	712.32	706.36	701.17	696.64	692.67	689.20	686.16	683.49	681.14
70,000	783.00	774.49	767.11	760.69	755.11	750.23	745.95	742.21	738.94	736.06	733.53
75,000	838.93	829.81	821.90	815.03	809.04	803.81	799.23	795.23	791.72	788.64	785.93
80,000	894.86	885.13	876.70	869.36	862.98	857.40	852.52	848.24	844.50	841.21	838.32
100,000	1118.57	1106.42	1095.87	1086.70	1078.72	1071.75	1065.65	1060.31	1055.63	1051.51	1047.90

MONTHLY PAYMENT

12½% Years / Amount	20	21	22	23	24	25	26	27	28	29	30
25	.29	.29	.28	.28	.28	.28	.27	.27	.27	.27	.27
50	.57	.57	.56	.55	.55	.55	.54	.54	.54	.54	.54
75	.86	.85	.84	.83	.83	.82	.81	.81	.81	.81	.81
100	1.14	1.13	1.11	1.10	1.10	1.10	1.08	1.08	1.08	1.08	1.07
200	2.28	2.25	2.23	2.21	2.20	2.19	2.17	2.16	2.15	2.15	2.14
300	3.41	3.38	3.34	3.31	3.30	3.28	3.25	3.24	3.23	3.22	3.21
400	4.55	4.50	4.46	4.42	4.39	4.37	4.34	4.32	4.30	4.29	4.27
500	5.69	5.63	5.57	5.52	5.49	5.46	5.42	5.40	5.38	5.36	5.34
600	6.82	6.75	6.68	6.66	6.59	6.55	6.51	6.48	6.45	6.43	6.41
700	7.96	7.87	7.80	7.73	7.69	7.64	7.59	7.55	7.53	7.50	7.48
800	9.09	9.00	8.91	8.84	8.78	8.73	8.68	8.63	8.60	8.57	8.54
900	10.23	10.12	10.03	9.94	9.88	9.82	9.76	9.71	9.68	9.64	9.61
1,000	11.37	11.25	11.14	11.05	10.98	10.91	10.84	10.79	10.75	10.71	10.68
2,000	22.73	22.49	22.28	22.10	21.95	21.81	21.69	21.58	21.50	21.42	21.35
3,000	34.09	33.73	33.42	33.15	32.92	32.72	32.53	32.38	32.25	32.13	32.02
4,000	45.45	44.97	44.56	44.20	43.89	43.62	43.38	43.17	42.99	42.83	42.70
5,000	56.81	56.22	55.69	55.25	54.86	54.52	54.22	53.96	53.74	53.54	53.37
6,000	68.17	67.46	66.83	66.57	65.83	65.43	65.07	64.75	64.49	64.25	64.04
7,000	79.53	78.70	77.97	77.35	76.81	76.33	75.91	75.55	75.23	74.96	74.71
8,000	90.90	89.94	89.11	88.39	87.78	87.23	86.75	86.34	85.98	85.66	85.39
9,000	102.26	101.18	100.25	99.44	98.75	98.14	97.60	97.13	96.73	96.37	96.06
10,000	113.62	112.43	111.39	110.49	109.72	109.04	108.44	107.92	107.48	107.08	106.73
15,000	170.43	168.64	167.08	165.74	164.58	163.56	162.66	161.89	161.21	160.61	160.09
20,000	227.23	224.85	222.78	220.99	219.43	218.08	216.89	215.85	214.95	214.15	213.46
25,000	284.04	281.06	278.47	276.48	274.29	272.59	271.11	269.81	268.68	267.69	266.82
30,000	340.85	337.27	334.17	331.48	329.15	327.11	325.33	323.77	322.42	321.23	320.18
35,000	397.65	393.48	389.86	386.73	384.01	381.63	379.55	377.74	376.15	374.76	373.55
40,000	454.46	449.69	445.56	441.97	438.86	436.15	433.77	431.70	429.89	428.30	426.91
45,000	511.27	505.90	501.25	497.22	493.72	490.66	487.99	485.66	483.63	481.84	480.27
50,000	568.08	562.11	556.95	552.47	548.58	545.18	542.21	539.62	537.36	535.38	533.63
55,000	624.88	618.32	612.64	607.72	603.43	599.70	596.44	593.59	591.10	588.91	587.00
60,000	681.69	674.54	668.34	665.66	658.29	654.22	650.66	647.55	644.83	642.45	640.36
65,000	738.50	730.75	724.03	718.21	713.15	708.74	704.88	701.51	698.57	695.99	693.72
70,000	795.30	796.96	779.73	773.46	768.01	763.25	759.10	755.47	752.30	749.52	747.09
75,000	852.11	843.17	835.42	828.70	822.86	817.77	813.32	809.44	806.04	803.06	800.45
80,000	908.92	899.38	891.12	883.95	877.72	872.29	867.54	863.40	859.79	856.60	853.81
100,000	1136.15	1124.22	1113.90	1104.94	1097.15	1090136	1084.43	1077.75	1074.72	1070.75	1067.26

MONTHLY PAYMENT

12 3/4% Years	20	21	22	23	24	25	26	27	28	12 3/4% 29	30
Amount											
25	.29	.29	.28	.28	.28	.28	.28	.28	.28	.28	.28
50	.58	.58	.57	.56	.56	.56	.55	.55	.55	.55	.55
75	.87	.86	.85	.84	.84	.84	.83	.83	.83	.82	.82
100	1.16	1.15	1.13	1.12	1.12	1.11	1.10	1.10	1.10	1.10	1.09
200	2.31	2.29	2.26	2.25	2.24	2.22	2.21	2.20	2.19	2.19	2.18
300	3.47	3.43	3.40	3.37	3.35	3.33	3.31	3.29	3.29	3.28	3.27
400	4.62	4.57	4.53	4.49	4.47	4.44	4.41	4.39	4.38	4.37	4.35
500	5.77	5.72	5.66	5.62	5.58	5.55	5.52	5.49	5.47	5.46	5.44
600	6.93	6.86	6.79	6.74	6.70	6.66	6.62	6.59	6.57	6.55	6.53
700	8.08	8.00	7.92	7.86	7.81	7.77	7.72	7.69	7.66	7.64	7.61
800	9.24	9.14	9.06	8.99	8.93	8.88	8.83	8.79	8.76	8.73	8.70
900	10.39	10.28	10.19	10.11	10.05	9.99	9.93	9.88	9.85	9.82	9.79
1,000	11.54	11.43	11.32	11.23	11.16	11.10	11.03	10.98	10.94	10.91	10.87
2,000	23.08	22.85	22.64	22.47	22.32	22.19	22.07	21.97	21.88	21.81	21.74
3,000	34.62	34.27	33.96	33.70	33.47	33.28	33.10	32.95	32.82	32.71	32.61
4,000	46.16	45.69	45.28	44.93	44.63	44.37	44.13	43.93	43.76	43.61	43.47
5,000	57.70	57.11	56.60	56.16	55.79	55.46	55.16	54.91	54.70	54.51	54.34
6,000	69.23	68.53	67.92	67.40	66.94	66.55	66.20	65.90	65.64	65.41	65.21
7,000	80.77	79.95	79.24	78.63	78.10	77.64	77.23	76.88	76.58	76.31	76.07
8,000	92.31	91.37	90.56	89.86	89.26	88.73	88.26	87.86	87.52	87.21	86.94
9,000	103.85	102.80	101.88	101.09	100.41	99.82	98.45	99.30	98.84	98.11	97.81
10,000	115.39	114.22	113.20	112.33	111.57	110.91	110.33	109.82	109.39	109.01	108.67
15,000	173.08	171.32	169.80	168.49	167.35	166.36	165.49	164.74	164.09	163.51	163.01
20,000	230.77	228.43	226.40	224.65	223.14	221.82	220.66	219.65	218.78	218.01	217.34
25,000	288.46	285.54	283.00	280.82	278.92	277.27	275.82	274.57	273.48	272.52	271.68
30,000	346.15	342.64	339.60	336.98	334.70	332.72	330.99	329.48	328.17	327.02	326.01
35,000	403.84	399.75	396.21	393.14	390.49	388.17	381.15	384.40	382.86	381.52	380.35
40,000	461.53	456.85	452.81	449.30	446.27	443.63	441.13	439.31	437.56	436.02	434.68
45,000	519.22	513.96	509.41	505.47	502.05	499.08	496.48	494.22	492.25	490.53	489.02
50,000	576.91	571.07	566.01	561.63	557.84	554.53	551.65	549.14	546.95	545.03	543.35
55,000	634.60	628.17	622.61	617.79	613.62	609.98	606.81	604.05	601.64	599.53	597.69
60,000	692.29	685.28	679.21	673.96	669.40	665.44	661.98	658.96	656.34	644.03	652.02
65,000	749.98	742.38	735.81	730.12	725.19	720.89	772.31	768.79	711.03	708.54	706.36
70,000	807.67	799.49	792.41	786.28	780.97	776.34	772.31	768.79	765.72	653.04	760.69
75,000	865.36	856.60	849.01	842.45	836.75	831.79	827.47	823.70	820.42	817.54	815.02
80,000	923.05	813.70	905.61	898.61	892.53	887.25	882.64	878.62	875.11	872.04	869.36
100,000	1153.82	1142.13	1132.02	1123.26	1115.67	1 109.06	1103.30	1098.27	1093.89	1090.05	1086.70

MONTHLY PAYMENT

13% | | | | | | | | | | 13%

Years Amount	20	21	22	23	24	25	26	27	28	29	30
25	.30	.30	.29	.29	.29	.29	.28	.28	.28	.28	.28
50	.59	.59	.58	.57	5.7	.57	.56	.56	.56	.56	.56
75	.88	.88	.86	.86	.86	.85	.84	.84	.84	.84	.83
100	1.18	1.17	1.15	1.14	1.14	1.13	1.12	1.12	1.12	1.11	1.11
200	2.35	2.33	2.30	2.28	2.27	2.26	2.24	2.23	2.23	2.22	2.22
300	3.52	3.49	3.45	3.43	3.41	3.39	3.37	3.35	3.34	3.33	3.32
400	4.69	4.68	4.60	4.57	4.54	4.52	4.49	4.47	4.46	4.44	4.43
500	5.86	5.81	5.75	5.71	5.68	5.64	5.61	5.59	5.57	5.55	5.54
600	7.03	6.97	6.90	6.85	6.81	6.77	6.73	6.70	6.68	6.66	6.64
700	8.21	8.13	8.05	7.99	7.94	7.90	7.86	7.82	7.80	7.77	7.75
800	9.38	9.29	9.20	9.13	9.08	9.03	8.98	8.94	8.91	8.88	8.85
900	10.55	10.45	10.35	10.28	10.21	10.16	10.10	10.06	10.02	9.99	9.96
1,000	11.72	11.61	11.50	11.42	11.35	11.28	11.22	11.17	11.14	11.10	11.07
2,000	23.44	23.21	23.00	22.83	22.69	22.56	22.44	22.35	22.27	22.10	22.13
3,000	35.15	34.81	34.51	34.25	34.03	33.84	33.67	33.52	33.40	33.29	33.19
4,000	46.87	46.41	46.01	45.68	45.38	45.12	44.89	44.70	44.53	44.38	44.25
5,000	58.58	58.01	57.51	57.08	56.72	56.40	56.11	55.87	55.66	55.48	55.31
6,000	70.30	69.61	69.01	68.50	68.06	67.68	67.33	67.04	66.79	66.57	66.38
7,000	82.02	81.20	80.52	79.92	79.40	78.95	78.57	78.22	77.92	77.67	77.44
8,000	93.73	92.81	92.02	91.33	90.75	90.23	89.78	89.39	89.06	88.76	88.50
9,000	105.45	104.42	103.52	102.75	102.09	101.51	101.00	100.56	100.19	99.85	99.56
10,000	117.16	116.02	115.02	114.17	113.43	112.79	112.22	111.74	111.32	110.95	110.62
15,000	175.74	174.02	172.53	171.25	170.15	169.18	168.34	167.61	389.60	388.31	387.17
20,000	234.32	232.03	230.04	228.34	226.86	225.57	224.45	223.48	445.26	443.78	442.48
25,000	292.90	290.03	287.56	285.42	283.57	281.96	280.56	279.34	500.92	499.25	497.79
30,000	351.48	348.04	345.07	342.50	340.29	338.36	336.67	335.21	556.57	554.72	553.10
35,000	410.06	406.04	402.58	399.59	397.00	394.75	392.79	391.08	612.23	610.19	608.41
40,000	468.64	464.05	460.10	456.67	453.71	451.14	448.90	446.95	667.89	665.66	663.72
45,000	527.21	522.06	517.60	513.75	510.43	507.53	505.01	502.82	723.54	721.14	719.03
50,000	585.79	580.06	575.11	570.84	567.14	563.92	561.12	558.69	779.20	776.61	774.34
55,000	644.37	638.07	632.62	627.92	623.85	620.31	617.23	614.56	834.86	832.08	829.65
60,000	702.95	696.07	690.14	685.01	680.57	676.71	673.35	670.43	890.51	887.55	884.96
65,000	761.53	754.08	747.65	742.09	737.28	733.10	729.46	726.30	1113.14	1109.44	1106.20
70,000	820.11	812.08	805.16	799.17	793.99	789.49	785.57	782.16			
75,000	878.69	870.09	862.67	856.26	850.71	845.88	841.68	838.03			
80,000	937.27	928.10	920.18	913.14	907.42	902.27	897.79	893.90			
100,000	1171.58	1160.12	1150.23	1141.68	1134.27	1127.84	1122.24	1117.38			

MONTHLY PAYMENT

13¼% Years	20	21	22	23	24	25	26	27	28	29	30
Amount											
25	.30	.30	.29	.29	.29	.29	.29	.29	.29	.29	.28
50	.60	.59	.58	.58	.58	.58	.57	.57	.57	.57	.57
75	.90	.89	.88	.87	.87	.87	.86	.85	.85	.85	.85
100	1.19	1.18	1.17	1.16	1.16	1.15	1.14	1.14	1.14	1.13	1.13
200	2.38	2.36	2.34	2.32	2.31	2.30	2.28	2.27	2.27	2.26	2.26
300	3.57	3.54	3.51	3.48	3.46	3.45	3.42	3.41	3.40	3.39	3.38
400	4.76	4.72	4.67	4.64	4.62	4.59	4.57	4.55	4.53	4.52	4.51
500	5.95	5.90	5.84	5.80	5.77	5.74	5.71	5.68	5.67	5.65	5.63
600	7.14	7.07	7.01	6.96	6.92	6.89	6.85	6.82	6.80	6.78	6.76
700	8.33	8.25	8.18	8.12	8.08	8.03	7.99	7.96	7.93	7.91	7.89
800	9.52	9.43	9.35	9.28	9.23	9.18	9.13	9.09	9.06	9.04	9.01
900	10.71	10.61	10.52	10.44	10.38	10.33	10.27	10.23	10.20	10.16	10.14
1,000	11.90	11.78	11.69	11.60	11.53	11.47	11.41	11.37	11.33	11.29	11.26
2,000	23.79	23.57	23.37	23.20	23.06	22.94	22.82	22.73	22.65	22.58	22.52
3,000	35.69	35.35	35.06	34.81	34.59	34.41	34.23	34.10	33.98	33.87	33.78
4,000	47.58	47.13	46.74	46.41	46.12	45.87	45.65	45.46	45.30	45.16	45.04
5,000	59.48	58.91	58.43	58.01	57.65	57.34	57.06	56.83	56.63	56.45	56.29
6,000	71.37	70.70	70.11	69.61	69.18	68.81	68.48	68.19	67.95	67.74	67.55
7,000	83.27	82.48	81.80	81.21	80.71	80.27	79.89	79.56	79.28	70.03	78.81
8,000	95.16	94.26	93.48	92.81	92.24	91.74	91.30	90.92	90.60	90.32	90.07
9,000	107.05	106.04	105.17	104.42	103.77	103.21	102.71	102.29	101.93	101.60	101.32
10,000	118.95	117.82	116.85	116.02	115.30	114.68	114.13	113.66	113.25	112.89	112.58
15,000	178.42	176.73	175.28	174.03	172.95	172.01	171.19	170.48	169.87	169.34	168.87
20,000	237.89	235.64	233.71	232.04	280.60	229.35	228.25	227.31	226.50	225.78	225.16
25,000	297.36	294.55	292.13	290.04	288.24	286.68	285.32	284.14	283.12	282.23	281.45
30,000	356.83	353.46	350.56	348.05	345.89	344.02	342.38	340.67	339.74	338.67	337.74
35,000	416.31	412.37	408.98	406.06	403.54	401.35	399.45	397.80	396.36	395.11	394.03
40,000	475.78	471.28	467.41	464.07	461.19	458.69	456.51	454.62	452.99	451.56	450.31
45,000	535.25	530.19	534.11	530.44	518.84	516.02	522.17	520.12	509.61	508.00	506.60
50,000	594.72	589.10	593.46	589.38	576.48	573.36	580.19	577.91	566.23	564.45	562.89
55,000	654.19	648.01	652.80	648.32	634.13	630.69	638.21	635.70	622.86	620.89	619.18
60,000	713.66	706.92	712.15	707.26	691.78	688.03	696.23	693.49	679.48	677.34	675.47
65,000	773.13	765.83	771.49	766.20	749.43	745.36	754.25	751.28	736.10	733.78	731.76
70,000	832.61	824.74	830.84	825.13	807.07	802.70	799,90	795.60	792.72	790.22	788.05
75,000	892.08	883.65	890.18	884.07	864.72	860.03	870.28	866.86	849.35	846.67	844.34
80,000	951.55	942.56	949.53	943.01	922.37	917.37	928.30	924.65	905.97	903.11	900.62
100,000	1189.44	1178.20	1186.91	1178.76	1152.96	1146.71	1160.38	1155.81	1132.46	1128.89	1125.78

13¼%

MONTHLY PAYMENT

13½% | | | | | | | | | 13½% |
|---|---|---|---|---|---|---|---|---|---|---|
| Years | 20 | 21 | 22 | 23 | 24 | 25 | 26 | 27 | 28 | 29 | 30 |
| Amount | | | | | | | | | | | |
| 25 | .31 | .30 | .30 | .30 | .30 | .30 | .29 | .29 | .29 | .29 | .29 |
| 50 | .71 | .60 | .60 | .59 | .59 | .59 | .58 | .58 | .58 | .58 | .58 |
| 75 | .91 | .90 | .89 | .88 | .88 | .88 | .87 | .87 | .87 | .87 | .86 |
| 100 | 1.21 | 1.20 | 1.19 | 1.18 | 1.18 | 1.17 | 1.16 | 1.16 | 1.16 | 1.15 | 1.15 |
| 200 | 2.42 | 2.40 | 2.37 | 2.36 | 2.35 | 2.34 | 2.32 | 2.31 | 2.31 | 2.30 | 2.30 |
| 300 | 3.63 | 3.59 | 3.56 | 3.54 | 3.52 | 3.50 | 3.48 | 3.47 | 3.46 | 3.45 | 3.44 |
| 400 | 4.83 | 4.79 | 4.75 | 4.72 | 4.69 | 4.67 | 4.64 | 4.62 | 4.61 | 4.60 | 4.59 |
| 500 | 6.04 | 5.99 | 5.93 | 5.89 | 5.86 | 5.83 | 5.80 | 5.78 | 5.76 | 5.75 | 5.73 |
| 600 | 7.25 | 7.18 | 7.12 | 7.07 | 7.04 | 7.00 | 6.96 | 6.93 | 6.92 | 6.90 | 6.88 |
| 700 | 8.46 | 8.38 | 8.31 | 8.25 | 8.21 | 8.16 | 8.12 | 8.09 | 8.07 | 8.04 | 8.02 |
| 800 | 9.66 | 8.58 | 9.50 | 9.43 | 9.38 | 9.33 | 9.28 | 9.25 | 9.22 | 9.19 | 1.17 |
| 900 | 10.87 | 10.77 | 10.68 | 10.61 | 10.55 | 10.50 | 10.44 | 10.40 | 10.37 | 10.34 | 10.31 |
| 1,000 | 12.08 | 11.97 | 11.87 | 11.79 | 11.72 | 11.66 | 11.60 | 11.56 | 11.52 | 11.49 | 11.46 |
| 2,000 | 24.15 | 23.93 | 23.74 | 23.58 | 23.44 | 23.32 | 23.21 | 23.12 | 23.04 | 22.97 | 22.91 |
| 3,000 | 36.23 | 35.90 | 35.61 | 35.36 | 35.16 | 34.97 | 34.81 | 34,67 | 34.56 | 34.46 | 34.37 |
| 4,000 | 48.30 | 47.86 | 47.48 | 47.15 | 46.87 | 46.63 | 46.42 | 46.23 | 46.08 | 45.94 | 45.82 |
| 5,000 | 60.37 | 59.82 | 59.35 | 58.94 | 58.59 | 58.29 | 58.02 | 57.79 | 57.60 | 57.43 | 57.28 |
| 6,000 | 72.45 | 71.79 | 71.21 | 70.73 | 70.31 | 69.94 | 69.62 | 69.35 | 69.12 | 68.91 | 68.73 |
| 7,000 | 84.52 | 83.75 | 83.18 | 82.51 | 82.03 | 81.60 | 81.23 | 80.91 | 80.63 | 80.39 | 80.18 |
| 8,000 | 96.59 | 95.71 | 94.95 | 94.30 | 93.74 | 93.26 | 92.83 | 92.47 | 92.15 | 91.88 | 91.64 |
| 9,000 | 108.67 | 107.68 | 106.82 | 106.09 | 105.46 | 104.91 | 104.43 | 104.02 | 103.67 | 103.36 | 103.09 |
| 10,000 | 120.74 | 119.64 | 118.69 | 117.88 | 117.18 | 116.57 | 116.04 | 115.58 | 115.19 | 114.85 | 114.55 |
| 15,000 | 181.11 | 179.46 | 178.04 | 176.81 | 175.76 | 174.85 | 174.06 | 173.37 | 172.78 | 172.27 | 171.82 |
| 20,000 | 241.48 | 239.28 | 237.38 | 235.75 | 234.35 | 233.13 | 232.08 | 231.16 | 230.37 | 229.69 | 229.09 |
| 25,000 | 301.85 | 299.10 | 296.73 | 294.69 | 292.94 | 291.42 | 290.09 | 288.95 | 287.97 | 287.11 | 286.36 |
| 30,000 | 362.22 | 358.92 | 356.07 | 353.63 | 351.52 | 349.70 | 348.11 | 346.74 | 345.56 | 344.53 | 343.63 |
| 35,000 | 422.59 | 418.73 | 415.42 | 412.57 | 410.11 | 407.98 | 406.13 | 404.53 | 403.15 | 401.95 | 400.90 |
| 40,000 | 482.95 | 478.55 | 474.76 | 471.50 | 468.70 | 466.26 | 464.15 | 462.33 | 460.74 | 459.37 | 458.17 |
| 45,000 | 543.32 | 538.37 | 534.11 | 530.44 | 527.28 | 524.55 | 522.17 | 520.12 | 518.34 | 516.79 | 515.44 |
| 50,000 | 603.69 | 598.19 | 593.46 | 589.38 | 585.87 | 582.83 | 580.19 | 577.91 | 575.93 | 574.21 | 572.71 |
| 55,000 | 664.06 | 658.01 | 652.80 | 648.32 | 644.45 | 641.11 | 638.21 | 635.70 | 633.52 | 631.63 | 329.98 |
| 60,000 | 724.43 | 717.83 | 712.15 | 707.26 | 703.04 | 699.39 | 696.23 | 693.49 | 691.11 | 689.05 | 687.25 |
| 65,000 | 784.80 | 777.65 | 771.49 | 766.20 | 761.63 | 757.67 | 754.25 | 751.28 | 748.71 | 746.47 | 744.52 |
| 70,000 | 845.17 | 837.46 | 830.84 | 825.13 | 820.21 | 815.96 | 812.27 | 809.07 | 806.30 | 803.89 | 801.79 |
| 75,000 | 905.54 | 897.28 | 890.18 | 884.07 | 878.80 | 874.24 | 870.28 | 866.86 | 863.89 | 861.31 | 859.06 |
| 80,000 | 965.90 | 957.10 | 949.53 | 943.01 | 937.39 | 932.52 | 928.30 | 924.65 | 921.48 | 918.73 | 916.33 |
| 100,000 | 1207.38 | 1196.37 | 1186.91 | 1178.76 | 1171.73 | 1165.65 | 1160.38 | 1155.81 | 1151.85 | 1148.41 | 1145.42 |

MONTHLY PAYMENT

13 3/4% | | | | | | | | | 13 3/4% |

Years	20	21	22	23	24	25	26	27	28	29	30
25	.31	.31	.30	.30	.30	.30	.30	.30	.30	.30	.30
50	.62	.61	.60	.60	.60	.60	.59	.59	.59	.59	.59
75	.92	.92	.90	.90	.90	.89	.88	.88	.88	.88	.88
100	1.23	1.22	1.21	1.20	1.20	1.19	1.18	1.18	1.18	1.17	1.17
200	2.46	2.43	2.41	2.39	2.39	2.37	2.36	2.35	2.35	2.34	2.34
300	3.68	3.65	3.62	3.59	3.58	3.56	3.54	3.53	3.52	3.51	3.50
400	4.91	4.86	4.82	4.79	4.77	4.74	4.72	4.70	4.69	4.68	4.67
500	6.13	6.08	6.03	5.99	5.96	5.93	5.90	5.88	5.86	5.84	5.83
600	7.36	7.29	7.23	7.18	7.15	7.11	7.08	7.05	7.03	7.01	7.00
700	8.58	8.51	8.44	8.38	8.34	8.30	8.26	8.23	8.20	8.18	8.16
800	9.81	9.72	9.64	9.58	9.53	9.48	9.44	9.40	9.38	9.35	9.33
900	11.03	10.94	10.85	10.78	10.72	10.67	10.62	10.58	10.55	10.52	10.49
1,000	12.26	12.15	12.05	11.97	11.91	11.85	11.80	11.75	11.72	11.68	11.66
2,000	24.51	24.30	24.11	23.95	23.82	23.70	23.59	23.50	23.43	23.36	23.31
3,000	36.77	36.44	36.16	35.92	35.72	35.54	35.39	35.26	35.14	35.04	34.96
4,000	49.02	48.59	48.22	47.90	47.63	47.39	47.18	47.01	46.86	46.72	46.61
5,000	61.28	60.74	60.27	59.87	59.53	59.24	58.98	58.76	58.57	58.40	58.26
6,000	73.53	72.88	72.32	71.85	71.44	71.08	70.77	70.51	70.28	70.08	69.91
7,000	85.78	85.03	84.38	83.82	83.35	82.93	82.57	82.26	82.00	81.76	81.56
8,000	98.04	97.18	96.43	95.79	95.25	94.78	94.36	94.01	93.71	93.44	93.21
9,000	110.29	109.32	108.48	107.77	107.16	106.62	106.16	105.76	105.42	105.12	104.87
10,000	122.55	121.47	120.54	119.74	119.06	118.47	117.96	117.51	117.14	116.80	116.52
15,000	183.82	182.20	180.81	179.61	178.59	177.70	176.93	176.27	175.70	175.20	174.77
20,000	245.09	242.93	241.08	239.49	238.12	236.94	235.91	235.03	234.27	233.60	233.03
25,000	306.36	303.66	301.35	299.36	297.65	296.17	294.89	293.78	292.83	292.00	291.28
30,000	367.63	364.39	361.61	359.23	357.18	355.40	353.87	352.60	351.40	350.40	349.54
35,000	428.90	425.12	421.88	419.10	416.71	414.64	412.85	411.30	409.96	408.80	407.79
40,000	490.17	485.86	482.15	479.97	476.24	473.87	471.82	470.06	468.52	467.20	466.05
45,000	551.44	546.59	542.47	538.84	535.76	533.10	530.80	528.81	527.09	525.60	524.31
50,000	612.71	607.32	602.69	598.71	595.29	592.34	589.78	587.57	585.66	584.00	582.56
55,000	673.98	668.05	662.96	658.59	654.82	651.57	648.76	646.33	644.23	642.40	640.82
60,000	735.25	728.78	723.23	718.46	714.35	710.80	707.73	705.08	702.79	700.80	699.07
65,000	796.52	789.51	783.50	778.33	773.88	770.04	766.71	763.84	761.36	759.20	757.33
70,000	857.79	850.24	843.77	838.20	833.41	829.27	825.69	822.60	819.92	817.60	815.58
75,000	919.06	910.98	904.04	898.07	892.94	888.50	884.67	881.35	878.49	875.00	873.84
80,000	980.33	971.71	964.30	957.94	952.47	947.74	943.65	940.11	937.05	934.40	932.10
100,000	1225.41	1214.63	1205.38	1197.43	1190.58	1184.67	1179.56	1175.14	1171.32	1168.00	1165.12

Years	20	21	22	23	24	25	26	27	28	29	30
25	.32	.31	.31	.30	.31	.31	.30	.30	.30	.30	.30
50	.63	.62	.61	.61	.61	.61	.60	.60	.60	.60	.60
75	.94	.93	.92	.91	.91	.91	.90	.90	.90	.90	.89
100	1.25	1.24	1.22	1.22	1.21	1.21	1.20	1.20	1.20	1.19	1.19
200	2.49	4.47	2.45	2.43	2.42	2.41	2.40	2.39	2.39	2.38	2.37
300	3.74	3.70	3.67	3.65	3.63	3.62	3.60	3.58	3.58	3.57	3.56
400	4.98	4.94	4.90	4.86	4.84	4.82	4.80	4.78	4.77	4.76	4.74
500	6.22	6.17	6.12	6.08	6.05	6.02	5.99	5.97	5.96	5.94	5.93
600	7.47	7.40	7.34	7.30	7.26	7.23	7.19	7.17	7.15	7.13	7.11
700	8.71	8.64	8.57	8.51	8.47	8.43	8.39	8.36	8.34	8.32	8.30
800	9.95	9.87	9.79	9.73	9.68	9.64	9.59	9.56	9.53	9.51	9.48
900	11.20	11.10	11.02	10.95	10.89	10.84	10.79	10.75	10.72	10.69	10.67
1,000	12.44	12.33	12.24	12.16	12.10	12.04	11.99	11.94	11.91	11.88	11.85
2,000	24.88	24.66	24.78	24.32	24.20	24.08	23.98	23.89	23.82	23.76	23.70
3,000	37.31	36.99	36.72	36.49	36.29	36.12	35.96	35.84	35.73	35.63	35.55
4,000	49.75	49.32	48.96	48.65	48.39	48.16	47.95	47.78	47.64	47.51	47.40
5,000	62.18	61.65	61.20	60.81	60.48	60.19	59.94	59.73	59.55	59.39	59.25
6,000	74.62	73.98	73.44	72.97	72.58	72.23	71.93	71.67	71.46	71.26	71.10
7,000	87.05	86.31	85.68	85.13	84.67	84.27	83.92	83.62	83.36	83.14	82.95
8,000	99.49	99.64	97.91	97.29	96.77	96.31	95.90	95.56	95.27	95.02	94.79
9,000	111.92	110.97	110.15	109.46	108.86	108.34	107.89	107.51	107.18	106.89	106.64
10,000	124.36	123.30	122.39	121.61	120.96	120.38	119.88	119.45	119.09	118.77	118.49
15,000	186.53	184.95	183.59	182.43	181.43	180.57	179.82	179.18	178.63	178.15	177.74
20,000	248.71	246.60	244.79	243.23	241.91	240.76	239.76	238.91	238.17	237.53	236.98
25,000	310.89	308.25	306.98	304.04	302.38	300.95	299.70	298.63	297.71	296.91	296.22
30,000	373.06	369.90	367.18	364.85	362.86	361.13	359.64	358.36	357.26	356.30	355.47
35,000	435.24	431.54	428.38	425.66	423.33	421.32	419.58	418.09	416.80	415.68	414.71
40,000	497.41	493.19	489.57	486.47	483.81	481.51	479.52	477.81	476.34	475.06	473.95
45,000	559.59	554.84	550.77	547.28	544.28	541.70	539.46	537.54	535.88	534.44	533.20
50,000	621.77	616.49	611.97	608.09	604.76	601.89	599.40	597.27	595.42	593.82	592.44
55,000	683.94	678.14	673.16	668.90	665.23	662.07	659.34	656.99	654.97	653.21	651.68
60,000	746.12	739.79	734.36	729.70	725.71	722.26	719.29	716.72	714.51	712.59	710.93
65,000	808.29	801.43	795.55	790.51	786.18	782.45	779.23	776.45	774.05	771.97	770.17
70,000	870.47	863.08	856.75	851.32	846.66	842.64	839.17	836.17	833.59	831.35	829.42
75,000	932.65	924.73	917.95	912.13	907.13	902.83	899.11	895.90	893.13	890.73	888.66
80,000	994.82	986.38	979.14	972.94	967.61	963.01	959.05	955.63	952.67	950.12	947.90
100,000	1243.53	1232.97	1223.93	1216.17	1209.51	1203.77	1198.81	1194.53	1190.84	1187.64	1184.88

MONTHLY PAYMENT

14¼%   14¼%

Years	20	21	22	23	24	25	26	27	28	29	30
Amount											
25	.32	.32	.31	.31	.31	.31	.31	.31	.31	.31	.31
50	.64	.63	.62	.62	.62	.62	.61	.61	.61	.61	.61
75	.95	.94	.93	.93	.93	.92	.92	.91	.91	.91	.91
100	1.27	1.26	1.24	1.23	1.23	1.23	1.22	1.22	1.22	1.21	1.21
200	2.53	2.51	2.49	2.47	2.46	2.45	2.44	2.43	2.43	2.42	2.41
300	3.79	3.76	3.73	3.70	3.69	3.67	3.65	3.64	3.64	3.63	3.62
400	5.05	5.01	4.97	4.94	4.92	4.90	4.87	4.86	4.85	4.83	4.82
500	6.31	6.26	6.21	6.17	6.15	6.12	6.10	6.07	6.06	6.04	6.03
600	7.58	7.51	7.46	7.41	7.38	7.34	7.31	7.28	7.27	7.25	7.23
700	8.84	8.76	8.70	8.64	8.60	8.57	8.53	8.50	8.48	8.46	8.44
800	10.10	10.02	9.94	9.88	9.83	9.79	9.75	9.71	9.69	9.66	9.54
900	11.36	11.27	11.18	11.11	11.06	11.01	10.96	10.93	10.90	10.87	10.85
1,000	12.62	12.52	12.43	12.35	12.29	12.23	12.18	12.14	12.11	12.08	12.05
2,000	25.24	25.03	24.85	24.70	24.58	24.46	24.36	24.28	24.21	24.15	24.10
3,000	37.86	37.55	37.28	37.05	36.86	36.69	36.54	36.42	36.32	36.23	36.15
4,000	50.47	50.05	49.70	49.40	49.15	48.92	48.73	48.56	48.42	48.30	48.19
5,000	63.09	62.57	62.13	61.75	61.43	61.15	60.91	60.70	60.53	60.37	60.24
6,000	75.71	75.09	74.55	74.10	73.72	73.38	73.09	72.84	72.63	72.45	72.29
7,000	88.33	87.60	86.98	86.45	86.00	85.61	85.27	84.98	84.73	84.52	84.33
8,000	100.94	100.12	99.40	98.80	98.29	97.84	97.45	97.12	96.84	96.59	96.38
9,000	113.56	112.63	111.83	111.15	110.57	110.07	109.63	109.26	108.94	108.67	108.43
10,000	126.18	125.14	124.26	123.50	122.86	122.30	121.81	121.40	121.05	120.74	120.47
15,000	189.26	187.71	186.38	185.24	184.28	183.44	182.72	182.10	181.57	181.11	180.71
20,000	252.35	250.28	248.51	247.00	245.71	244.59	243.63	242.80	242.09	241.47	240.94
25,000	315.43	312.85	310.64	308.75	307.13	305.74	304.53	303.50	302.61	301.84	301.18
30,000	378.52	375.42	372.77	370.50	368.56	366.88	365.44	364.20	363.13	362.21	361.41
35,000	441.61	437.99	434.90	432.25	429.98	428.03	426.34	424.90	423.65	422.58	421.65
40,000	504.69	500.56	498.02	494.00	491.41	489.18	487.25	485.60	484.18	482.94	481.88
45,000	567.78	563.13	559.15	555.75	552.83	550.32	548.16	546.30	544.70	543.31	542.11
50,000	630.86	625.70	621.28	617.50	614.26	611.47	609.06	607.00	605.22	603.68	602.35
55,000	693.95	688.27	683.41	679.25	675.68	672.62	669.97	667.70	665.74	664.05	662.58
60,000	757.04	750.84	745.54	741.00	737.11	733.76	730.88	728.40	726.26	724.41	722.82
65,000	820.12	813.41	807.66	802.75	798.53	794.91	791.78	789.09	786.78	784.78	783.05
70,000	883.21	875.98	869.79	864.50	859.96	856.05	852.69	849.79	847.30	845.13	843.29
75,000	946.29	938.55	931.92	926.25	921.38	917.20	913.60	910.49	907.82	905.51	903.52
80,000	1009.38	1001.12	994.05	988.00	982.81	878.35	974.50	971.20	968.35	965.88	963.75
100,000	1261.72	1251.39	1242.56	1235.00	1228.51	1222.93	1218.13	1213.99	1210.43	1207.35	1204.69

MONTHLY PAYMENT

14½% Years	20	21	22	23	24	25	26	27	28	29	30
Amount											
25	.32	.32	.32	.32	.32	.31	.31	.31	.31	.31	.31
50	.64	.64	.63	.63	.63	.63	.62	.62	.62	.62	.62
75	.96	.96	.95	.94	.94	.94	.93	.93	.93	.93	.92
100	1.28	1.27	1.26	1.25	1.25	1.25	1.24	1.24	1.24	1.23	1.23
200	2.56	2.54	2.52	2.51	2.50	2.49	2.48	2.47	2.47	2.46	2.45
300	3.84	3.81	3.78	3.76	3.75	3.73	3.71	3.70	3.70	3.69	3.68
400	5.12	5.08	5.05	5.02	5.00	4.97	4.95	4.93	4.93	4.91	4.90
500	6.40	6.35	6.31	6.27	6.24	6.22	6.19	6.17	6.16	6.14	6.13
600	7.68	7.62	7.57	7.52	7.49	7.46	7.43	7.40	7.39	7.37	7.35
700	8.96	8.89	8.83	8.78	8.74	8.70	8.66	8.63	8.62	8.59	8.58
800	10.24	10.16	10.09	10.03	9.99	9.94	9.90	9.87	9.85	9.82	9.80
900	11.52	11.43	11.35	11.29	11.23	11.18	11.14	11.10	11.08	11.05	11.03
1,000	12.80	12.70	12.61	12.54	12.48	12.43	12.38	12.34	12.31	12.28	12.25
2,000	25.60	25.40	25.23	25.08	24.96	24.85	24.75	24.67	24.61	24.55	24.50
3,000	38.40	38.10	37.84	37.62	37.43	37.27	37.13	37.01	36.91	36.82	36.74
4,000	51.20	50.80	50.45	50.16	49.91	49.69	49.50	49.34	49.21	49.09	48.99
5,000	64.00	63.50	63.06	62.69	62.38	62.11	61.88	61.68	61.51	61.36	61.23
6,000	76.80	76.20	75.68	75.23	74.86	74.53	74.25	74.01	73.81	73.63	73.48
7,000	89.60	88.90	88.29	87.77	87.34	86.96	86.63	86.35	86.11	85.90	85.72
8,000	102.40	101.60	100.90	100.31	99.81	99.38	99.00	98.68	98.41	98.17	97.97
9,000	115.20	114.29	113.51	112.85	112.29	111.80	111.38	111.02	110.71	110.44	110.22
10,000	128.00	126.99	126.13	125.39	124.76	124.22	123.75	123.35	123.01	122.72	122.46
15,000	192.00	190.49	189.19	188.08	187.14	186.33	185.63	185.03	184.52	184.07	183.69
20,000	256.00	253.98	252.25	250.78	249.52	248.44	247.50	246.70	246.02	245.43	244.92
25,000	320.00	317.48	315.32	313.47	311.90	310.55	309.38	308.38	307.52	306.78	306.14
30,000	384.00	380.97	378.38	376.17	374.28	372.65	371.25	370.05	369.03	368.14	367.37
35,000	460.80	457.16	441.44	438.86	436.66	434.76	433.13	431.73	430.53	429.49	428.60
40,000	512.00	507.96	504.51	501.56	499.04	496.87	495.01	493.41	492.03	490.85	489.83
45,000	576.00	571.45	567.57	564.25	561.42	558.98	556.88	555.08	553.54	552.20	551.06
50,000	640.00	634.95	630.63	626.95	623.79	621.09	618.76	616.76	615.04	613.56	612.28
55,000	704.00	698.44	693.70	689.64	686.17	683.19	680.63	678.43	676.55	674.92	673.51
60,000	768.00	761.94	756.76	752.35	748.55	745.30	742.51	740.11	738.05	736.27	734.74
65,000	832.00	825.43	819.82	815.03	810.93	807.41	804.38	801.78	799.55	797.63	795.97
70,000	896.00	888.93	882.89	877.72	873.31	869.52	866.26	863.46	861.06	858.98	857.19
75,000	960.00	952.42	945.95	940.42	935.69	931.63	928.13	925.14	922.56	920.34	918.42
80,000	1024.00	1015.92	1009.01	1003.11	998.07	993.74	990.01	986.81	984.06	981.69	979.65
100,000	1280.00	1269.89	1261.27	1253.89	1247.58	1242.17	1237.51	1233.52	1230.08	1227.12	1224.56

14 3/4% Years	20	21	22	23	24	25	26	27	28	14 3/4% 29	30
Amount											
25	.33	.33	.32	.32	.32	.32	.32	.32	.32	.32	.32
50	.65	.65	.64	.64	.64	.64	.63	.63	.63	.63	.63
75	.98	.97	.96	.96	.96	.95	.94	.94	.94	.94	.94
100	1.30	1.29	1.28	1.27	1.27	1.27	1.26	1.25	1.25	1.25	1.25
200	2.60	2.58	2.56	2.55	2.54	2.53	2.51	2.51	2.50	2.50	2.49
300	3.90	3.87	3.84	3.82	3.81	3.79	3.77	3.76	3.75	3.75	3.74
400	5.20	5.16	5.12	5.09	5.07	5.05	5.03	5.01	5.00	4.99	4.98
500	6.50	6.45	6.40	6.36	6.34	6.31	6.28	6.27	6.25	6.24	6.23
600	7.80	7.74	7.68	7.64	7.61	7.57	7.54	7.52	7.50	7.49	7.47
700	9.09	9.02	8.96	8.91	8.87	8.84	8.80	8.77	8.75	8.73	8.72
800	10.39	10.31	10.24	10.18	10.14	10.10	10.06	10.02	10.00	9.98	9.96
900	11.69	11.60	11.52	11.46	11.41	11.36	11.31	11.28	11.25	11.23	11.21
1,000	12.99	12.89	12.80	12.73	12.67	12.62	12.57	12.53	12.50	12.47	12.45
2,000	25.97	25.77	25.60	25.46	25.34	25.23	25.14	25.06	25.00	24.94	24.89
3,000	38.96	38.66	38.40	38.19	38.01	37.85	37.71	37.59	37.50	37.41	37.34
4,000	51.94	51.54	51.20	50.91	50.67	50.46	50.28	50.12	50.00	49.88	49.78
5,000	64.92	64.43	64.00	63.64	63.34	63.08	62.85	62.65	62.49	62.35	62.23
6,000	77.91	77.31	76.80	76.37	76.01	75.69	75.42	75.19	74.99	74.82	74.67
7,000	90.89	90.20	89.60	89.10	88.68	88.31	87.99	87.72	87.49	87.29	87.12
8,000	103.87	103.08	102.40	101.83	101.34	100.92	100.56	100.25	99.99	99.76	99.56
9,000	116.86	115.97	115.20	114.56	114.01	113.54	113.13	112.78	112.49	112.23	112.01
10,000	129.84	128.85	128.00	127.29	126.68	126.15	125.70	125.31	124.98	124.70	124.45
15,000	194.76	193.27	192.01	190.93	190.01	189.22	188.54	187.96	187.47	187.04	186.68
20,000	259.68	257.70	256.01	254.57	253.35	252.30	251.39	250.62	249.96	249.39	248.90
25,000	324.59	322.12	320.01	318.22	316.69	315.37	314.24	313.27	312.45	311.74	311.12
30,000	389.51	386.54	384.01	381.86	380.02	378.44	377.09	375.93	374.94	374.08	373.35
35,000	454.43	450.97	448.02	445.50	443.35	441.52	439.94	438.58	437.43	436.43	435.57
40,000	519.35	515.39	512.02	509.14	506.69	504.59	502.78	501.24	499.92	498.78	497.80
45,000	584.26	579.81	576.02	572.79	570.03	567.66	565.63	563.90	562.41	561.12	560.02
50,000	649.18	644.24	640.02	636.43	633.37	630.74	628.48	626.55	624.89	623.47	622.24
55,000	714.10	708.66	704.02	700.07	696.70	693.81	691.33	689.20	687.38	685.82	684.47
60,000	779.02	773.08	768.03	763.72	760.04	756.88	754.18	751.86	749.87	748.16	746.69
65,000	843.94	837.51	832.03	827.36	823.37	819.96	817.02	814.51	812.36	810.51	808.91
70,000	908.85	901.93	896.03	891.00	886.71	883.03	879.87	877.17	874.85	872.85	871.14
75,000	973.77	966.35	960.03	954.65	950.05	946.10	942.72	939.82	937.34	935.20	933.36
80,000	1038.69	1030.78	1024.04	1018.29	1013.38	1009.18	1005.57	1002.48	999.83	997.55	995.59
100,000	1298.36	1288.47	1280.04	1272.86	1266.73	1261.47	1256.96	1253.10	1249.79	1246.93	1244.48

MONTHLY PAYMENT

15% Years	20	21	22	23	24	25	26	27	28	29	30
Amount											
25	.33	.33	.33	.33	.33	.33	.32	.32	.32	.32	.32
50	.66	.66	.65	.65	.65	.65	.64	.64	.64	.64	.64
75	.99	.99	.97	.97	.97	.97	.96	.96	.96	.96	.95
100	1.32	1.31	1.29	1.29	1.29	1.29	1.28	1.27	1.27	1.27	1.27
200	2.64	2.62	2.60	2.58	2.58	2.57	2.55	2.55	2.54	2.54	2.53
300	3.96	3.93	3.90	3.88	3.86	3.85	3.83	3.82	3.81	3.81	3.80
400	5.27	5.23	5.20	5.17	5.15	5.13	5.10	5.09	5.08	5.07	5.06
500	6.59	6.54	6.49	6.46	6.43	6.41	6.38	6.36	6.35	6.34	6.33
600	7.91	7.85	7.79	7.75	7.72	7.69	7.66	7.64	7.62	7.61	7.59
700	9.22	9.15	9.09	9.04	9.01	8.97	8.94	8.91	8.89	8.87	8.86
800	10.54	10.46	10.39	10.34	10.29	10.25	10.21	10.18	10.16	10.14	10.12
900	11.86	11.77	11.69	11.62	11.58	11.53	11.49	11.45	11.43	11.41	11.38
1,000	13.17	13.08	12.99	12.92	12.86	12.81	12.76	12.73	12.70	12.67	12.65
2,000	26.34	26.15	25.98	25.84	25.72	25.62	25.53	25.45	25.40	25.34	25.29
3,000	39.51	39.22	38.97	38.76	38.58	38.43	38.29	38.18	38.09	38.01	37.94
4,000	52.68	52.29	51.96	51.68	51.44	51.24	51.06	50.91	50.79	50.68	50.58
5,000	65.84	65.36	64.95	64.59	64.30	64.05	63.82	63.64	63.48	63.34	63.23
6,000	79.01	78.43	77.93	77.51	77.16	76.85	76.59	76.36	76.18	76.01	75.87
7,000	92.18	91.50	90.92	90.43	90.02	89.66	89.35	89.09	88.87	88.68	88.52
8,000	105.35	104.57	103.91	103.35	102.88	102.47	102.12	101.82	101.57	101.35	101.16
9,000	118.52	117.65	116.90	116.18	115.74	115.28	114.88	114.55	114.26	114.02	113.80
10,000	131.68	130.72	129.89	129.19	128.60	128.09	127.65	127.27	126.96	126.68	126.45
15,000	197.52	196.07	194.83	193.78	192.89	192.13	191.47	190.91	190.44	190.02	189.67
20,000	263.36	261.43	259.78	258.40	257.19	256.17	255.29	254.55	253.91	253.36	252.89
25,000	329.20	326.78	324.72	322.97	321.49	320.21	319.12	318.18	317.39	316.70	316.12
30,000	395.04	392.14	389.67	387.57	385.78	384.25	382.94	381.82	380.87	380.04	379.34
35,000	460.88	457.50	454.61	452.16	450.08	448.30	446.76	445.46	444.34	443.38	442.58
40,000	526.72	522.85	519.56	516.76	514.38	512.34	510.59	509.10	507.82	506.72	505.78
45,000	592.56	588.21	584.50	581.35	578.67	576.38	574.41	572.73	571.30	570.06	569.00
50,000	658.40	653.56	649.49	545.95	642.97	640.42	638.24	636.37	634.77	633.40	632.23
55,000	724.24	718.92	714.39	710.54	707.27	704.46	702.06	700.01	698.25	696.74	695.45
60,000	790.08	784.28	779.34	775.14	771.56	768.50	765.88	763.64	761.73	760.08	758.67
65,000	855.92	849.63	844.28	839.73	835.86	832.54	829.71	827.28	825.21	823.42	821.89
70,000	921.76	914.99	909.23	904.33	900.16	896.59	893.53	890.92	888.68	886.76	885.12
75,000	987.60	980.34	974.17	968.92	964.45	960.63	957.35	954.55	952.16	950.10	948.34
80,000	1053.44	1045.70	1039.12	1033.50	1028.75	1024.67	1021.18	1018.19	1015.64	1013.44	1011.56
100,000	1316.79	1307.12	1298.90	1291.90	1285.93	1280.84	1276.47	1272.74	1269.54	1266.80	1264.45